Fodor's
New Edition

Seattle & Vancouver

Portions of this book appear in *Fodor's Pacific North Coast*

Fodor's Travel Publications, Inc.
New York • Toronto • London • Sydney • Auckland

ISBN 0-679-02587-1

Fodor's Seattle & Vancouver

Editor: Larry Peterson
Contributors: Steven K. Amsterdam, Robert Brown, Susan Brown, Ray Chatelin, John Doerper, Mary Engel, Alison Hoffman, Eve Johnson, Laura M. Kidder, Mike Miller, Glenn W. Sheehan, Loralee Wenger, Adam Woog
Creative Director: Fabrizio La Rocca
Cartographer: David Lindroth
Illustrator: Karl Tanner
Cover Photograph: Eddie Hironaka/Image Bank

Design: Vignelli Associates

Special Sales

Fodor's Travel Publications are available at special discounts for bulk purchases for sales promotions or premiums. Special editions, including personalized covers, excerpts of existing guides, and corporate imprints, can be created in large quantities for special needs. For more information, contact your local bookseller or write to Special Markets, Fodor's Travel Publications, 201 East 50th Street, New York, NY 10022. Inquiries from Canada should be directed to your local Canadian bookseller or sent to Random House of Canada, Ltd., Marketing Dept., 1265 Aerowood Drive, Mississauga, Ontario L4W 1B9. Inquiries from the United Kingdom should be sent to Fodor's Travel Publications, 20 Vauxhall Bridge Road, London, England SWIV 2SA.

MANUFACTURED IN THE UNITED STATES OF AMERICA

10 9 8 7 6 5 4 3 2

Contents

Foreword *v*

Highlights *viii*

Fodor's Choice *ix*

Introduction *xiv*

1 **Essential Information** *1*

Before You Go *2*

Visitor Information *2*
Tours and Packages *2*
When to Go *4*
Festivals and Seasonal Events *5*
What to Pack *6*
Taking Money Abroad *7*
Getting Money from Home *7*
Currency *8*
What It Will Cost *8*
Passports and Visas *9*
Customs *10*
Traveling with Cameras, Camcorders, and Laptops *10*
Language *11*
Insurance *11*
Car Rentals *13*
Rail Passes *14*
Student and Youth Travel *14*
Traveling with Children *15*
Hints for Travelers with Disabilities *16*
Hints for Older Travelers *18*
Further Reading *18*

Arriving and Departing *19*

From North America by Plane *19*
From the U.S. by Car *21*
From the U.S. by Train *22*
From the U.S. by Bus *22*
From the U.K. by Plane *22*

Staying in Seattle and Vancouver *23*

Getting Around *23*
Telephones *26*
Radio Stations *26*
Mail *27*
Tipping *27*
Opening and Closing Times *27*
Shopping *27*
Participant Sports and Outdoor Activities *28*
Spectator Sports *31*

Beaches *31*
Dining *32*
Lodging *33*
Credit Cards *35*

2 Portrait of Seattle and Vancouver *37*

"In the Footsteps of the First Settlers,"
by Glenn W. Sheehan *38*

3 Seattle *44*

4 Vancouver *109*

Index *172*

Maps

Seattle and Vancouver *xi*
World Time Zones *xii–xiii*
Downtown Seattle *52–53*
Metropolitan Seattle *55*
Downtown Seattle Dining *66–67*
Metropolitan Seattle Dining *68*
Seattle Lodging *76–77*
Puget Sound *92*
Vancouver Exploring *112–113*
Tour 1: Downtown Vancouver *118*
Tour 2: Stanley Park *123*
Tour 3: Granville Island *126*
Downtown Vancouver Dining *137*
Greater Vancouver Dining *138*
Vancouver Lodging *146*
Downtown Victoria *157*

Foreword

We wish to express our gratitude to those who have helped with this guide, including Seattle/King County News Bureau, especially Barry Anderson and David Blandford; Elvira Quarin at Tourism Vancouver; Robert Brown with the Canadian Consulate General; and Hinda Simon.

While every care has been taken to ensure the accuracy of the information in this guide, the passage of time will always bring change, and consequently, the publisher cannot accept responsibility for errors that may occur.

All prices and opening times quoted here are based on information supplied to us at press time. Hours and admission fees may change, however, and the prudent traveler will avoid inconvenience by calling ahead.

Fodor's wants to hear about your travel experiences, both pleasant and unpleasant. When a hotel or restaurant fails to live up to its billing, let us know and we will investigate the complaint and revise our entries where the facts warrant it.

Send your letters to the editors of Fodor's Travel Publications, 201 E. 50th Street, New York, NY 10022.

Highlights and Fodor's Choice

Highlights

Seattle Although Seattle may not be quite as "hot" a destination as it was over the past few years, it still ranks way up there among U.S. cities to visit. A recent survey of 30,000 *Conde Nast Traveler* magazine readers pegged Seattle as the **fourth-favorite metropolitan destination** in the country. Although some locals say that greater Seattle has sprawled itself right out of its charm, there are still plenty of reasons to visit, and some of the most appealing are everyday local phenomena rather than official tourist sites—sidewalk espresso stands, microbrews, micropubs, and a lively nightlife scene that ranges from opera to grunge rock, Shakespeare to improvisation.

A must-see in town is Woodland Park Zoo's **tropical rain forest exhibit,** which opened in 1992. The exhibit, which takes visitors through the complex layers of a rain forest, was named the best in the country in 1993 by the American Association of Zoological Parks and Aquariums.

In the fall of 1993, the **Seattle Children's Theatre** opened the **Charlotte Martin Theatre,** a $10 million facility adjacent to the Pacific Science Center at the Seattle Center. SCT is the second-largest professional resident children's theater company in the country, and has commissioned more than 55 new plays, adaptations, and musicals, many of which have gone on to be produced by theater companies across the United States.

Vancouver The high-speed ferry service **Sealink Express,** carrying passengers only, continues to effortlessly transport visitors from downtown Vancouver to downtown Victoria, allowing visitors to take in both towns without the long trip to and from the regular car-ferry terminals. Another ferry company, Sea Containers, Ltd., is currently refurbishing its ***Princess Marguerite*** ferry with possible plans to put it to work on the Vancouver–Prince Rupert route along the Inside Passage.

Local Vancouver sightseeing has been improved, too, thanks to the **Vancouver Trolleys,** like old-fashioned streetcars, that take you on a guided tour of all the major attractions (Stanley Park, English Bay, Gastown, Robson Street, Granville Island, the Vancouver Museum, Queen Elizabeth Park, Chinatown, and Science World) for an all-day unlimited-stop ticket.

Fodor's Choice

No two people will agree on what makes a perfect vacation, but it's fun and helpful to know what others think. We hope you'll have a chance to experience some of Fodor's Choices yourself in Seattle and Vancouver. For detailed information about each entry, refer to the appropriate chapter.

Seattle

Attractions

International District

Pike Place Market

Seattle Aquarium

Space Needle

Woodland Park Zoo

Special Moments

Sitting in on the "Out to Lunch" concert series at one of Seattle's parks

Seeing Seattle at night from the Space Needle's observation deck

Reading the hundreds of name tiles on the floor of the Pike Place Market

Seeing Mt. Rainier looming above Puget Sound on a clear day when "the mountain comes out"

Hotels

Alexis (*Very Expensive*)

Four Seasons Olympic Hotels (*Very Expensive*)

Edgewater (*Expensive*)

Sorrento (*Expensive*)

Inn at the Market (*Moderate–Expensive*)

Meany Tower Hotel (*Inexpensive*)

Restaurants

Fuller's (*Expensive*)

The Painted Table (*Expensive*)

Wild Ginger (*Moderate*)

Saigon Gourmet (*Inexpensive*)

Vancouver

Attractions

Butchart Gardens, Victoria

Dr. Sun-yat Sen Classical Garden, Stanley Park

Granville Public Market, Granville Island

Vancouver Aquarium

Shopping

Fourth Avenue (between Burrard and Balsam streets)

Government Street, Victoria

Market Square, Victoria

Robson Street

Restaurants Les Deux Gros, Whistler (*Expensive*)

Tojo's (*Expensive*)

English Bay Café (*Moderate*)

The Raintree (*Moderate*)

Six Mile House, Victoria (*Inexpensive*)

Phnom Penh (*Inexpensive*)

Hotels Le Chamois, Whistler (*Very Expensive*)

Hotel Grand Pacific, Victoria (*Very Expensive*)

Le Meridien (*Very Expensive*)

Wedgewood Hotel (*Expensive*)

Hotel Georgia (*Moderate*)

Craigmyle Guest House, Victoria (*Inexpensive–Moderate*)

Sylvia Hotel (*Inexpensive*)

Seattle and Vancouver

World Time Zones

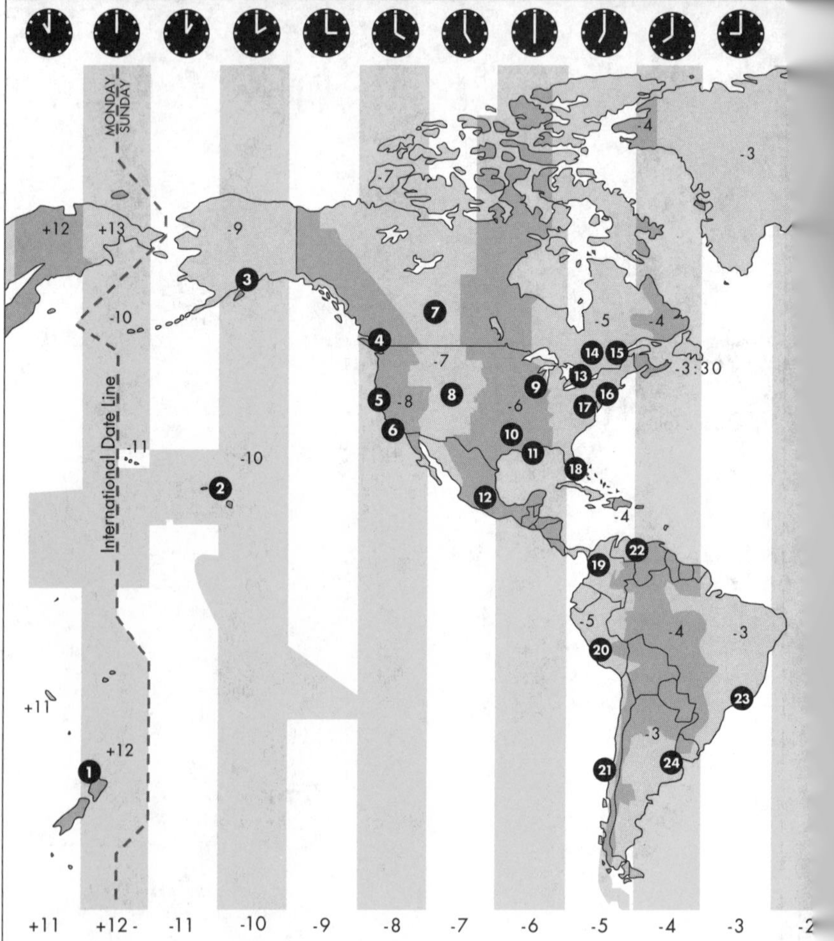

Numbers below vertical bands relate each zone to Greenwich Mean Time (0 hrs.).
Local times frequently differ from these general indications,
as indicated by light-face numbers on map.

Algiers, **29**
Anchorage, **3**
Athens, **41**
Auckland, **1**
Baghdad, **46**
Bangkok, **50**
Beijing, **54**
Berlin, **34**
Bogotá, **19**
Budapest, **37**
Buenos Aires, **24**
Caracas, **22**
Chicago, **9**
Copenhagen, **33**
Dallas, **10**
Delhi, **48**
Denver, **8**
Djakarta, **53**
Dublin, **26**
Edmonton, **7**
Hong Kong, **56**
Honolulu, **2**
Istanbul, **40**
Jerusalem, **42**
Johannesburg, **44**
Lima, **20**
Lisbon, **28**
London (Greenwich), **27**
Los Angeles, **6**
Madrid, **38**
Manila, **57**

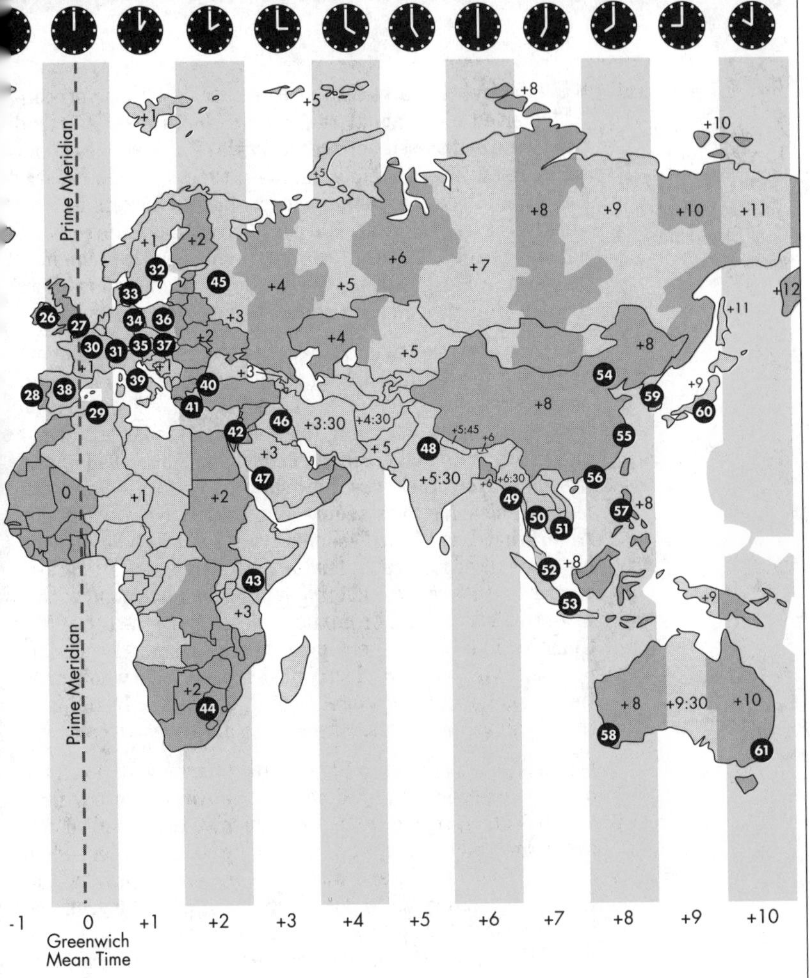

Mecca, **47**
Mexico City, **12**
Miami, **18**
Montréal, **15**
Moscow, **45**
Nairobi, **43**
New Orleans, **11**
New York City, **16**
Ottawa, **14**
Paris, **30**
Perth, **58**
Reykjavík, **25**
Rio de Janeiro, **23**
Rome, **39**
Saigon (Ho Chi Minh City), **51**
San Francisco, **5**
Santiago, **21**
Seoul, **59**
Shanghai, **55**
Singapore, **52**
Stockholm, **32**
Sydney, **61**
Tokyo, **60**
Toronto, **13**
Vancouver, **4**
Vienna, **35**
Warsaw, **36**
Washington, D.C., **17**
Yangon, **49**
Zürich, **31**

Introduction

By Philip Joseph

A native New Yorker, Phil has found his way to Seattle where he is a freelance writer and editor.

The first time I visited Seattle, I took with me preconceived ideas about the Pacific Northwest. A friend who had moved here recently was full of stories about camping on the weekends, biking after work, and theater tickets that cost the same price as movies tickets in New York. Articles in the national press raved about the region's natural beauty, cultural vibrancy, and healthy economy. "America's Most Livable City," they touted, referring to Seattle. So I arrived with high expectations.

The weather was ideal. We went to Orcas Island—a short drive and ferry ride from Seattle—and camped on a bluff overlooking Puget Sound. My friend fell asleep, and I lay on my back in front of a dying fire, beneath stellar patterns I had rarely noticed before, and considered how inadequate my life in New York was, how suited I was to the natural, more wholesome lives people led in the Great Northwest. All of what I had heard seemed true: I felt I had found the ideal blend of natural splendor and urban sophistication, where a rain forest could mingle in perfect harmony with a modern metropolis. The next day we drove to the top of Mt. Constitution, the highest peak on the island. From this privileged perspective, I surveyed virtually the whole pristine region, including Puget Sound, Vancouver Island, and the Olympic Mountains. I decided to move west.

Needless to say, I suffered some disillusionment. I can remember waiting for a taxi at Sea-Tac Airport on my first day in Seattle, trying to decide if the mist demanded an umbrella and wondering why everything suddenly looked so dreary. Two days later I made my first major purchase in Seattle—a mountain bike. Eager to prove myself an outdoorsman, that evening I pedaled to a party on Queen Anne Hill; the terrain—typical for Seattle—was a little steeper than I had expected. Cursing every step, I ended up climbing the arduous hill, with bike alongside me. I was beginning to learn that, while the image of the great outdoors meeting the great metropolis evokes drama, if not romance, the two forces don't always create the most comfortable situations.

Last December, for instance, a snowstorm hit Seattle, leaving the steep hills sheathed in ice. As a New York native, I expected salt on the sidewalks, sand on the streets, and a fairly active city the next day. Not a chance. Many of the busiest streets hadn't been plowed, cars were abandoned by the side of the road, and businesses and schools were shut down. The message was clear: If you live on the Pacific North Coast, you must accept nature's tendency to disrupt and inconvenience you. Houses slide down eroded slopes into Puget Sound, volcanoes erupt, and it rains and rains and rains. Rigidity, outrage, obstinate determination, or any other form of hubris can get you into trouble. I was the only passenger on a bus one night, and the bus driver drove three blocks off his route to drop me at the door of my destination. Sure, he was being kind, but it's more than that. Native northwesterners are used to adjustments, and they make them without thinking twice.

My enchanted experience on Orcas Island was no fluke. If nature disrupts, its grace and power also inspires. On a clear day in Seattle, Mt. Rainier floats, dreamlike, over the industrial southern end of the city; the Cascade Mountains reign in the east, looming over Lake Washington; in the west, the Olympics rise over Bainbridge Island and Elliott Bay, and ragged clouds turn an evening sky into an explosion of color. Standing at the seawall in Vancouver's Stanley Park, the mountains rest at what seems like just an arm's reach across Burrard Inlet. Take just a few steps onto one of the park trails and you feel as though you're lost in a virgin forest, with no sign of city life.

If the weather has been especially depressing, I seize the first clear day and rent a canoe at the University of Washington waterfront in Seattle. The channels at the University Arboretum give way to Lake Washington, fringed by the Cascade Mountains. Inevitably, I feel serene, as I did on Orcas Island, and the Northwest once again becomes the ideal place to live.

But residents of Seattle and Vancouver don't just paddle away their days. Politics run hot here, and local leaders work hard to maintain legislation that has helped to protect the environment of the cities and their surroundings. Likewise, advocates deserve kudos for their efforts to restore some of the history that went into the makings of Seattle and Vancouver. In 1971, the Canadian Government bought Granville Island, which was originally used to store logging supplies. Today, only businesses that deal with maritime activities, the arts, and a public market are permitted to set up shop on the island. A walk around the island will lead you past produce stalls, crafts merchants, food vendors, and artists' studios. Around the same time as the Granville Island purchase, Vancouver embarked on the restoration of Gastown, a historic area by the waterfront and named for "Gassy" Jack Deighton, who opened the settlement's first saloon. By the time Deighton died in 1875, a bawdy and sometimes lawless townsite had sprouted in the vicinity of his saloon. In one way, the area remained faithful to his vision, as it proceeded for the next 100 years to attract an abundance of drunks. In 1960, more than two-thirds of all arrests in Vancouver were made in the vicinity of the old Deighton House. Some of the old buildings remain, but until the rehabilitation the squalor of the neighborhood was more prominent than its history. Today boutiques, galleries, restaurants, and a steam-powered clock line the cobblestone streets of this touted tourist spot—a worthy tribute to the old codger.

Vancouver's history predates Gassy Jack Deighton and the first white entourage. When the settlers arrived in Vancouver, there were, according to one witness, 10 Suquamish villages in the area. A few years later, most of the land had been claimed by the newcomers, and the villages had vanished. Fortunately, the native culture survived, and today Vancouver is the center for producing and selling native Pacific Coast crafts. Local Haida carver Bill Reid has his studio on Granville Island; galleries display the works of Inuit, Tlingit, Tsimshian, Kwakiutl, Haida, and Salish artisans; students can study the craft at the University of British Columbia; and the university's Museum of Anthropology houses one of the finest collections of native art in the world. Western techniques have been studied and incorporated into the works, but the dominant styles and the mythological references—usually related to the animal wildlife of the region—are firmly rooted in Pacific Coast cultures.

Seattle's early history began with the native Suquamish people, and the city has devoted much energy to preserving its historic neighborhoods. In the late 1800s, Seattle began to expand around a steam-powered lumber mill at the foot of a hill, in the area of what is now called Pioneer Square. Loggers cut the trees near the hilltop and skidded them down to the mill along a road that came to be known as "skid road." "Road" soon became "row," and the term lost its original significance.

By the early 1960s, Pioneer Square had lost its historic character, going the same sordid route as Gastown had in Vancouver. So Seattle undertook a massive rehabilitation of its own. Historic buildings were restored, shops and galleries moved in, and, in keeping with the theme, the city put 1890s-style uniforms on the police officers who walked the local beat.

Fortunately, Pioneer Square hasn't become overly sanitized. On my first visit to Seattle, a friend took me to a small bar on the block between the square and the waterfront. A quiet place to have a beer, she said. Soon after we sat down, a man with a gruff voice broke into a chorus of "Barnacle Bill the Sailor." When a younger man dressed in black told him to be quiet, a fight broke out. So much for the quiet beer. Most urban rehabilitations leave only the pure and clean, but Pioneer Square retains its old rowdiness, lending authenticity to the restoration. A church that feeds the homeless is right across the street from the Elliott Bay Bookstore, where well-known writers read from their latest works. On weekend nights, the OK Hotel (not really a hotel) may have slam dancing that appeals to a young, leather-adorned crowd, and just a few blocks away the busy Trattoria Mitchelli offers late-night pasta to a mixed-bag clientele. Seattle's unrefined elements nicely balance all the historical charm, making this part of town feel lived-in and real.

The city's other major restoration project was the Pike Place Market, which was originally built in 1907. The complex of lofts and stalls overlooking Elliott Bay nearly faced the demolition ball in the 1960s, but was saved by a voter referendum. Amid a maze of ramps and hallways, today's visitors shop for gourmet foods, spices, posters, jewelry, crafts, clothes, fish, and produce.

I go down to the market to get my hair cut. On my way, I pass a fish stall that's on the first level. A seller—I call him the fish-thrower—stands before an array of sea creatures displayed on beds of ice. Hoarsely, the man calls out the specials and jokes with a few potential customers. No takers, yet. Now the man is discussing a particualr salmon with an older woman. He holds up the fish and lets it fly, over the heads of potential customers and into a piece of wax paper held by one of the counter merchants. Successful completion, as usual.

Now I walk down to the barbershop. Kim, my barber of choice, raises the radio volume, prattles for a while about her love life, and needles the owner, who is tending to the customer in the only other chair. He takes her ribbing in stride. The cut costs $7, and without fail there's a line out the door. My impulse is to ask the owner why he doesn't expand—get a bigger shop, with room for a new chair and another assistant. Clearly, there's a demand for it. But I can imagine his response: "You transplants are all the same, all bent on expansion." In this city, I remind myself, two chairs can be better than three. It's the same message that the Pike Place merchants are now sending to the Preservation and Development Authority, which manages the complex and nearly allowed it to slip into the control of a New York investor group. The market remains in the hands of the PDA, but merchants still worry about the future of the complex.

Of course, no one can deny that both cities have reaped at least some economic and cultural benefits from all the growth and renewal of the past few decades. Vancouver is among the busiest ports in North America, and Seattle—recognized in the past as the home of airline manufacturer Boeing—is now a center for computer technology as well, thanks to Bill Gates's Microsoft company. You can go to the theater for less than $10 in Seattle and, while a chandelier may not fall from the ceiling à la *Phantom of the Opera,* the performance is generally first-rate. Vancouver's Jazz Festival ranks among the best in the world.

All the success is also making people think. Highways are more crowded; sprawling suburbs encroach on the forests;

and homelessness, drugs, and street gangs are on the rise. In Seattle, some locals have responded by forming a group called Lesser Seattle, devoted to discouraging people from moving here. "Keep the Bastards Out," they say, only half-jokingly. But beneath the tough talk lies a simple wish they share with Vancouverites: to maintain at least some control over the recent changes in their cities. If you plan on spending some time in either Seattle or Vancouver, don't be too concerned with this talk. No one will blame you outright for all the congestion and untrammelled growth; folks out here are too polite for that. They may instead hint at it, or bait you into a statement that you'll later regret. "This rain can be depressing, huh?" A resident might feel you out with this kind of question, to see what kind of appreciation you really have. Keep your answers short, and remember that out here, two chairs are often better than three.

1 Essential Information

Before You Go

Visitor Information

For free travel information, contact the following tourism offices:

In the U.S. **Washington Tourism Development Division** (Box 45213, Olympia, WA 98504, tel. 206/586–2088, 206/586–2102, or 800/544–1800).

In Canada **Tourism British Columbia** (1117 Wharf St., Victoria, B.C. V8W 2Z2, tel. 800/663–6000).

In the U.K. For touring tips and brochures, contact the **United States Travel and Tourism Administration** (Box 1EN, London WIA 1EN, tel. 071/495–4466), **Canadian High Commission, Tourism Division** (Canada House, Trafalgar Sq., London SW1Y 5BJ, tel. 071/930–6857), or **Tourism British Columbia** (1 Regent St., London SW1Y 4NS, tel. 071/930–6857).

Tours and Packages

Should you buy your travel arrangements to Seattle and Vancouver packaged or do it yourself? There are advantages either way. Buying packaged arrangements saves you money, particularly if you can find a program that includes exactly the features you want. You also get a pretty good idea of what your trip will cost from the outset. Generally, you have two options: fully escorted tours and independent packages. Escorted tours are most often via motorcoach, with a tour director in charge. They're ideal if you don't mind having limited free time and traveling with strangers. Your baggage is handled, your time rigorously scheduled, and most meals planned. Such tours are therefore the most hassle-free way to see a destination, as well as generally the least expensive. Independent packages allow plenty of flexibility. They generally include airline travel and hotels, with certain options available, such as sightseeing, car rental, and excursions. Such packages are usually more expensive than escorted tours, but your time is your own.

While you can book directly through tour operators, you will pay no more to go through a travel agent, who will be able to tell you about tours and packages from a number of operators. Whatever program you ultimately choose, be sure to find out exactly what is included: taxes, tips, transfers, meals, baggage handling, ground transportation, entertainment, excursions, sports or recreation (and rental equipment if necessary). Ask about the level of hotel used, its location, the size of its rooms, the kind of beds, and its amenities, such as pool, room service, or programs for children, if they're important to you. Find out the operator's cancellation penalties. Nearly everyone charges them, and the only way to avoid them is to buy trip-cancellation insurance (*see* Trip Insurance, *below*). Also ask about the single supplement, a surcharge assessed to solo travelers. Some operators do not make you pay it if you agree to be matched up with a roommate of the same sex, even if one is not found by departure time. Remember that a program that has features you won't use may not be the most cost-wise choice for you.

Fully Escorted Tours

Escorted tours are usually sold in three categories: deluxe, first-class, and tourist or budget class. The most important differences are the price, of course, and the level of accommodations. Some operators specialize in one category, while others offer a range.

Contact **Maupintour** (Box 807, Lawrence, KS 66044, tel. 913/843–1211 or 800/255–4266) and **Tauck Tours** (11 Wilton Rd., Westport, CT 06881, tel. 203/226–6911 or 800/468–2825) in the deluxe category; **Brendan Tours** (15137 Califa St., Van Nuys, CA 91411, tel. 818/985–9696 pr 800/421–8446), **Brennan Tours** (1402 3rd Ave., Suite 717, Seattle, WA 98101, tel. 206/622–9155 or 800/237–7249), **Caravan Tours** (401 N. Michigan Ave., Chicago, IL 60611, tel. 312/321–9800 or 800/227–2826), **Gadabout Tours** (700 E. Tahquitz Way, Palm Springs, CA 92262, tel. 619/325–5556 or 800/952–5068), **Globus** (150 S. Los Robles Ave., Pasadena, CA 91101, tel. 818/449–0919 or 800/556–5454), **Holland American Westours** (300 Elliott Ave. W., Seattle, WA 98119, tel. 206/281–3535 or 800/426–0327), and **Princess Tours** (2815 2nd Ave., Suite 400, Seattle, WA 98121, tel. 206/728–4202) in the first-class category; and **Cosmos,** a division of Globus (at the same number), and **Gray Line of Seattle** (720 S. Forest St., Seattle, WA 98134, tel. 206/624–5813) in the budget category.

Most itineraries are jam-packed with sightseeing, so you see a lot in a short amount of time (usually one place per day). To judge just how fast-paced the tour is, review the itinerary carefully. If you are in a different hotel each night, you will be getting up early each day to head out, travel to your next destination, do some sightseeing, have dinner, and go to bed; then you'll start all over again. If you want some free time, make sure it's mentioned in the tour brochure; if you want to be escorted to every meal, confirm that any tour you consider does that. Also, when comparing programs, be sure to find out if the motorcoach is air-conditioned and has a rest room on board. Make your selection based on price and stops on the itinerary.

Independent Packages

Independent packages are usually offered by airlines, tour operators who may also do escorted programs, and any number of other companies from large, established firms to small, new entrepreneurs. Most packages to Seattle and Vancouver are through the major airlines that service the Pacific North Coast.

Contact **American Airlines Fly AAway Vacations** (tel. 800/321–2121) and **United Airlines' Vacation Planning Center** (tel. 800/328–6877).

Programs come in a wide range of prices based on levels of luxury and options—in addition to hotel and airfare, sightseeing, car rental, transfers, admission to local attractions, and other extras. Note that when pricing different packages, it sometimes pays to purchase the same arrangements separately, as when a rock-bottom promotional airfare is being offered, for example. Again, base your choice on what's available in your budget for the destinations you want to visit.

Special-Interest Travel

Special-interest programs may be fully escorted or independent. Some require a certain amount of expertise, but most are for the average traveler with an interest and are usually hosted by experts in the subject matter. When the program is escorted, it enjoys the advantages and disadvantages of all escorted programs; because your fellow travelers are apt to be passionate or knowledgeable about the subject, they can prove as enjoyable a part of your travel experience as the destination itself. The price range is wide, but the cost is usually higher—sometimes a lot higher—than for ordinary escorted tours and packages, because of the expert guidance and special activities.

Biking **Backroads** (1516 5th St., Suite Q333, Berkely, CA 94710, tel. 510/527–1555 or 800/245–3874) offers a variety of biking programs throughout the Northwest, including Washington and Vancouver.

Nature **Oceanic Society Expeditions** (Fort Mason Center, Bldg. E, San Francisco, CA 94123, tel. 415/441–1106 or 800/326–7491) offers a "Killer Whales" expedition off Vancouver Island, with accommodations aboard its 68-foot boat.

When to Go

The Pacific North Coast's mild, pleasant climate is best from June through September. Hotels in the major tourist destinations are often filled in July and August, so it's important to book reservations in advance. Summer temperatures generally range in the 70s, and rainfall is usually minimal. Nights, however, can be cool, so if you're going to enjoy the nightlife, take along a sweater or jacket.

Spring and fall are also excellent times to visit. The weather usually remains quite good, and the prices for accommodations, transportation, and tours can be lower (and the crowds much smaller!) in the most popular destinations.

In winter, the coastal rain turns to snow in the nearby mountains, making the region a skier's dream. World-class ski resorts such as British Columbia's Whistler Village are luring a growing number of winter visitors from around the world.

Climate Tempered by a warm Japan current and protected by the mountains from the extreme weather conditions found inland, the coastal regions of Oregon, Washington, British Columbia, and Southeast Alaska experience a uniformly mild climate.

Average daytime summer highs are in the 70s; winter temperatures are generally in the 40s. Snow is uncommon in the lowland areas. If it does snow (usually in December or January), everything grinds to a halt—but children love it!

Seattle has an average of only 36 inches of rainfall a year—less than New York, Chicago, or Miami. The wetness, however, is concentrated during the winter months, when cloudy skies and drizzly weather persist. More than 75% of Seattle's annual precipitation occurs from October through March.

The following are average daily maximum and minimum temperatures for Seattle and Vancouver.

Seattle

Jan.	45F	7C	**May**	66F	19C	**Sept.**	69F	20C
	35	2		47	8		52	11
Feb.	50F	10C	**June**	70F	21C	**Oct.**	62F	16C
	37	3		52	11		47	8
Mar.	53F	12C	**July**	76F	24C	**Nov.**	51F	10C
	38	3		56	13		40	4
Apr.	59F	13C	**Aug.**	75F	24C	**Dec.**	47F	8C
	42	5		55	13		37	3

Vancouver

Jan.	41F	5C	**May**	63F	17C	**Sept.**	64F	18C
	32	0		46	8		50	10
Feb.	46F	8C	**June**	66F	19C	**Oct.**	57F	14C
	34	1		52	11		43	6
Mar.	48F	9C	**July**	72F	22C	**Nov.**	48F	9C
	36	2		55	13		37	3
Apr.	55F	13C	**Aug.**	72F	22C	**Dec.**	45F	7C
	41	5		55	13		34	1

Information Sources For current weather conditions for cities in the United States and abroad, plus the local time and helpful travel tips, call the **Weather Channel Connection** (tel. 900/932–8437; 95¢ per minute) from a touch-tone phone.

Festivals and Seasonal Events

Seattle and Vancouver come alive each year in a burst of colorful festivities. The following is a sample of noteworthy seasonal events. For dates and more details, contact the local tourism departments.

Seattle **Late May. Northwest Folklife Festival** lures musicians and artists to Seattle for one of the largest folkfests in the United States. Tel. 206/684–7300.

Mid-July. Bite of Seattle serves up sumptuous specialties from the city's finest restaurants. Tel. 206/232–2982.

Mid-July–early Aug. Seafair, Seattle's biggest event of the year, kicks off with a torchlight parade through downtown and culminates in the Blue Angels air show and hydroplane races on Lake Washington. Tel. 206/728–0123.

Late Aug.–early Sept. Bumbershoot, a Seattle festival of the arts, presents more than 400 performers in music, dance, theater, comedy, and the visual and literary arts. Tel. 206/684–7200.

Vancouver **Mid-May. Vancouver Children's Festival,** the largest event of its kind in the world, presents dozens of performances in mime, puppetry, music, and theater. Tel. 604/687–7697.

Late May. Swiftsure Race Weekend draws more than 300 competitors to Victoria's harbor for an international yachting event. Tel. 604/592–2441.

Late May. Victoria Day, a national holiday, is usually celebrated throughout Canada on the penultimate weekend in May.

Late June. Canadian International Dragon Boat Festival, Vancouver is a multicultural festival featuring dragon boat races based on Chinese legend. Community and children's activities, dance, and visual arts are featured. Tel. 604/684–5151.

Late June. Du Maurier International Jazz Festival celebrates a broad spectrum of jazz, blues, and related improvised music, with more than 200 performances in 20 locations in Vancouver. Tel. 604/682–0706.

Late June–early July. Fort Vancouver Days in Vancouver is a citywide celebration with rodeo, a bluegrass festival, a chili cook-off, and the largest fireworks display west of the Mississippi. Tel. 206/693–1313.

July 1. Canada Day inspires celebrations around the country in honor of Canada's birthday.

Mid-July. Harrison Festival of the Arts, in Harrison Hot Springs, offers a spectrum of artistic expression with a unique blend of international, national, and regional artists and performers. Tel. 604/796–3664.

Mid-July. Vancouver Sea Festival features water-related activities, such as a wooden- and heritage-boat festival, plus a parade, fireworks, entertainment, and a carnival. Tel. 604/684–3378.

Late July. International Bathtub Race takes to the high seas, from Nanaimo to Vancouver. Tel. 604/754–8474.

Mid-Aug.–early Sept. Pacific National Exhibition, western Canada's biggest annual fair, brings top-name entertainment and a variety of displays to Vancouver. Tel. 604/253–2311.

What to Pack

Clothing Residents of Seattle and Vancouver are generally informal by nature and wear clothing that reflects their disposition. Summer days are warm but evenings can cool off substantially. Layered clothing is the local preference—sweatshirts, sweaters, and jackets are removed or put on as the day progresses. If you plan to explore the cities on foot, or if you choose to hike along mountain trails or beaches, bring comfortable walking shoes.

Dining out is usually an informal affair, although some restaurants require a jacket and tie for men and dresses for women. Residents tend to dress conservatively when going to the theater or symphony, but it's not uncommon to see some patrons wearing jeans. In other words, almost anything is acceptable for most occasions.

Miscellaneous Bring an extra pair of eyeglasses or contact lenses. If you have a health problem that may require you to purchase a prescription drug, pack enough to last the duration of the trip, or have your doctor write a prescription using the drug's generic name, since brand names vary from country to country. And don't forget to pack a list of the addresses of offices that supply refunds for lost or stolen traveler's checks.

Luggage

Regulations Free baggage allowances on an airline depend on the airline, the route, and the class of your ticket. In general, on domestic flights you are entitled to check two bags—neither exceeding 62 inches, or 158 centimeters (length + width + height), or weighing more than 70 pounds (32 kilograms). A third piece may be brought aboard as a carryon; its total dimensions are generally limited to less than 45 inches (114 centimeters), so it will fit easily under the seat in front of you or in the overhead compartment. There are variations, so ask in advance. The single rule, a Federal Aviation Administration safety regulation that pertains to carry-on baggage on U.S. airlines, requires that carryons be properly stowed and allows the airline to limit allowances and tailor them to different aircraft and operational conditions. Charges for excess, oversize, or overweight pieces vary, so inquire before you pack.

Safeguarding Your Luggage Before leaving home, itemize your bags' contents and their worth; this list will help you estimate the extent of your loss if your bags go astray. To minimize that risk, tag them inside and out with your name, address, and phone number. (If you use your home address, cover it so that potential thieves can't see it.) At check-in, make sure that the tag attached by baggage handlers bears the correct three-letter code for your destination. If your bags do not arrive with you, or if you detect damage, do not leave the airport until you've filed a written report with the airline.

Taking Money Abroad

Traveler's Checks Although you will want plenty of cash when visiting small cities or rural areas, traveler's checks are usually preferable. The most widely recognized are **American Express, Citicorp, Thomas Cook,** and **Visa,** which are sold by major commercial banks. American Express also issues *Traveler's Cheques for Two*, which can be countersigned and used by you or your traveling companion. Some checks are free; usually the issuing company or the bank at which you make your purchase charges 1%–2% of the checks' face value as a fee. Be sure to buy a few checks in small denominations to cash toward the end of your trip, when you don't want to be left with more foreign currency than you can spend. Always record the numbers of checks as you spend them, and keep this list separate from the checks.

Currency Exchange American money is readily accepted in much of Canada (especially in communities near the border), but it is advisable to convert U.S. dollars to Canadian dollars at a bank or foreign-exchange office in order to get the most favorable rate. Traveler's checks and major U.S. credit cards are accepted in larger cities and resorts, but in smaller towns and rural areas, you may need cash.

Getting Money from Home

Cash Machines Automated-teller machines (ATMs) are proliferating; many are tied to international networks such as **Cirrus** and **Plus.** You can use your bank card at ATMs away from home to withdraw money from an account and get cash advances on a credit-card account (providing your card has been programmed with a personal identification number, or PIN). Check in advance on limits on withdrawals and cash advances within specified periods. Remember that on cash advances you are charged interest from the day you get the money from ATMs as well as from tellers. And note that transaction fees for ATM withdrawals outside your home turf will probably be higher than for withdrawals at home.

For specific Cirrus locations in the United States and Canada, call 800/424–7787 (for U.S. Plus locations, 800/843–7587), and press the area code and first three digits of the number you're calling from (or the calling area where you want an ATM).

American Express Cardholder Services The company's **Express Cash** system lets you withdraw cash and/or traveler's checks from a worldwide network of 57,000 American Express dispensers and participating bank ATMs. You must *enroll first* (call 800/227–4669 for a form and allow two weeks for processing). Withdrawals are charged not to your card but to a designated bank account. You can withdraw up to $1,000 per seven-day period on the basic card, more if your card is gold or platinum. There is a 2% fee (minimum $2.50, maximum $10) for each cash transaction, and a 1% fee for traveler's checks (except for the platinum card), which are available only from American Express dispensers.

At AmEx offices, cardholders can also cash personal checks for up to $1,000 in any seven-day period; of this, $200 can be in cash, more if available, with the balance paid in traveler's checks, for which all but platinum cardholders pay a 1% fee. Higher limits apply to the gold and platinum cards.

Wiring Money You don't have to be a cardholder to send or receive an **American Express MoneyGram** for up to $10,000. To send one, go to an American Express MoneyGram agent, pay up to $1,000 with a credit card and anything over that in cash, and phone a transaction reference number to your intended recipient, who needs only present identification and the reference number to the nearest MoneyGram agent to pick up the cash. There are MoneyGram agents in more than 60 countries (call 800/543–4080 for locations). Fees range from 5%–10%, depending on the amount and how you pay. You can't use American Express, which is really a convenience card—only Discover, MasterCard, and Visa credit cards.

You can also use **Western Union.** To wire money, take either cash or a check to the nearest office. (Or you can call and use a credit card.) Fees are roughly 5%–10%. Money sent from the United States or Canada will be available for pick up at agent locations within minutes. (Note that once the money is in the system it can be picked up at *any* location. You don't have to miss your train waiting for it to arrive in City A, because if there's an agent in City B, where you're headed, you can pick it up there, too.) There are approximately 20,000 agents worldwide (call 800/325–6000 for locations).

Currency

The United States and Canada both use the same currency denominations—dollars and cents—although each currency has a different value on the world market. In the United States, the most common paper currency comes in $1, $5, $10, and $20 bills. Common notes in Canada include the $2, $5, $10, and $20 bills. (Canada recently phased out its $1 bill, replacing it with a $1 gold-colored coin nicknamed the "loonie" by Canadians because it contains a picture of a loon on one side.) Coins in both countries come in denominations of 1¢ (penny), 5¢ (nickel), 10¢ (dime), 25¢ (quarter), and 50¢.

What It Will Cost

Prices for meals and accommodations in the Pacific North Coast are generally lower than in other major North American regions. Prices for first-class hotel rooms in Seattle and Vancouver range from $100 to $200 a night, although you can still find some "value" hotel rooms for $65 to $90 a night. Most hotels offer weekend packages that offer discounts of up to 50%. Don't look for these special deals during the peak summer season, however, when hotels are nearly filled to capacity.

As a rule, costs outside the major cities are lower, but prices for rooms and meals at some of the major deluxe resorts can rival those at the best big-city hotels.

Compared with many other parts of the world, the Pacific Northwest is a travel bargain. The region is becoming increasingly popular with Japanese visitors, for example, who find prices for hotels, meals, and commodities to be quite a steal.

Prices in Canada are always quoted in Canadian dollars. When comparing prices with those in the United States, costs should be calculated via the current rate of exchange. At press time (fall 1993), the Canadian dollar was worth US$.75, but this exchange rate can vary considerably. Check with a bank or other financial institution for the current rate. A good way to be sure you're getting the best exchange rate is by using your credit card. The issuing bank will convert your bill at the current rate.

Sales tax varies among areas. The sales tax in Washington is 7.9%. Seattle adds 5% to the rate for hotel rooms. Canada's 7% Goods & Services Tax (GST) is added to hotel bills but will be rebated to foreign visitors. (*See* Shopping in Staying in Seattle and Vancouver, *below*). In British Columbia, consumers pay an 8%–10% provincial and municipal tax. The percentage varies from one municipality to another.

Passports and Visas

U.S. and Canadian Citizens Citizens and permanent residents of the United States and Canada are not required to have passports or visas to visit each other's country. However, native-born citizens should carry identification showing proof of citizenship, such as a birth certificate, a voter-registration card, or a valid passport. Naturalized citizens should carry a naturalization certificate or some other proof of citizenship. Individuals under the age of 18 who are not accompanied by their parents should bring a letter from a parent or guardian giving them permission to travel in another country. Permanent residents of the United States who are not U.S. citizens should carry their Alien Registration Receipt Cards. U.S. citizens interested in visiting Canada for more than 90 days may apply for a visa that allows them to stay for six months. For more information, contact the Canadian Embassy (501 Pennsylvania Ave. NW, Washington, DC 20001, tel. 202/682–1740).

U.K Citizens To enter the United States or Canada, you will need a valid, 10-year British passport (£15 for a standard 32-page passport, £30 for a 94-page passport). Note that a one-year British passport is not acceptable for entry under any circumstances. You can obtain passport application forms from most travel agents and major post offices, or from the **Passport Office** (Clive House, 70 Petty France, London SW1H 9HD, tel. 071/279–3434 or 071/279–4000).

You will not need a visa if you are staying in the United States for 90 days or less, have a return or onward ticket on a major airline, and complete a visa waiver form and an arrival/departure card. There are some exceptions to this, so check with your travel agent or with the Visa Unit of the **United States Embassy** (Visa and Immigration Dept., 5 Upper Grosvenor St., London W1A 2JB, tel. 071/499–3443 for recorded information or 071/499–7010). Visa applications must be made by mail. If you will be entering from Canada, you can complete the visa waiver form at the port of entry.

British visitors are not required to have a visa to enter Canada. Their stay in Canada, however, cannot exceed six months without authorization from Canadian immigration.

Customs

Americans may bring home from Canada $400 in foreign goods, as long as you've been out of the United States for at least 48 hours and you haven't made an international trip in 30 days. Each member of the family is entitled to the same exemption regardless of age, and exemptions may be pooled. Visitors to Canada who meet the minimum-age requirements of the province of entry (19 years in British Columbia) may take in either 1.1 liters (40 ounces) of liquor or wine or 24 12-ounce cans or bottles of beer. Visitors over 16 may take in 50 cigars, 200 cigarettes, and 400 grams (14 ounces) of manufactured tobacco. Gifts valued at less than $40 each can also be brought into Canada, providing they do not contain tobacco or alcohol. Gifts valued at more than $40 are subject to regular import duty on the excess amount.

Visitors age 21 or over can take into the United States 200 cigarettes or 50 cigars, or two kilograms of tobacco; one liter of alcohol; and duty-free gifts to a value of $100. For further information on United States customs regulations consult the brochure "Know Before You Go," which carefully outlines what returning U.S. residents may and may not bring back into the country, and at what cost. Contact U.S. Customs Service (1301 Constitution Ave., Washington, DC 20229).

British citizens may import from countries outside the EC such as the United States and Canada 200 cigarettes, 100 cigarillos, 50 cigars or 250 grams of tobacco; 1 liter of spirits or 2 liters of fortified or sparkling wine; 2 liters of still table wine; 60 milliliters of perfume; 250 milliliters of toilet water; plus £36 worth of other goods, including gifts and souvenirs. For further information or a copy of "A Guide for Travellers," which details standard customs procedures as well as what you may bring into the United Kingdom from abroad, contact **HM Customs and Excise** (New King's Beam House, 22 Upper Ground, London SE1 9PJ, tel. 071/620–1313).

Canada has very strict gun-control laws. Firearms with no legitimate sporting or recreational use are not allowed into the country. This includes all handguns, automatic weapons, and any rifle or shotgun that has been modified. For further information on Canadian customs regulations, write to **Revenue Canada** (Customs and Excise, Ottawa, Ont. K1A 0L5, tel. 613/993–6220).

Traveling with Cameras, Camcorders, and Laptops

Film and Cameras If your camera is new or if you haven't used it for a while, shoot and develop a few rolls of film before leaving home. Pack some lens tissue and an extra battery for your built-in light meter and invest in an inexpensive skylight filter, to both protect your lens and provide some definition in hazy shots. Store film in a cool, dry place—never in the car's glove compartment or on the shelf under the rear window.

Films above ISO 400 are more sensitive to damage from airport security X-rays than others; very high speed films, ISO 1000 and above, are exceedingly vulnerable. To protect your film, don't put it in checked luggage; carry it with you in a plastic bag and ask for a hand inspection. Such requests are honored at American airports. Don't depend on a lead-lined bag to protect film in checked luggage—the airline may very well turn up the dosage of radiation to see what you've got in there. Airport metal detectors do not harm film, although you'll set off the alarm if you walk through one with a roll in your pocket. Call the Kodak Information Center (tel. 800/242–2424) for details.

Camcorders Before your trip, put new or long-unused camcorders through their paces, and practice panning and zooming. Invest in a skylight filter to protect the lens, and check the lithium battery that lights up the LCD (liquid crystal display) modes. Take along an extra pair of the rechargeable nickel-cadmium batteries that are the camera's power source, so while you're using your camcorder you'll have one battery ready and another recharging.

Videotape Unlike still-camera film, videotape is not damaged by X-rays. However, it may well be harmed by the magnetic field of a walk-through metal detector. Airport security personnel may want you to turn the camcorder on to prove that it is a camera, so make sure the battery is charged when you get to the airport.

Laptops Security X-rays do not harm hard-disk or floppy-disk storage. Most airlines allow you to use your laptop aloft but request that you turn it off during takeoff and landing so as not to interfere with navigation equipment. Make sure the battery is charged when you arrive at the airport, because you may be asked to turn on the computer at security checkpoints to prove that it is what it appears to be. If you're a heavy computer user, consider traveling with a backup battery.

Language

Canada is officially a bilingual country (English and French). You will see many signs and services offered in both languages; however, little French is spoken on Canada's west coast.

Insurance

For U.S. Residents Most tour operators, travel agents, and insurance agents sell specialized health-and-accident, flight, trip-cancellation, and luggage insurance as well as comprehensive policies with some or all of these features. Before you make any purchase, review your existing health and homeowner policies to find out whether they cover expenses incurred while traveling.

Health-and-Accident Insurance Supplemental health-and-accident insurance for travelers is usually a part of comprehensive policies. Specific policy provisions vary, but they tend to address three general areas, beginning with reimbursement for medical expenses caused by illness or an accident during a trip. Such policies may reimburse anywhere from $1,000 to $150,000 worth of medical expenses; dental benefits may also be included. A second common feature is the personal-accident, or death-and-dismemberment, provision, which pays a lump sum to your beneficiaries if you die or to you if you lose one or both limbs or your eyesight. This is similar to the flight insurance described below, although it is not necessarily limited to accidents involving airplanes or even other "common carriers" (buses, trains, and ships) and can be in effect 24 hours a day. The lump sum awarded can range from $15,000 to $500,000. A third area generally addressed by these policies is medical assistance (referrals, evacuation, or repatriation and other services). Some policies reimburse travelers for the cost of such services; others may automatically enroll you as a member of a particular medical-assistance company.

Flight Insurance This insurance, often bought as a last-minute impulse at the airport, pays a lump sum to a beneficiary when a plane crashes and the insured dies (and sometimes to a surviving passenger who loses eyesight or a limb); thus it supplements the airlines' own coverage as described in the limits-of-liability paragraphs on your ticket (up to $75,000 on international flights, $20,000 on domestic ones—and that is generally subject to litigation). Charging an airline ticket to a major credit card often automatically signs you up for flight insurance; in this case, the coverage may also embrace travel by bus, train, and ship.

Baggage Insurance In the event of loss, damage, or theft on international flights, airlines limit their liability to $20 per kilogram for checked baggage (roughly about $640 per 70-pound bag) and $400 per passenger for unchecked baggage. On domestic flights, the ceiling is $1,250 per passenger. Excess-valuation insurance can be bought directly from the airline at check-in but leaves your bags vulnerable on the ground.

Trip Insurance There are two sides to this coin. **Trip-cancellation-and-interruption insurance** protects you in the event you are unable to undertake or finish your trip. **Default** or **bankruptcy insurance** protects you against a supplier's failure to deliver. Consider the former if your airline ticket, cruise, or package tour does not allow changes or cancellations. The amount of coverage to buy should equal the cost of your trip should you, a traveling companion, or a family member get sick, forcing you to stay home, plus the nondiscounted one-way airline ticket you would need to buy if you had to return home early. Read the fine print carefully; pay attention to sections defining "family member" and "preexisting medical conditions." A characteristic quirk of default policies is that they often do not cover default by travel agencies or default by a tour operator, airline, or cruise line if you bought your tour and the coverage directly from the firm in question. To reduce your need for default insurance, give preference to tours packaged by members of the United States Tour Operators Association (USTOA), which maintains a fund to reimburse clients in the event of member defaults. Even better, pay for travel arrangements with a major credit card, so you can refuse to pay the bill if services have not been rendered—and let the card company fight your battles.

Comprehensive Policies Companies supplying comprehensive policies with some or all of the above features include **Access America, Inc.,** underwritten by BCS Insurance Company (Box 11188, Richmond, VA 23230, tel. 800/284–8300); **Carefree Travel Insurance,** underwritten by The Hartford (Box 310, 120 Mineola Blvd., Mineola, NY 11501, tel. 516/294–0220 or 800/323–3149); **Tele-Trip** (Mutual of Omaha Plaza, Box 31762, Omaha, NE 68131, tel. 800/228–9792), a subsidiary of Mutual of Omaha; **The Travelers Companies** (1 Tower Sq., Hartford, CT 06183, tel. 203/277–0111 or 800/243–3174); **Travel Guard International,** underwritten by Transamerica Occidental Life Companies (1145 Clark St., Stevens Point, WI 54481, tel. 715/345–0505 or 800/782–5151); and **Wallach and Company, Inc.** (107 W. Federal St., Box 480, Middleburg, VA 22117, tel. 703/687–3166 or 800/237–6615).

These companies may also offer the above types of insurance separately.

U.K. Residents Most tour operators, travel agents, and insurance agents sell specialized policies covering accident, medical expenses, personal liability, trip cancellation, and loss or theft of personal property. Some policies include coverage for delayed departure and legal expenses, winter sports, accidents, or motoring abroad. You can also purchase an annual travel-insurance policy valid for every trip you make during the year in which it's purchased (usually only trips of less than 90 days). Before you leave, make sure you will be covered if you have a preexisting medical condition or are pregnant; your insurers may not pay for routine or continuing treatment, or may require a note from your doctor certifying your fitness to travel.

The **Association of British Insurers,** a trade association representing 450 insurance companies, advises extra medical coverage for visitors to the United States.

For advice by phone or a free booklet, "Holiday Insurance," that sets out what to expect from a holiday-insurance policy and gives price guidelines, contact the Association of British Insurers (51 Gresham St., London EC2V 7HQ, tel. 071/600–3333; 30 Gordon St., Glasgow G1 3PU, tel. 041/226–3905; Scottish Provincial Bldg., Donegall Sq. W, Belfast BT1 6JE, tel. 0232/249176; call for other locations).

Car Rentals

All major car-rental companies are represented in the Pacific Northwest, including **Avis** (tel. 800/331–1212 or 800/879–2847 in Canada); **Budget** (tel. 800/527–0700); **Dollar** (tel. 800/800–4000); **Hertz** (tel. 800/654–3131 or 800/263-0600 in Canada); and **National** (tel. 800/227–7368). In cities, unlimited-mileage rates range from about $26 per day for an economy car to $50 for a large car; weekly unlimited-mileage rates range from $105 to $230. Rates are higher in some rural areas.

Requirements Your own U.S., Canadian, or U.K. driver's license is acceptable. If you are taking a rental car across the United States–Canada border, keep a copy of the rental contract with you. It should bear an endorsement stating that the vehicle is permitted entry into the other country.

Extra Charges Picking up the car in one city or country and leaving it in another may entail drop-off charges or one-way service fees, which can be substantial. The cost of a collision or loss-damage waiver (*see below*) may also be high.

Cutting Costs If you know you will want a car for more than a day or two, you can save by planning ahead. Major international companies have programs that discount their standard rates by 15%–30% if you make the reservation before departure (anywhere from two to 14 days), rent for a minimum number of days (typically three or four), and prepay the rental. Ask about these advance-purchase schemes when you call for information. More economical rentals are those that come as part of fly/drive or other packages, even those as bare-bones as the rental plus an airline ticket (*see* Tours and Packages, *above*).

Other sources of savings are the companies that operate as wholesalers—companies that do not own their own fleets but rent in bulk from those that do and offer advantageous rates to their customers. Rentals through such companies must be arranged and paid for in advance. Among them are **Auto Europe** (Box 1097, Camden, ME 04843, tel. 207/236–8235, 800/223–5555, or 800/458–9503 in Canada), **Connex International** (23 N. Division St., Peekskill, NY 10566, tel. 914/739–0066, 800/333–3949, or 800/843–5416 in Canada), and **Europe by Car** (mailing address: 1 Rockefeller Plaza, New York, NY 10020; walk-in address: 14 W. 49th St., New York, NY 10020, tel. 212/581–3040 or 212/245–1713; 9000 Sunset Blvd., Los Angeles, CA 90069, tel. 213/252–9401 or 800/223–1516 in CA). You won't see these wholesalers' deals advertised; they're even better in summer, when business travel is down. Always ask whether unlimited mileage is available. Find out about any required deposits, cancellation penalties, and drop-off charges, and confirm the cost of the collision damage waiver (CDW).

One last tip: Remember to fill the tank when you turn in the vehicle, to avoid being charged for refueling at what you'll swear is the most expensive pump in town.

Insurance and Collision Damage Waiver

The standard rental contract includes liability coverage (for damage to public property, injury to pedestrians, etc.) and coverage for the car against fire, theft (not included in certain countries), and collision damage with a deductible—most commonly \$2,000–\$3,000, occasionally more. In the case of an accident, you are responsible for the deductible amount unless you've purchased the CDW, which costs an average \$12 a day, although this varies depending on what you've rented, where, and from whom.

Because this adds up quickly, you may be inclined to say "no thanks"—and that's certainly your option, although the rental agent may not tell you so. Note before you decline that deductibles are occasionally high enough that totaling a car would make you responsible for its full value. Planning ahead will help you make the right decision. By all means, find out if your own insurance covers damage to a rental car while traveling (not simply a car to drive when yours is in for repairs). And check whether charging car rentals to any of your credit cards will get you a CDW at no charge. In many states, laws mandate that renters be told what the CDW costs, that it's optional, and that their own auto insurance may provide the same protection.

Rail Passes

VIA Rail Canada (tel. 800/665–0200) offers a **Canrailpass** that is good for 30 days. System-wide passes cost \$282 (Jan. 6–June 6 and Oct. 1–Dec. 14) and \$420 (June 7–Sept. 30). Youth passes (age 24 and under) are \$377 in peak season and \$257 during the off-season. Prices are quoted in U.S. dollars. Tickets can be purchased in the United States or the United Kingdom from a travel agent, from **Long Haul Leisurail** (Box 113, Peterborough PE1 1LE, tel. 0733/51780), or upon arrival in Canada. This offer does not apply to Canadian citizens.

Student and Youth Travel

Travel Agencies

The foremost U.S. student travel agency is **Council Travel,** a subsidiary of the nonprofit Council on International Educational Exchange (CIEE). It specializes in low-cost travel arrangements, is the exclusive U.S. agent for several discount cards, and, with its sister CIEE subsidiary, **Council Charter,** is a source of airfare bargains. The Council Charter brochure and CIEE's twice-yearly *Student Travels* magazine, which details its programs, are available at the Council Travel office at CIEE headquarters (205 E. 42nd St., New York, NY 10017, tel. 212/661–1450) and at 37 branches in college towns nationwide (free in person, $1 by mail). The **Educational Travel Center** (ETC, 438 N. Francis St., Madison, WI 53703, tel. 608/256–5551) also offers low-cost rail passes, domestic and international airline tickets (mostly for flights departing from Chicago), and other budgetwise travel arrangements. Other travel agencies catering to students include **Travel Management International** (TMI, 18 Prescott St., Suite 4, Cambridge, MA 02138, tel. 617/661–8187) and **Travel Cuts** (187 College St., Toronto, Ont. M5T 1P7, tel. 416/979–2406).

Discount Cards For discounts on transportation and on museum and attractions admissions, buy the **International Student Identity Card** (ISIC) if you're a bona fide student, or the **International Youth Card** (IYC) if you're under 26. In the United States, the ISIC and IYC cards cost $15 each and include basic travel accident and sickness coverage. Apply to **CIEE** (*see* address *above*, tel. 212/661–1414; the application is in *Student Travels*). In Canada, the cards are available for $15 each from **Travel Cuts** (*see above*). In the United Kingdom, the cards cost £5 and £4 respectively at student unions and student travel companies, including Council Travel's London office (28A Poland St., London W1V 3DB, tel. 071/437–7767).

Hosteling An **International Youth Hostel Federation** (IYHF) membership card is the key to more than 5,300 hostel locations in 59 countries; the sex-segregated, dormitory-style sleeping quarters, including some for families, go for $7–$20 a night per person. Membership is available in the United States through **American Youth Hostels** (AYH, 733 15th St. NW, Washington, DC 20005, tel. 202/783–6161), the American link in the worldwide chain, and costs $25 for adults 18–54, $10 for those under 18, $15 for those 55 and over, and $35 for families. Volume 2 of the two-volume *Guide to Budget Accommodation* lists hostels in Asia and Australasia as well as in Canada and the United States ($13.95 including postage). IYHF membership is available in Canada through the **Canadian Hosteling Association** (1600 James Naismith Dr., Suite 608, Gloucester, Ont. K1B 5N4, tel. 613/748–5638) for $26.75, and in the United Kingdom through the **Youth Hostel Association of England and Wales** (8 St. Stephen's Hill, St. Albans, Herts. AL1 2DY, tel. 0727/55215) for £9.

Traveling with Children

Many local organizations, such as public libraries, museums, parks and recreation departments, and YMCA/YWCAs, have special events throughout the year for children of all ages. Check local newspaper listings for such activities as plays, storytelling, sporting events, and so forth.

Publications *Newsletter* *Family Travel Times*, published 10 times a year by **Travel With Your Children** (TWYCH, 45 W. 18th St., 7th Floor Tower, New York, NY 10011, tel. 212/206–0688; annual subscription $55), covers destinations, types of vacations, and modes of travel.

Books *Traveling with Children—And Enjoying It*, by Arlene K. Butler ($11.95 plus $3 shipping per book; Globe Pequot Press, Box 833, Old Saybrook, CT 06475, tel. 800/243–0495 or 800/962–0973 in CT) helps plan your trip with children, from toddlers to teens. From the same publisher is *Recommended Family Resorts in the United States, Canada, and the Caribbean*, by Jane Wilford with Janet Tice ($12.95).

Tour Operators **GrandTravel** (6900 Wisconsin Ave., Suite 706, Chevy Chase, MD 20815, tel. 301/986–0790 or 800/247–7651) offers international and domestic tours for grandparents traveling with their grandchildren. The catalogue, as charmingly written and illustrated as a children's book, positively invites armchair traveling with lap-sitters aboard. **Rascals in Paradise** (650 5th St., Suite 505, San Francisco, CA 94107, tel. 415/978–9800, or 800/872–7225) specializes in programs for families.

Getting There

Airfares On domestic flights, children under 2 not occupying a seat travel free, and older children currently travel on the "lowest applicable" adult fare.

Baggage The adult baggage allowance applies for children paying half or more of the adult fare. Check with the airline for particulars.

Safety Seats The FAA recommends the use of safety seats aloft and details approved models in the free leaflet ""**Child/Infant Safety Seats Recommended for Use in Aircraft**" (available from the Federal Aviation Administration, APA–200, 800 Independence Ave. SW, Washington, DC 20591, tel. 202/267–3479). Airline policy varies. U.S. carriers must allow FAA-approved models, but because these seats are strapped into a regular passenger seat, they may require that parents buy a ticket even for an infant under 2 who would otherwise ride free.

Facilities Aloft Airlines provide other facilities and services for children, such as children's meals and freestanding bassinets (to those sitting in seats on the bulkhead, where there's enough legroom to accommodate them). Make your request when reserving. The annual February/March issue of *Family Travel Times* gives details of the children's services of dozens of airlines ($10; *see above*). "Kids and Teens in Flight" (free from the U.S. Department of Transportation, tel. 202/366–2220) offers tips for children flying alone.

Baby-Sitting Services Most large hotels offer licensed baby-sitters or referrals. Resorts are more likely to provide children's services than are downtown hotels, which are geared to business travelers. Contact individual hotels for specifics, as facilities vary widely.

Hints for Travelers with Disabilities

Organizations Several organizations provide travel information for people with disabilities, usually for a membership fee, and some publish newsletters and bulletins. Among them are the **Information Center for Individuals with Disabilities** (Fort Point Pl., 27–43 Wormwood St., Boston, MA 02210, tel. 617/727–5540 or 800/462–5015 in MA between 11 and 4, or leave message; TDD/TTY tel. 617/345–9743); **Mobility International USA** (Box 3551, Eugene, OR 97403, voice and TDD tel. 503/343–1284), the U.S. branch of an international organization based in Britain (*see below*) and present in 30 countries; **MossRehab Hospital Travel Information Service** (1200 W. Tabor Rd., Philadelphia, PA 19141, tel. 215/456–9603, TDD tel. 215/456–9602); the **Society for the**

Advancement of Travel for the Handicapped (SATH, 347 5th Ave., Suite 610, New York, NY 10016, tel. 212/447–7284, fax 212/725–8253); the **Travel Industry and Disabled Exchange** (TIDE, 5435 Donna Ave., Tarzana, CA 91356, tel. 818/368–5648); and **Travelin' Talk** (Box 3534, Clarksville, TN 37043, tel. 615/552–6670).

In Canada The **Canadian Paraplegic Association** (780 S.W. Marine Dr., Vancouver, BC V6P 5Y7, tel. 604/324–3611) provides information on touring British Columbia for travelers with disabilities. Information for the hearing-impaired is available from the **Western Institute for the Deaf** (2125 W. 7th Ave., Vancouver, BC V6K 1X9, tel. 604/736–7391, TDD 604/736–2527). The annual *British Columbia Accommodation Guide* (tel. 800/663–6000) includes a list of hotel facilities for individuals who are disabled.

In the United Kingdom Main information sources include the **Royal Association for Disability and Rehabilitation** (RADAR, 25 Mortimer St., London W1N 8AB, tel. 071/637–5400), which publishes travel information for the disabled in Britain, and **Mobility International** (228 Borough High St., London SE1 1JX, tel. 071/403–5688), the headquarters of an international membership organization that serves as a clearinghouse of travel information for people with disabilities.

Travel Agencies and Tour Operators **Directions Unlimited** (720 N. Bedford Rd., Bedford Hills, NY 10507, tel. 914/241–1700), a travel agency, has expertise in tours and cruises for the disabled. **Evergreen Travel Service** (4114 198th St. SW, Suite 13, Lynnwood, WA 98036, tel. 206/776–1184 or 800/435–2288) operates Wings on Wheels Tours for those in wheelchairs, White Cane Tours for the blind, and tours for the deaf and makes group and independent arrangements for travelers with any disability. **Flying Wheels Travel** (143 W. Bridge St., Box 382, Owatonna, MN 55060, tel. 800/535–6790 or 800/722–9351 in MN), a tour operator and travel agency, arranges international tours, cruises, and independent travel itineraries for people with mobility disabilities. **Nautilus,** at the same address as TIDE (*see above*), packages tours for the disabled internationally.

Publications The Easter Seal Society (521 2nd Ave. W, Seattle, WA 98119, tel. 206/281–5700) publishes ***Access Seattle,*** a free guide to the city's services for the disabled.

Several free publications are available from the Consumer Information Center (Pueblo, CO 81009): "New Horizons for the Air Traveler with a Disability," a U.S. Department of Transportation booklet describing changes resulting from the 1986 Air Carrier Access Act and those still to come from the 1990 Americans with Disabilities Act (include Department 608Y in the address), and the Airport Operators Council's *Access Travel: Airports* (Dept. 5804), which describes facilities and services for the disabled at more than 500 airports worldwide.

Twin Peaks Press (Box 129, Vancouver, WA 98666, tel. 206/694–2462 or 800/637–2256) publishes the *Directory of Travel Agencies for the Disabled* ($19.95), listing more than 370 agencies worldwide; *Travel for the Disabled* ($19.95), listing some 500 access guides and accessible places worldwide; the *Directory of Accessible Van Rentals* ($9.95) for campers and RV travelers worldwide; and *Wheelchair Vagabond* ($14.95), a collection of personal travel tips. Add $2 per book for shipping. The Sierra Club publishes *Easy Access to National Parks* ($16 plus $3 shipping; 730 Polk St., San Francisco, CA 94109, tel. 415/776-2211).

Hints for Older Travelers

Organizations The **American Association of Retired Persons** (AARP, 601 E St. NW, Washington, DC 20049, tel. 202/434-2277) provides independent travelers the Purchase Privilege Program, which offers discounts on hotels, car rentals, and sightseeing, and the AARP Motoring Plan, provided by Amoco, which furnishes domestic trip-routing information and emergency road-service aid for an annual fee of $39.95 per person or couple ($59.95 for a premium version). AARP also arranges group tours, cruises, and apartment living through AARP Travel Experience from American Express (400 Pinnacle Way, Suite 450, Norcross, GA 30071, tel. 800/927-0111); these can be booked through travel agents, except for the cruises, which must be booked directly (tel. 800/745-4567). AARP membership is open to those 50 and over; annual dues are $8 per person or couple.

Two other membership organizations offer discounts on lodgings, car rentals, and other travel products, along with such nontravel perks as magazines and newsletters. The **National Council of Senior Citizens** (1331 F St. NW, Washington, DC 20004, tel. 202/347-8800) is a nonprofit advocacy group with some 5,000 local clubs across the United States; membership costs $12 per person or couple annually. **Mature Outlook** (6001 N. Clark St., Chicago, IL 60660, tel. 800/336-6330), a Sears Roebuck & Co. subsidiary with 800,000 members, charges $9.95 for an annual membership.

Note: When using any senior-citizen identification card for reduced hotel rates, mention it when booking, not when checking out. At restaurants, show your card before you're seated; discounts may be limited to certain menus, days, or hours. If you are renting a car, ask about promotional rates that might improve on your senior-citizen discount.

Educational Travel **Elderhostel** (75 Federal St., 3rd floor, Boston, MA 02110, tel. 617/426-7788) is a nonprofit organization that has offered inexpensive study programs for people 60 and older since 1975. Programs are held at more than 1,800 educational institutions in the United States, Canada, and 45 other countries; courses cover everything from marine science to Greek myths and cowboy poetry. Participants generally attend lectures in the morning and spend the afternoon sightseeing or on field trips; they live in dorms on the host campuses. Fees for programs in the United States and Canada, which usually last one week, run about $300, not including transportation.

Tour Operators **Saga International Holidays** (222 Berkeley St., Boston, MA 02116, tel. 800/343-0273), which specializes in group travel for people over 60, offers a selection of variously priced tours and cruises covering five continents. If you want to take your grandchildren, look into **GrandTravel** (*see* Traveling with Children, *above*).

Further Reading

History The late Bill Spiedel, one of Seattle's most colorful characters, wrote about the early history of the city in books replete with lively anecdotes and legends; *Sons of the Profits* and *Doc Maynard* are two of his best. *Washingtonians, A Biographical Portrait of the State,* edited by David Brewster and David M. Buerge, is a series of essays on well-known and influential residents who have left their mark on the state.

At the Field's End, by Nicolas O'Connell, features interviews with 20 leading writers who are all closely connected to the Pacific Northwest and reflect the character of the region. *Whistlepunks and Geoducks—Oral Histories from the Pacific Northwest,* by Ron Strickland, is a collection of stories told by old-timers from all walks of life in Washington State. Gloria Snively's *Exploring the Seashore* offers a guide to shorebirds and intertidal plants and animals in Washington, Oregon, and British Columbia. The *Northwest Sportsman Almanac,* edited by Terry W. Sheely, provides an in-depth guide to fishing and hunting in the Pacific North Coast.

Fiction Well-known fiction writers of the region include Raymond Carver, Ursula LeGuin, Jean Auel, Aaron Elkin, Frank Herbert, J. A. Jance, Ken Kesey, W. P. Kinsella, Jack Hodgin, Tom Robbins, Willo Davis Roberts, William Stafford, Walt Morey, and Norman Maclean.

Arriving and Departing

From North America by Plane

Flights are either nonstop, direct, or connecting. A **nonstop** flight requires no change of plane and makes no stops. A **direct** flight stops at least once and can involve a change of plane, although the flight number remains the same; if the first leg is late, the second waits. This is not the case with a **connecting** flight, which involves a different plane and a different flight number.

Airports and Airlines There are international airports in Seattle and Vancouver. All major U.S. carriers—**Alaska** (tel. 800/426–0333), **American** (tel. 800/433–7300), **Continental** (tel. 800/525–0280), **Delta** (tel. 800/221–1212), **Northwest** (tel. 800/225–2525), **TWA** (tel. 800/221–2000), **United** (tel. 800/241–6522), and **USAir** (tel. 800/428–4322)—offer regular flights into Seattle from points throughout the United States. **American Airlines, Delta,** and **United** fly direct to Vancouver from various points in the United States. **Air Canada** (tel. 800/663–8868) and **Canadian Airlines International** (tel. 800/426–7000) offer frequent service from all major Canadian cities to Vancouver.

Flying Time Nonstop flying time from New York to Seattle is approximately 5 hours; flights from Chicago are about 4–4½ hours; flights between Los Angeles and Seattle take 2½ hours. Flights from New York to Vancouver take about 8 hours with connections; from Chicago, about 4½ hours nonstop; and from Los Angeles, about 3 hours nonstop.

Cutting Flight Costs The Sunday travel section of most newspapers is a good source of deals. When booking, particularly through an unfamiliar company, call the Better Business Bureau to find out whether any complaints have been registered against the company, pay with a credit card if you can, and consider trip-cancellation and default insurance.

Promotional Airfares All the less expensive fares, called promotional or discount fares, are round-trip and involve restrictions. The exact nature of the restrictions depends on the airline, the route, and the season and on whether travel is domestic or international, but you must usually buy the ticket—commonly called an APEX (advance purchase excursion) when it's for international travel—in advance (seven, 14, or 21 days are usual). You must also respect certain minimum- and maximum-stay requirements (for instance, over a Saturday night or at least seven and no more than 30, 45, or 90 days), and you must be willing to pay penalties for changes. Airlines generally allow some changes for a fee. But the cheaper the fare, the more likely the ticket is to be nonrefundable; it would take a death in the family for the airline to give you any of your money back if you had to cancel. The lowest fares are also subject to availability; because only a certain percentage of the plane's total seats will be sold at that price, they may go quickly.

Consolidators Consolidators or bulk-fare operators—also known as bucket shops—buy blocks of seats on scheduled flights that airlines anticipate they won't be able to sell. They pay wholesale prices, add a markup, and resell the seats to travel agents or directly to the public at prices that still undercut the airline's promotional or discount fares. You pay more than on a charter but ordinarily less than for an APEX ticket, and, even when there is not much of a price difference, the ticket usually comes without the advance-purchase restriction. Moreover, although tickets are marked nonrefundable so you can't turn them in to the airline for a full-fare refund, some consolidators sometimes give you your money back. Carefully read the fine print detailing penalties for changes and cancellations. If you doubt the reliability of a company, call the airline once you've made your booking and confirm that you do, indeed, have a reservation on the flight.

The biggest U.S. consolidator, C.L. Thomson Express, sells only to travel agents. Well-established consolidators selling to the public include **Council Charter** (205 E. 42nd St., New York, NY 10017, tel. 212/661–0311 or 800/800–8222), a division of the Council on International Educational Exchange and a longtime charter operator now functioning more as a consolidator; **Travac** (989 6th Ave., New York, NY 10018, tel. 212/563–3303 or 800/872–8800), also a former charterer; and **UniTravel** (Box 12485, St. Louis, MO 63132, tel. 314/569–0900 or 800/325–2222).

Charter Flights Charters usually have the lowest fares and the most restrictions. Departures are limited and seldom on time, and you can lose all or most of your money if you cancel. (Generally, the closer to departure you cancel, the more you lose, although sometimes you will be charged only a small fee if you supply a substitute passenger.) The charterer, on the other hand, may legally cancel the flight for any reason up to 10 days before departure; within 10 days of departure, the flight may be canceled only if it becomes physically impossible to operate it. The charterer may also revise the itinerary or increase the price after you have bought the ticket, but if the new arrangement constitutes a "major change," you have the right to a refund. Before buying a charter ticket, read the fine print for the company's refund policy and details on major changes. Money for charter flights is usually paid into a bank escrow account, the name of which should be on the contract. If you don't pay by credit card, make your check payable to the escrow account (unless you're dealing with a travel agent, in which case, his or her check should be payable to the escrow account). The Department of Transportation's Consumer Affairs Office (I–25, Washington, DC 20590, tel. 202/366–2220) can answer questions on charters and send you its "Plane Talk: Public Charter Flights" information sheet.

Charter operators may offer flights alone or with ground arrangements that constitute a charter package. Well-established charter operators include **Council Charter** (205 E. 42nd St., New York, NY 10017, tel. 212/661–0311 or 800/800–8222), now largely a consolidator, despite its name, and **Travel Charter** (1120 E. Long Lake Rd., Troy, MI 48098, tel. 313/528–3500 or 800/521–5267), with Midwestern departures. **DER Tours** (Box 1606, Des Plains, IL 60017, tel. 800/782–2424), a charterer and consolidator, sells through travel agents.

Discount Travel Clubs

Travel clubs offer their members unsold space on airplanes, cruise ships, and package tours at nearly the last minute and at well below the original cost. Suppliers thus receive some revenue for their "leftovers," and members get a bargain. Membership generally includes a regular bulletin or access to a toll-free telephone hot line giving details of available trips departing anywhere from three or four days to several months in the future. Packages tend to be more common than flights alone, so if airfares are your only interest, read the literature before joining. Reductions on hotels are also available. Clubs include **Discount Travel International** (114 Forrest Ave., Suite 203, Narberth, PA 19072, tel. 215/668–7184; $45 annually, single or family), **Moment's Notice** (425 Madison Ave., New York, NY 10017, tel. 212/486–0503; $45 annually, single or family), **Travelers Advantage** (CUC Travel Service, 49 Music Sq. W, Nashville, TN 37203, tel. 800/548–1116; $49 annually, single or family), and **Worldwide Discount Travel Club** (1674 Meridian Ave., Miami Beach, FL 33139, tel. 305/534–2082; $50 annually for family, $40 single).

Smoking

Smoking is now banned on all domestic flights of less than six hours' duration in the United States, and on all Canadian flights, including flights to and from Europe and the Far East.

From the U.S. by Car

The U.S. interstate highway network provides quick and easy access to the Pacific North Coast in spite of imposing mountain barriers. From the south, I–5 runs from the U.S.–Mexican border through California, into Oregon and Washington, and ends at the U.S.–Canadian border. Most of the population is clustered along this corridor. From the east, I–90 stretches from Boston to Seattle.

The main entry point into Canada by car is on I–5 at Blaine, Washington, 30 miles south of Vancouver. Two major highways enter British Columbia from the east: the Trans-Canada Highway (the longest highway in the world, running more than 5,000 miles from St. John's, Newfoundland, to Victoria, British Columbia) and the Yellowhead Highway, which runs through northern British Columbia from the Rocky Mountains to Prince Rupert.

Border-crossing procedures are usually quick and simple (*see* Passports and Visas *and* Customs, *above*). The I-5 border crossing at Blaine, WA, is open 24 hours a day and is one of the busiest border crossings anywhere between the United States and Canada. Peak traffic times at the border northbound into Canada are daily at 4 PM. Southbound, delays can be expected evenings and weekend mornings. Try to plan on reaching the border at off-peak times. There are smaller highway border stations at various other points between Washington and British Columbia, but they may be closed at night.

From the U.S. by Train

Amtrak (tel. 800/872–7245), the U.S. passenger rail system, has daily service to the Pacific North Coast from the midwestern United States and California. The *Empire Builder* takes a northern route from Chicago to Seattle. The *Coast Starlight* begins in Los Angeles, makes stops throughout western Oregon and Washington, and terminates its route in Seattle. At present, there are no trains that cross the border from Seattle into Canada.

Canada's passenger service, **VIA Rail Canada** (tel. 800/665–0200), operates transcontinental routes on the *Canadian* three times weekly between eastern Canada and Vancouver. During the summer months, this service expands to six weekly trips on the western leg of the trip between Jasper, Alberta, and Vancouver.

From the U.S. by Bus

Greyhound Lines (tel. 800/231–2222) operates bus service to Washington and British Columbia from various points in the United States and Canada. Bus service in North America—though fairly economical—has not been a first-class means of travel in recent years. But Greyhound and other bus companies are taking great pains to improve service. New amenities may include an on-board host/hostess, meals, and VCRs.

From the U.K. by Plane

Airlines and Airfares British travelers reach the Pacific North Coast via the main international gateways of Seattle and Vancouver.

British Airways (tel. 081/897–4000) services Seattle and Vancouver from Heathrow. **KLM** (tel. 081/751–9000; in U.S. tel. 800/777–5553) travels to Vancouver from 25 U.K. and Irish airports via Amsterdam. **Air Canada** (tel. 081/759–2636) flies from Heathrow to Vancouver; **Canadian Airlines International** (tel. 081/667–0666 or 0345/616767 outside London) services Vancouver from Gatwick.

Fares on scheduled flights vary considerably. January to March are the cheapest months to fly, and midweek flights nearly always offer some reductions.

Charters With weekly flights to Vancouver, **Globespan Ltd.** (tel. 0293/562690), **ASAT** (tel. 0737/778560), and **Unijet** (tel. 0444/459100) offer sizable reductions on fares. At press time, prices began at £425 round-trip. You can also find good deals through specialized ticket agencies such as **Travel Cuts** (tel. 071/637–3161).

Staying in Seattle and Vancouver

Getting Around

By Plane Regional air travel has changed considerably in the past few years. National carriers have given up many of their shorter routes to secondary cities, but smaller, regional companies have taken up the slack. These companies are often owned by, or have joint marketing and reservation systems with, larger airlines. Instead of operating jets, they often fly turboprop planes that hold 10–50 passengers.

Leading regional carriers in the Pacific North Coast are **Horizon Air** (tel. 800/547–9308) and **United Express** (tel. 800/241–6522). The two airlines provide frequent service between cities in Washington. Horizon Air also flies internationally from Seattle to Vancouver and Victoria.

The two major regional carriers in Canada are **Air BC** (tel. 800/663–8868 or 800/776–3000) and **Canadian Partner** (tel. 800/426–7000). They serve communities throughout western Canada and have daily flights from Vancouver and Victoria into Seattle. **Helijet Airways** (tel. 604/273–1414) provides jet helicopter service from Vancouver to Victoria as well as Whistler ski resort.

With all the water surrounding the Pacific North Coast, float planes are a common and convenient means of transportation. Accommodating 5–15 passengers, the planes fly at fairly low elevations and provide a great way to see the scenery.

In addition to its regular airport service, Air BC has float-plane service between Vancouver and Victoria harbors. **Kenmore Air** (tel. 800/543–9595) has scheduled flights from Seattle's Lake Union to Victoria and points in the San Juan Islands. Along with several other float-plane companies, Kenmore provides fly-in service to remote fishing resorts along the coast of British Columbia.

By Train The Pacific North Coast has a number of scenic train routes in addition to those operated by Amtrak and VIA Rail Canada. The **Rocky Mountaineer** (Great Canadian Railtour Co., Ltd., 340 Brooksbank Ave., Suite 104, North Vancouver, BC V7J 2C1, tel. 800/665–7245) is a two-day rail cruise between Vancouver and the Canadian Rockies, May–October. There are two routes—one to Banff/Calgary and the other to Jasper—through landscapes considered to be the most spectacular in the world. An overnight hotel stop is made in Kamloops.

On Vancouver Island, VIA Rail (tel. 604/383–4324) runs the *E&N Railway* daily from Victoria north to Nanaimo. **BC Rail** (Box 8770, Vancouver, B.C. V6B 4X6, tel. 604/631–3500) operates daily service from its North Vancouver terminal to the town of Prince George. At Prince George, it is possible to connect with VIA Rail's *Skeena* service east to Jasper and Alberta or west to Prince Rupert. BC Rail also operates a summertime excursion steam train, the *Royal Hudson*, between North Vancouver and Squamish, at the head of Howe Sound.

By Bus

Scheduled Service **Greyhound Lines** (tel. 800/231–2222) operates regular intercity bus routes to points throughout the region. **Gray Line of Seattle** (tel. 206/624–5077) has daily bus service between Seattle and Victoria via the Washington State ferry at Anacortes. Smaller bus companies provide service within local areas. One such service, **Pacific Coach Lines** (tel. 800/661–1725), runs from downtown Vancouver to Victoria (via the British Columbia ferry system). **Quick Coach Lines** (tel. 604/244–3744, 800/655–2122 in U.S.) provides bus service from Seattle's Sea-Tac Airport to Vancouver, stopping at major hotels and the cruise terminal.

Charters Several companies operate charter bus service and scheduled sightseeing tours that last from a few hours to several days. Most tours can be booked locally and provide a good way for visitors to see the sights comfortably within a short period of time. **Gray Line** companies in Seattle (tel. 206/624–5077), Vancouver (tel. 604/681–8687), and Victoria (tel. 604/388–5248) run such sightseeing trips.

By Car

Highway travel in the Pacific North Coast is largely determined by the geography of the region. In Washington and British Columbia, roads that run east to west are limited to a few mountain passes.

Speed Limits The speed limit on U.S. interstate highways is 65 miles per hour in rural areas and 55 miles per hour in urban zones and on secondary highways. In Canada (where the metric system is used), the speed limit is usually 100 kilometers per hour on expressways and 80 kilometers per hour on secondary roads.

Insurance Vehicle insurance is compulsory in the United States and Canada. Motorists are required to produce evidence of insurance if they become involved in an accident. Upon arrival, visitors from foreign countries should contact an insurance agent or broker to obtain the necessary insurance for North America.

Winter Driving Winter driving in the Pacific North Coast can sometimes present some real challenges. In coastal areas, the mild, damp climate contributes to roadways that are frequently wet. Winter snowfalls are not common (generally only once or twice a year), but when snow does fall, traffic grinds to a halt and the roadways become treacherous and stay that way until the snow melts.

Tire chains, studs, or snow tires are essential equipment for winter travel in mountain areas. If you're planning to drive into high elevations, be sure to check the weather forecast beforehand. Even the main-highway mountain passes can be forced to close because of snow conditions. During the winter months, state and provincial highway departments operate snow advisory telephone lines that give pass conditions.

Auto Clubs The **American Automobile Association** (AAA) and the **Canadian Automobile Association** (CAA) provide full services to members of any of the Commonwealth Motoring Conference (CMC) clubs, including the Automobile Association, the Royal Automobile Club, and the Royal Scottish Automobile Club. Services are also available to members of the Alliance Internationale de l'Automobile (AIT), the Federation Internationale de l'Automobile (FIA), and the Federation of Interamerican Touring and Automobile Clubs (FITAC). Members receive travel information, itineraries, maps, tour books, information about road and weather conditions, emergency road services, and travel-agency services.

By Ferry Ferries play an important part in the transportation network of the Pacific North Coast. In some areas, ferries provide the only form of access into and out of communities. In other places, ferries transport thousands of commuters a day to and from work in the cities. For visitors, ferries are one of the best ways to get a feel for the region and its ties to the sea.

British Columbia The **British Columbia Ferry Corporation** (1112 Fort St., Victoria, B.C. V8V 4V2, tel. 604/386–3431 in Victoria or 604/669–1211 in Vancouver; for recorded schedule information, tel. 604/656–0757 in Victoria or 604/685–1021 in Vancouver) operates one of the largest and most modern ferry fleets in the world, with 38 ships serving 42 ports of call along the coast of British Columbia. More than 15 million passengers ride this fleet each year.

The busiest ferries operate between the mainland and Vancouver Island, carrying passengers, cars, campers, RVs, trucks, and buses. Peak traffic times are Friday afternoons, Saturday mornings, and Sunday afternoons, especially during summer months and holiday weekends. The company also provides scheduled service on the *Queen of the North* between Port Hardy at the northern end of Vancouver Island and the port city of Prince Rupert. From there, connections can be made to Alaskan ferries that travel still farther north, or to a VIA Rail train heading east through the Canadian Rockies. Connections to the Queen Charlotte Islands (reservations strongly recommended) can also be made via another British Columbia ferry.

The *Queen of the North* sails every two days during the summer and once a week during the winter. Summer cruises (June–Sept.) take 15 hours (all in daylight), so passengers can enjoy every bit of the spectacular coastal scenery. Reservations are strongly recommended. For reservations, contact British Columbia Ferry Corporation (*see above*).

Clipper Navigation (2701 Alaskan Way, Pier 69, Seattle, WA 98121, tel. 800/888–2535) operates three passenger-only jet catamarans between Seattle and Victoria; the largest holds 300 people, the smallest 250. Each boat makes the scenic crossing in just under three hours. A longer run (five hours) that includes stops in Friday Harbor and Port Townsend has recently been added.

Black Ball Transport's (430 Belleville St., Victoria, B.C. V8V 1W9, tel. 604/386–2202 in Victoria or 206/457–4491 in Port Angeles) MV *Coho* makes daily crossings year-round, from Port Angeles to Victoria. The *Coho* can carry 800 passengers and 100 cars across the Strait of Juan de Fuca in 1½ hours. Advance reservations are not accepted.

Gray Line Cruises (tel. 206/738–8099) operates the 200 passenger-only *Victoria Star,* which provides boat service between Bellingham and Victoria from mid-May to mid-October.

Victoria Rapid Transit operates the passenger-only *Victoria Express* (Box 1928, Port Angeles, WA 98362, tel. 206/452–8088 or 800/633–1589 for reservations in Washington) and offers a one-hour crossing of the Strait of Juan de Fuca between Port Angeles and Victoria from the end of May through the end of October.

Washington The **Washington State Ferry System** (Colman Dock, Seattle, WA 98104, tel. 206/464-6400 or 800/843-3779 in WA) has 25 ferries in its fleet, which carries more than 23 million passengers a year between points on Puget Sound and the San Juan Islands. Reservations are not available on any domestic routes.

If you are planning to take a ferry, try to avoid peak commuter hours. The heaviest traffic flows are eastbound in the mornings and on Sunday evenings, and westbound on Saturday mornings and weekday afternoons. The best times for travel are 9–3 and after 7 PM on weekdays. In July and August, you may have to wait up to two hours to take a car aboard one of the popular San Juan Islands ferries. Walk-on space is always available; if possible, leave your car behind.

By Cruise Ship Cruise ships travel British Columbia's Inside Passage to Alaska from mid-May through early October. Most ships start or end their seven-day journeys in Vancouver, making stops at several Alaskan ports along the way. A few companies provide land tours in conjunction with their week-long cruises into the Yukon Territory and other parts of Alaska.

Telephones

The telephone area codes in the Pacific North Coast are 206 for western Washington, including Seattle, and 604 for British Columbia.

Pay telephones cost 25¢ for local calls. Charge phones are also found in many locations. These phones can be used to charge a call to a telephone-company credit card, your home phone, or the party you are calling: You do not need to deposit 25¢. For directory assistance, dial 1, the area code, and 555–1212. For local directory assistance, dial 1 followed by 555–1212. You can dial most international calls direct. Dial "0" to reach an operator.

Many hotels place a surcharge on local calls made from your room and include a service charge on long-distance calls. It may be cheaper for you to make your calls from a pay phone in the hotel lobby rather than from your room.

Radio Stations

The air waves are packed in Seattle and Vancouver, but the following are the top stations.

Seattle **KBSG-AM (1210)/FM (97.3)**, '50s, '60s, and '70s music; **KING-FM (98.1)**, classical; **KIRO-AM (710)**, news, sports, and features; **KMPS-AM (1300)/FM (94.1)**, country music; **KUOW-FM (94.9)**, National Public Radio—news, classical music, and features; and **KUBE-FM (93.3)**, contemporary rock.

Vancouver **CFOX-FM (99.3)**, contemporary rock; **CFUN-AM (1410)/FM (100.1)**, oldies and hits; **CBU-AM (1370)**, CBC Radio—news and features; and **CJJR-FM (93.7)**, country music.

Mail

Postal Rates Postage rates vary for different classes of mail and destinations. Check with the local post office for rates before mailing a letter or parcel. At press time, it cost 29¢ to mail a standard letter anywhere within the United States. Mail to Canada cost 40¢ per first ounce, and 23¢ for each additional ounce; mail to Great Britain and other foreign countries cost 50¢ per half-ounce.

First-class rates in Canada are 46¢ for up to 30 grams of mail delivered within Canada, 52¢ for up to 30 grams delivered to the United States, 70¢ for up to 50 grams. International mail and postcards run 92¢ for up to 20 grams, $1.26 for 20–50 grams.

Receiving Mail Visitors can have letters or parcels sent to them while they are traveling by using the following address: Name of addressee, c/o General Delivery, Main Post Office, City and State/Province, U.S./Canada, Zip Code (U.S.) or Postal Code (Canada). Contact the nearest post office for further details. Any item mailed to "General Delivery" must be picked up by the addressee in person within 15 days or it will be returned to the sender.

Tipping

Tips and service charges are usually not automatically added to a bill in the United States or Canada. If service is satisfactory, customers generally give waiters, waitresses, taxi drivers, barbers, hairdressers, and so forth, a tip of 15%–20% of the total bill. Bellhops, doormen, and porters at airports and railway stations are generally tipped $1 for each item of luggage.

Opening and Closing Times

British Columbia In British Columbia, many stores close on Sunday. Outlets that cater to tourists are the notable exception. Normal banking hours in Canada are 10–3 on weekdays, with extended hours in many locations. Some banks in major cities are now open on Saturday morning.

Washington Most retail stores in Washington are open 9:30–6 seven days a week in downtown locations and later at suburban shopping malls. Downtown stores sometimes stay open late Thursday and Friday nights. Normal banking hours are weekdays 9–6; some branches are also open on Saturday morning.

Shopping

What to Buy The Pacific North Coast offers shoppers quite a selection of locally made crafts and souvenirs. Some of the most distinctive items are produced by Native American artists, who manufacture prints, wood carvings, boxes, masks, and other items. Shops in Seattle and Vancouver carry a wide variety of these objects, but collectors can find the best selection and prices in the small communities located on Vancouver Island.

Another popular "souvenir" for visitors is freshly caught salmon. Fish vendors can pack a recent catch in a special airlines-approved box that will keep the fish fresh for a couple of days. A package of smoked salmon—which will keep even longer—is another alternative.

Public markets are among the best places to purchase salmon and other gifts. Seattle's historic Pike Place Market and Vancouver's Granville Island Market offer a wonderful array of fish stalls, fresh fruit and vegetable stands, arts and crafts vendors, and small shops that sell practically everything.

Because residents of the Pacific North Coast have such an active lifestyle, many leading manufacturers and retailers of outdoor equipment and apparel have their headquarters there. Recreation Equipment Inc. (REI) has several stores in the Seattle area that sell everything from high-quality sleeping bags and backpacks to freeze-dried food and mountain-climbing equipment. Eddie Bauer, the famous recreational clothing and equipment catalog distributor and retailer, was founded in Seattle and still has outlets there.

Taxes Washington's tax is 7%–8.2%, depending on municipality; provincial sales tax in British Columbia is 6%. Canada's Goods and Services Tax (GST) is 7%, applicable on virtually every purchase except basic groceries and a small number of other items. Visitors to Canada may claim a full rebate of the GST on any goods taken out of the country as well as on short-term accommodations. Rebates can be claimed either immediately on departure from Canada at participating duty-free shops or by mail. Rebate forms can be obtained at most stores and hotels in Canada or by writing to **Revenue Canada** (Visitor's Rebate Program, Ottawa, Ontario, Canada K1A 1J5, tel. 613/991–3346 or 800/668–4748 in Canada). Claims must be for a minimum of $7 worth of tax and can be submitted up to a year from the date of purchase. Purchases made during multiple visits to Canada can be grouped together for rebate purposes.

Participant Sports and Outdoor Activities

Bicycling Bicycling is a popular sport in the Pacific North Coast, appealing to both families out for a leisurely ride and avid cyclists seeking a challenge on rugged mountain trails.

Several cycling organizations sponsor trips of various lengths and degrees of difficulty, both on- and off-road. For further information, contact **Washington State Bicycle Association** (tel. 206/329–2453), **Cascade Bicycle Club** (tel. 206/522–2453), and **Bicycling Association of British Columbia** (1200 Hornby St., Vancouver, B.C. V6Z 2E2, tel. 604/669–2453).

Rentals are available from bicycle shops in most cities.

Boating The sheltered waters of Puget Sound plus the area's many freshwater lakes, make boating one of the most popular outdoor activities in the Pacific North Coast. On sunny days, a virtual fleet of boats dots the waterways; in fact, some experts say that there are more boats per capita in the Puget Sound area than anywhere else in the world.

Because of the region's mild climate, it is possible to enjoy boating throughout the year. Charters, which are available with or without a skipper and crew, can be rented for a period of a few hours to several days. The calm waterways are also rated among the best in the world for sea kayaking, an appealing way to explore the intertidal regions. **The Trade Association of Sea**

Kayaking (TASK) (Box 84144, Seattle, WA 98124, tel. 206/621–1018) provides information on outfitters, rentals, seminars, and safety.

Cruising and particularly deep-sea-fishing charters are available from many ports throughout the Pacific North Coast. The area's swift rivers also provide challenges to avid canoers and kayakers. A word of warning, however: Many of these rivers should be attempted only by experienced boaters. Check with local residents or outfitters to find out what dangers may lie downstream before taking to the waterways.

Climbing/ Mountaineering The mountains of the Pacific North Coast have given many an adventurer quite a challenge. It is no coincidence that many members of the U.S. expedition teams to Mt. Everest have come from this region.

With expert training and advanced equipment, mountaineering can be a safe sport, but you should never go climbing without an experienced guide. Classes are available from qualified instructors. For more information, contact **The Mountaineers** (300 3rd Ave. W, Seattle, WA 98119, tel. 206/284–8484), and **Rainier Mountaineering Inc.** (Paradise, WA 98397, tel. 206/569–2227).

Fishing The coastal regions and inland lakes and rivers of the Pacific Northwest are known for their excellent fishing opportunities. Fishing lodges, many of which are accessible only by float plane, cater to anglers in search of the ultimate fishing experience.

Visiting sportsmen must possess a nonresident license for the state or province in which they plan to fish. Licenses are easily obtainable at sporting-goods stores, bait shops, and other outlets in popular fishing areas.

For information on fishing regulations, contact **Washington Department of Fisheries** (Administration Bldg., Room 115, Olympia, WA 98504, tel. 206/586–1425 for Washington salmon fishing or marine licenses) or the **Washington State Department of Wildlife** (600 Capitol Way N, Olympia, WA 98501, tel. 206/753–5700 for freshwater fishing). In British Columbia, separate licenses are required for saltwater and freshwater fishing. Information and licenses for saltwater fishing can be obtained from the **Department of Fisheries and Oceans** (555 W. Hastings St., Suite 400, Vancouver, BC V6B 5G3, tel. 604/666–0384). For freshwater fishing, contact the **Ministry of Environment, Fish and Wildlife Information** (Parliament Bldgs., Victoria, BC V8V 1X5, tel. 604/387–9740).

Golf The Pacific North Coast has many excellent golf courses, but not all of them are open to the public. Consequently, visitors may find it difficult to arrange a tee time at a popular course. If you are a member of a golf club at home, check to see if your club has a reciprocal playing arrangement with any of the private clubs in the areas that you will be visiting.

Hiking There are many trails in the Pacific North Coast that are geared to both beginning and experienced hikers. The **National Parks and Forests Outdoor Recreation Information Center** (915 2nd Ave., Room 442, Seattle, WA 98174, tel. 206/220–7450) can provide maps of trails that are well marked and well maintained. Guidebooks that describe the best trails in the area are readily available in local bookstores. The *Footsore* series of books, published by The Mountaineers (306 2nd Ave. W, Seattle, WA 98119, tel. 206/285–2665), are among the best.

Hunting An autumn visit to the Pacific North Coast yields opportunities for hunting deer and waterfowl in the coastal areas and around inland lakes. Big-game hunters, who are on the trail for elk, moose, and bear, should go to British Columbia, where outfitters are available to act as guides.

For more information on hunting facilities and licenses, contact **Washington State Department of Wildlife** (600 Capitol Way N, Olympia, WA 98501, tel. 206/753–5700) or the **British Columbia Ministry of Environment, Wildlife Branch** (810 Blanshard St., Victoria, BC V8W 2H1, tel. 604/387–9740).

Sailboarding Puget Sound and some of the area's inland lakes are popular venues for this sport. Sailboard rentals and lessons are available from local specialty shops. In British Columbia, the town of Squamish is quickly becoming another major windsurfing destination.

Scuba Diving The crystal-clear waters of Puget Sound—with their diversity of marine life—present excellent opportunities for scuba diving and underwater photography. For information on dive shops, equipment rentals, and charter boats in British Columbia, contact **Dive B.C.** (707 Westminster Ave., Powell River, B.C. V8A 1C5, tel. 604/485–6267).

Skiing
Downhill Skiing is by far the most popular winter activity in the area. Moist air off the Pacific Ocean dumps snow on the coastal mountains, providing excellent skiing from November through the end of March and sometimes into April. Local newspapers regularly list snow conditions for ski areas throughout the region during the winter season. Resort and lift-ticket prices tend to be less expensive here than at the internationally known ski destinations. Most Washington ski resorts cater to those who've come for a day of skiing rather than a longer stay.

The Whistler and Blackcomb mountains, north of Vancouver, comprise the biggest ski area in the region. Whistler Village resort boasts the longest and second-longest vertical drops (more than a mile each) of any ski area in North America. Aside from Whistler/Blackcomb, British Columbia has many other excellent ski resorts scattered throughout the province, including several that are only minutes from downtown Vancouver.

Washington has 20 ski areas, several of which are located just east of Seattle in the Cascade Mountains. Snoqualmie Pass, the ski area closest to Seattle—about 45 minutes east—contains three ski areas: Snoqualmie, Ski Acres, and Alpental. Other major ski resorts nearby include Mt. Baker, Crystal Mountain, Stevens Pass, and Mission Ridge.

Cross-Country Cross-country skiing is a popular and less expensive way to enjoy the winter wilderness. Many downhill ski resorts also have well-marked and well-groomed cross-country trails. Washington operates a system of more than 40 **SnoParks** (Office of Winter Recreation, Parks and Recreation Commission, 7150 Cleanwater La., KY-11, Olympia, WA 98504, tel. 206/586–0185) that are a series of groomed cross-country trails within state parks in which, for the price of a one-day ($7), three-day ($10), or seasonal ($20) pass, skiers have access to trails in 70 locations statewide.

Wildlife Viewing The Pacific North Coast offers ample opportunities for viewing wildlife, both on land and on water. Bald eagles, sea lions, dolphins, and whales are just a few of the animals that can be observed in the region. The best way to identify native creatures is with a pair of binoculars and a good nature guide at hand. Books on regional wildlife can be found in local bookstores.

Northwest Interpretive Association (83 S. King St., Suite 212, Seattle, WA 98104, tel. 206/553–2636), in cooperation with the **National Park and Forest Services,** operates *Pacific Northwest Field Seminars*. This nonprofit program offers outdoor courses from April through October covering topics such as nature writing and photography, wildlife, ecology, birding, geology, volcanology, and backpacking. Fees average about $35 per day for one- to four-day seminars.

Spectator Sports

Baseball The **Seattle Mariners** (tel. 206/628–0888 for tickets) of the American League play in the 60,000-seat indoor Kingdome. Tickets are almost always available. The baseball season runs from April to early October.

Several minor league teams play in smaller outdoor stadiums, including the **Vancouver Canadians** (tel. 604/872–5232), the **Tacoma Tigers** (tel. 206/752–7707), and the **Everett Giants** (tel. 206/258–3673).

Basketball Washington fields a big-league basketball team: the **Seattle SuperSonics** (tel. 206/281–5850) at the Seattle Coliseum.

Football The **Seattle Seahawks** (tel. 206/827–9766 for tickets) of the National Football League play in the Kingdome during the fall, but games are almost always sold out. Tickets are usually available for the **British Columbia Lions** (tel. 604/685–4344) of the Canadian Football League, who play in the indoor British Columbia Place Stadium in Vancouver.

Hockey The **Vancouver Canucks** (tel. 604/254–5141) of the National Hockey League hit the ice at the Pacific Coliseum. Minor-league "junior" hockey has a strong following in Seattle.

Horse Racing Thoroughbred horse racing takes place at **Exhibition Park** (tel. 604/254–1631) in Vancouver from April to October. Harness racing occurs from April to October at the **Cloverdale Raceway** (tel. 604/576–9141), located south of Vancouver near the U.S. border.

Powerboating Each year thousands of spectators watch unlimited-class hydroplanes, or "thunder boats," race on Seattle's Lake Washington in early August as the grand finale of **Seafair** (*see* Festivals and Seasonal events in Before You Go, *above*).

Beaches

The Pacific coasts of Washington and British Columbia have long, sandy beaches that run for miles at a stretch. But the waters are often too cold or treacherous for swimming. Even in summertime, beach goers must be prepared to dress warmly.

The beaches of Washington are more remote from the major centers of population. Seattle is a two- to three-hour drive from the nearest ocean beaches. Even in summer, the beaches are never crowded.

Most of the west coast of Vancouver Island is totally isolated. Pacific Rim National Park is one of the few places where ocean beaches are accessible. On the eastern coast of Vancouver Island, there are a number of good swimming beaches around the town of Parksville.

The gravel beaches of Washington's Puget Sound and British Columbia's Inside Passagé attract few swimmers or sunbathers, but the beaches are popular for beachcombing and viewing abundant marine life.

Dining

Many restaurants in the Pacific North Coast serve local specialties such as salmon, crab, oysters, and other seafood delicacies. Seattle's Pike Place Market and Vancouver's Granville Island Market display bountiful supplies of local seafood and produce, and these are good places to scan what you might find on restaurant menus. Ethnic foods are also becoming increasingly popular, especially Asian cuisines such as Japanese, Korean, and Thai.

There is tremendous emphasis on and enjoyment of the hearty and savory fare available in this area. Chefs of all stripes key their menus to the seasonal availability of local produce. In June strawberries are in season, July brings in Walla Walla Sweets (a softball-size mild onion and a local delicacy), blackberries (which grow wild, and can be picked from the roadside) take the forefront in August, and the Washington apple crop comes in in the fall.

Portions of the Pacific North Coast are major wine-producing regions. Local wines are often featured in the best restaurants. Beer, too, is a popular local product, and microbreweries have enjoyed increasing popularity throughout the Northwest. Often located in or connected with a local pub, some of these breweries produce only enough specialty beers (called microbrews) for their own establishments. Some, however, such as Red Hook Ale, Ballard Bitter, and Anchor Ale, are also available from regular beer outlets. Some wineries and microbreweries offer tours and tastings.

Coffee has become a passion in Seattle. Lattés (the local version of café au lait), cappuccinos, and espressos are the beverages of choice in the finer—and even not so fine—restaurants around town (you can get a latté at the downtown McDonald's). Espresso stands do a brisk business on almost every other downtown corner. The latest phenomenon are drive-through espresso stands that are popping up in suburban areas. The coffee craze is also spreading to Vancouver. Enjoy!

As a general rule, restaurants in metropolitan areas are more expensive than those outside the city. But many city establishments, especially those that feature foreign cuisines, are surprisingly inexpensive. Because of space limitations, we have listed only restaurants recommended as the best within each price range.

Lodging

Rates Although the names of the various hotel and motel price categories are standard, the prices listed under each may vary from one area to another. This variation reflects local price standards: For example, a Moderate price in a large urban area might be considered Expensive in a rural region. In all cases, price ranges for each category are clearly stated before each listing.

Hotels Most big-city hotels cater primarily to business travelers, with such facilities as restaurants, cocktail lounges, swimming pools, exercise equipment, and meeting rooms. Room rates often reflect the range of amenities offered. Most cities also have less expensive hotels, which are clean and comfortable but have fewer upscale facilities. A new accommodations trend is all-suite hotels, which offer more intimate facilities and are gaining popularity with business travelers. Examples are **Courtyard By Marriott** (tel. 800/321–2211) and **Embassy Suites Hotels** (tel. 800/362–2779).

Many properties offer special weekend rates, sometimes up to 50% off regular prices. However, these deals are usually not extended during peak summer months, when hotels are normally full.

Vancouver and Seattle have all experienced major hotel building booms during the past 10 years. Most of the major chains have properties in one of these cities. For more information, contact **Canadian Pacific** (tel. 800/828–7447), **Delta** (tel. 800/877–1133), **Doubletree** (tel. 800/528–0444), **Four Seasons** (tel. 800/332–3442), **Hilton** (tel. 800/445–8667), **Holiday Inn** (tel. 800/465–4329), **Hyatt** (tel. 800/233–1234), **Marriott** (tel. 800/228–9290), **Ramada** (tel. 800/228–2828), **Red Lion Hotels and Inns** (tel. 800/547–8010), **Sheraton** (tel. 800/325–3535), **Stouffer** (tel. 800/468–3571), **West Coast Hotels/Coast Hotels** (tel. 800/426–0670), and **Westin** (tel. 800/228–3000).

Motels/Motor Inns The familiar roadside motel of the past is fast disappearing from the landscape. In its place are economical chain-run motor inns that are strategically located at highway intersections. Some of these establishments offer very basic facilities; others provide restaurants, swimming pools, and other amenities.

Nationally recognized chains include **Best Western** (tel. 800/528–1234), **Days Inn** (tel. 800/325–2525), **La Quinta Inns** (tel. 800/531–5900), **Motel 6** (tel. 800/437–7486), **Quality Inns** (tel. 800/228–5151), **Super 8 Motels** (tel. 800/848–8888), and **Travelodge** (tel. 800/255–3050). **Nendel's** (tel. 800/547–0106) and **Shilo Inns** (tel. 800/222–2244) are regional chains.

Inns These establishments generally are located outside cities and have anywhere from 8 to 20 rooms. Lodging is often in an old restored building with some historical or architectural significance. Inns are sometimes confused with bed-and-breakfasts because they may include breakfast in their basic rate.

Bed-and-Breakfasts Bed-and-breakfasts are private homes that reflect the personalities and tastes of their owners. Generally, B&Bs have 2–10 rooms, some with private baths and others with shared facilities. Breakfast is always included in the price of the room.

B&Bs have flourished in recent years. Some homes advertise to the public, while others maintain a low profile. Most belong to a reservation system through which you can book a room.

Reservation services in the Pacific North Coast include **Best Canadian Bed & Breakfast Network** (1090 W. King Edward Ave., Vancouver, B.C. V6H 1Z4, tel. 604/738–7207), **Hometours International, Inc.** (1170 Broadway, Suite 614, New York, NY 10001, tel. 212/689–0851 or 800/367–4668), **Northwest Bed & Breakfast Travel Unlimited** (610 S.W. Broadway, Portland, OR 97205, tel. 503/243–7616), and **Traveller's Bed & Breakfast** (Box 492, Mercer Island, WA 98040, tel. 206/232–2345). Before leaving the United Kingdom, you can book a B&B through **American Bed & Breakfast, Inter-Bed Network** (31 Ernest Rd., Colchester, Essex CO7 9LQ, tel. 0206/223162).

Resorts The Pacific North Coast has quite a variety of resorts—from rural fishing lodges to luxury destination showpieces.

The Whistler Village resort in British Columbia is best known for its world-class skiing. But Whistler is equally impressive as a year-round destination for golf, tennis, swimming, mountain biking, and horseback riding.

Camping Camping is a popular and inexpensive way to tour the Pacific Northwest. Washington and British Columbia all have networks of excellent government-run parks that offer camping and organized activities. A few state and provincial parks will accept advance camping reservations, but most do not. Privately operated campgrounds sometimes have extra amenities such as laundry rooms and swimming pools. For more information, contact the local state or provincial tourism department.

YMCAs/YWCAs YMCAs or YWCAs are usually a good bet for clean, no-frills, reliable lodging in large towns and cities. These buildings are often centrally located, and their rates are significantly lower than those at city hotels. Nonmembers are welcome, but they may pay slightly more than members. A few very large Ys have accommodations for couples, but sleeping arrangements are usually segregated.

Home Exchange This is obviously an inexpensive solution to the lodging problem, because house-swapping means living rent-free. You find a house, apartment, or other vacation property to exchange for your own by becoming a member of a home-exchange organization, which then sends you its annual directories listing available exchanges and includes your own listing in at least one of them. Arrangements for the actual exchange are made by the two parties to it, not by the organization. Principal clearinghouses include **Intervac U.S./International Home Exchange** (Box 590504, San Francisco, CA 94159, tel. 415/435–3497), the oldest, with thousands of foreign and domestic homes for exchange in its three annual directories; membership is $62, or $72 if you want to receive the directories but remain unlisted. The **Vacation Exchange Club** (Box 650, Key West, FL 33041, tel. 800/638–3841), also with thousands of foreign and domestic listings, publishes four annual directories plus updates; the $50 membership includes your listing in one book. **Loan-a-Home** (2 Park La., Apt. 6E, Mount Vernon, NY 10552, tel. 914/664–7640) specializes in long-term exchanges; there is no charge to list your home, but the directories cost $35 or $45 depending on the number you receive.

Apartment and Villa Rentals If you want a home base that's roomy enough for a family and comes with cooking facilities, a furnished rental may be the solution. It's generally cost-wise, too, although not always—some rentals are luxury properties (economical only when your party is large). Home-exchange directories do list rentals—often second homes owned by prospective house swappers—and there are services that can not only look for a house or apartment for you (even a castle if that's your fancy) but also handle the paperwork. Some send an illustrated catalogue and others send photographs of specific properties, sometimes at a charge; up-front registration fees may apply.

Among the companies is **Rent a Home International** (7200 34th Ave. NW, Seattle, WA 98117, tel. 206/789-9377 or 800/488-7368). **Hideaways International** (767 Islington St., Box 4433, Portsmouth, NH 03802, tel. 603/430-4433 or 800/843-4433) functions as a travel club. Membership ($79 yearly per person or family at the same address) includes two annual guides plus quarterly newsletters; rentals are arranged directly between members, not by the club staff.

Credit Cards

The following credit card abbreviations have been used in this book: AE, American Express; D, Discover; DC, Diners Club; MC, MasterCard; and V, Visa.

2 Portrait of Seattle and Vancouver

In the Footsteps of the First Settlers

By Glenn W. Sheehan

A principal investigator at SJS Archaeological Services, Inc., in Bridgeport, PA, Glenn W. Sheehan has worked extensively in the Pacific Northwest and Arctic regions.

There's a sort of primeval mystery about the majestic landscapes of the Pacific Northwest Coast, something elemental and ancient that can give you a strange sense of being dislocated in time. Drive along the coastal roads of Washington's Olympic Peninsula, for example, and you'll pass magnificent rain forest, pounding surf, and partially submerged chunks of headland stranded at sea. Every bridge you cross takes you over an ancient fishing stream where prehistoric Indians harvested salmon. The oldest trees along the road bear scars where these Indians pulled off bark strips dozens of feet long, which they used for clothing, construction work, and rope making. Stop to look out over the water, and you feel the presence of ancient whale hunters scanning the horizon for spouts among the waves.

It isn't just a question of landscape, either. Elders in the Eskimo (Inuit is the preferred term in Canada) and Indian communities along the coast still pass on stories told to them by their ancestors, stories that can sometimes be traced as far back as 1,000 years, and their tribal art is a living expression of cultures whose origins are lost in the mists of prehistory.

Despite a lack of hard evidence, many archaeologists believe the first people to inhabit the New World arrived by way of the Pacific North Coast. Unlike Columbus and the seafaring Vikings, Polynesians, Chinese, and Japanese, all of whom crossed oceans to arrive at different points in North and South America, it is believed that the first Americans came on foot. If these pioneers had boats at all, they were small ones, not designed for long-distance travel across oceans. They came via Alaska and traveled through Canada into the western United States.

Although these assertions sound feasible, there aren't any known archaeological sites to support them. The oldest documented sites in the New World are believed to be 20,000–13,000 years old; the oldest known sites in the Pacific Northwest are Indian settlements that fall at the younger end of this range, at about 13,000 years old. Why then is the Pacific Northwest Coast believed to be the point of entry for the earliest settlers? Because it's the only place where people could have walked into the New World or used their small boats to travel along the coast without excessive danger. The last Ice Age tied up so much water that ocean levels probably dropped by hundreds of feet around the world. On certain winter days today, a person can walk between Alaska and the Soviet Union on ice when the oceans freeze over. But during the Ice Age the oceans were so reduced that the seabed was temporarily exposed as dry land, supporting vegetation and game, with fish in the rivers and sea mammals on the coast. So much ground was exposed, in fact, that the Old World and the New were connected by dry land. And though their languages and blood types differ, evidence strongly suggests that both the Eskimos and Indians have their roots somewhere in Asia. As one Eskimo friend of mine once said, "You know, those Chinese look an awful lot like us. They must be descended from Eskimos."

Why then aren't there any sites to prove this migration theory? All human activity may have been confined to lower ground levels now hidden under the ocean, reason the archaeologists. Or people may have traveled in small numbers, so their remains aren't easily detected. Or we may have already found these sites without recognizing them as such. Even though the two American continents were not inhabited with people at the outset, they did have abundant herds of large game, animals that had no fear of humans. Hunters with such easy prey wouldn't stay in one place for long; as they killed off their local supply of meat, or as the animals learned how to avoid people, the hunters moved on. So it is possible that the settlers arrived in the Pacific Northwest, lived a nomadic life there for a while, and then roamed on to other parts of North America and into South America.

The first Americans came to a land we wouldn't recognize today. Most of Canada, Alaska, and the northern United States were still under ice. Arctic weather and the forests, animals, and plants that are found in today's far north were prevalent halfway down the lower 48 states. Then the weather changed: The ice sheets melted and the ice receded north. The animal and plant distributions we see today started to become established about 10,000 years ago. Rivers and streams that were previously frozen started to run fast and clear at low temperatures. Conditions for pioneering salmon became so ideal that by 5,000 or so years ago, there were huge runs extending hundreds of miles inland.

For hunters it was a revolutionary time. Herds of large animals started to diminish or disappear, and the big-game hunters were increasingly confronted with more work and less to show for their efforts. Many hunters in the Pacific Northwest Coast, particularly those in Washington, British Columbia, and southeastern Alaska, turned to fishing instead. Their nomadic life following the herds became a more settled one as they switched to fishing. And as they started to settle down, they were able to accumulate more material things.

The first Americans moved north to south, from Alaska to Canada and then to the lower 48 states and finally into Central America and South America. The more recent inhabitants who made their living from salmon fishing, however, headed in the opposite direction, from the lower Pacific Northwest up into Canada and Alaska. The art and culture of these people spread and flourished in the Pacific Northwest and continued to do so in the centuries preceding their contact with European explorers. Archaeological sites of these fishing peoples date back 2,500 years and more.

Native Americans often moved when they felt their villages had grown too big. According to stories told by Indian elders, entire clans would depart and make new settlements along the Pacific Coast. Battles between Indian tribes, and warfare between the Eskimos and Indians, also prompted the relocation of some villages. And eventually, as the native and Euro-American economies became entwined, some Indians and Eskimos abandoned their villages. Many of these villages can still be seen today: Houses may have fallen, totem poles may have been reduced by museum acquisitions, and the forest is once again dense, but the villages are there. Not only can archaeologists find and excavate the abandoned sites of these people, they also can talk to their descendants. When an archaeologist is puzzled by an object he digs out of the ground, he can consult the elders of various Indian and Eskimo groups, who can often identify it and describe its use. And when the elders can't identify an object, they can often point researchers in the right direction.

During this prehistoric fishing era, the most prosperous natives were those of Washington, British Columbia, and southern Alaska. They had the good life, and they flaunted it. Their art was larger than life, while their potlatches (celebratory feasts) gave new meaning to the words conspicuous consumption. The success of the fishing peoples led to imitation. The natives of Kodiak Island were Eskimo, for example, and their ancestors came to the New World to fish and hunt sea mammals along the coast, rather than hunt the big land-bound game as the Indians' ancestors did. Surprising enough, however, the Kodiak people achieved a society in many ways remarkably similar to that of Indian tribes living to the east and south. Their art, archaeology, and legends demonstrate the connections.

Indian groups were open to the ways of others too. In the far north of Alaska, where trees don't grow and fish runs can be counted in dozens instead of millions, Eskimo hunters had great success in capturing large whales. Indian groups of the lower Pacific Northwest did the same, using many of the whale-hunting techniques and rituals employed by people as far away as Point Barrow on the Arctic Coast.

Although the native groups along the Pacific Northwest Coast were lucky enough to avoid outright war with the European and American settlers, they did suffer some adversity. The natives of Kodiak, for example, were viciously attacked by Russians, and many natives eventually lost land in Canada and the United States. All the natives suffered when commercial fishing and river dams reduced salmon runs, and again when Yankee whalers destroyed whales in huge numbers. Despite these setbacks, however, both the Indians and Eskimos have retained much of their culture and way of life into the present.

One of the best-known archaeological sites of these settlers is Ozette, located on the Makah Reservation in Washington's Olympic Peninsula. The finds of the site can be viewed by the public, and visitors can request permission to visit the site itself. Call the Makah Reservation (tel. 206/645–2711) for information. The village of Ozette was partially covered by a mud slide several hundred years ago. This apparent catastrophe ironically turned out to preserve the village, however, for the wet mud provided an anaerobic environment hostile to most decay-causing organisms. As a result, the mud-covered section of Ozette was preserved in its entirety, a kind of New World Pompeii.

Archaeologists usually excavate with masons' trowels because they generally dig up stone and ceramics, objects that a skillfully handled trowel won't harm. But at Ozette in the 1970s, there was a delightful obstacle to overcome. Basketry, cordage, clothing, and all kinds of soft materials had been preserved, but since they were preserved wet, they were particularly soft, and the trowels cut through them like mud. Even experienced excavators couldn't feel the damage they were doing to the objects.

A whole new excavation approach was undertaken, called "wet site" archaeology. Using water hoses to excavate the village, the archaeologists discovered that mud and debris could be washed away, leaving artifacts intact. During the handlers' first clumsy attempts at hosing down the mud, artifacts could be seen tumbling downhill with the water, but after some trial and error, the workers were able to keep even small finds in place.

One of the most exciting aspects of the Ozette excavation was the support archaeologists received from Indians living in the region. The Makah tribe encouraged archaeologists to excavate Ozette and assisted in the fieldwork; tribal members provided logistical support and helped interpret finds. And the tribe even built a museum based on the artifacts on its grounds at Neah Bay.

The Indians also helped prepare artifacts for public display, which turned out to be quite a challenge. Generally, archaeological finds of stone and ceramic pieces are preserved simply by being cleaned first in water and then glued together. But Ozette produced all kinds of perishable artifacts, objects that quickly started to deteriorate once they were removed from their muddy entombment. So the Makah Tribe provided laboratory space and helped the archaeologists preserve and stabilize the finds.

These descendants of the ancient Indians went one step further and created a living experiment on the site. The Makah people worked outside to build a plank house, like those in Ozette, and then attempted to use the interior in the same ways their ancestors did. Life in the house was set up based upon the directions of tribal elders, historic accounts, and archaeological interpretations. In the end, the house looked as if one good mud slide would turn it into another ruined Ozette home. After this experimental period, the tribe dismantled the house and rebuilt it inside the Makah museum.

A large dugout canoe was also built for the museum. The art of making canoes had almost died out, but it was revived to capture an important part of life in Ozette. Young and old worked together to build the boat and to pass on these ancient skills.

Other archaeological sites in the area require a bit more effort to explore. From southern Alaska to Oregon, you can find hundreds of petroglyphs (rock carvings) and pictographs (rock paintings). Only a handful of them can be dated, however, so they can't be attributed to any particular group of people. Some are easily accessible, and seen by the public every day. Others are so hidden you can only find them if you happen to stumble upon them. Still other carvings are positioned at the tidal zone and consequently are under water at high tide. One worthwhile guide to the many accessible rock carvings is Beth and Ray Hill's *Indian Petroglyphs of the Pacific Northwest.*

Prehistoric Indians also carved petroglyphs on land, although mostly facing the ocean, or else overlooking a river or waterway. Pictographs, on the other hand, can be seen throughout the Northwest Coast. Some of these detailed rocks have been jackhammered from their embedded frames and carted away; others have eroded, and still others lie beneath reservoirs. But the vast majority are right where they were created, and with permission from native or nonnative landowners, or government agencies, visitors can examine them. More than 500 sites are known. One protected site open to the public is Petroglyph Park in the town of Nanaimo, on Vancouver Island. Petroglyphs at Wrangell, Alaska, are also open to the public.

The ancient craft of carving giant totem poles out of trees has survived as a living art form, with plenty of demand for new poles. Carvers today often work in public throughout the Pacific Northwest, at museums or on the grounds of institutions that have commissioned their artwork. Young workers aspire to apprentice with master carvers, and gift shops all over the region offer miniature reproductions.

The totem pole is the best-known example of current Northwest Coast tribal art, but masks, tools, and a variety of paintings and prints also continue the artistic tradition of the area. Artwork can be purchased at local galleries, many of which are located on Indian lands and are run by Indians. The choices are broader and the prices lower here than they are in the native art galleries of New York and California. The Dukuah Gallery (1971 Peninsula Rd., Ocluelet, B.C., V0R 3A0, tel. 604/726–7223) is run by native Lillian Mac and her husband, Bert Mac, the hereditary Chief of the Toquant tribe. Native artists visit and work in the gallery year-round.

The British Columbia Provincial Museum in Victoria, with its unique collection of prehistoric fish bones, is an outstanding research center, with representation from all five species of salmon and almost every other fish that might have been harvested by prehistoric natives. Each fish skeleton has been mounted on wires, with all the bones together in proper anatomical order. While this is a scientific collection, it verges on being a work of art in itself, with skeletal fish elongating and compressing into fantastic shapes.

In Vancouver, at the University of British Columbia's Museum of Anthropology, there's an excellent archaeological collection that's very accessible to the public. Visitors can open any of the Plexiglas-covered drawers to examine even the most delicate artifacts. Other artifacts can be seen at the Thomas Burke Memorial Washington State Museum at the University of Washington in Seattle, and at the Alaska State Museum in Juneau, where they also have a first-rate collection of historic baleen (fibrous plates that hang from the roof of the whale's mouth) baskets. Only native hunters and artisans are legally permitted to own unprocessed baleen.

Any overview of Northwest Coast archaeology inevitably leaves out more than it includes. Paleo-Indian sites, Russian fur-hunting activities, cave sites in Washington's channeled scablands, mastodons and mammoths, and cairns dug up 100 years ago can all be found along the Pacific Northwest Coast. And if you visit the area searching for a glimpse of the past, native people will share their stories, researchers may invite you to observe their work, artisans will explain their ancient crafts, and the museums will let you view even the most fragile artifacts. For here, one thing remains constant: the people's eagerness to document and understand the past.

3 Seattle

By Adam Woog and Loralee Wenger

Adam Woog is a Seattle-based freelance writer whose works have appeared in the Village Voice, Seattle Times, *and* Japan Times. *Loralee Wenger is the former travel editor for* Pacific Northwest *magazine and a freelance writer whose articles have appeared in the* San Francisco Examiner, Washington Post, Parade *magazine, and* Glamour *magazine.*

Seattle is defined by water. There's no use denying the city's damp weather, or the fact that its skies are cloudy for much of the year. People in Seattle don't tan—goes the joke—they rust. Vendors at the city's waterfront Public Market sell T-shirts that read "Seattle Rain Festival: January through December."

But Seattle is also defined by a different kind of water. A variety of rivers, lakes, and canals bisect steep hills, creating a series of distinctive areas along the water's edge that provide for a wide range of activities. Funky fishing boats and floating homes, swank yacht clubs and waterfront restaurants, exist side by side.

But a city is defined by people as well as by its geography, and the people of Seattle—some half million within the city proper, another 2 million in the surrounding Puget Sound region—are a diversified bunch. Seattle has long had an active Asian and Asian-American population, as well as being home to well-established communities of Scandinavians, African Americans, Jews, Native Americans, Hispanics, and other ethnic groups.

Although it's impossible to accurately generalize about such a varied group, the prototypical Seattleite was once pithily summed up by a *New Yorker* cartoon in which one arch-eyebrowed East Coast matron says to another, "They're backpacky, but nice." And it's true, nearly everyone in Seattle shares a love for the outdoors.

Aided by the proximity of high mountains (the Cascades to the east, the Olympics to the west) and water (both salt water and fresh water are everywhere), Seattle's vigorous outdoor sports are perennial favorites. The city's extensive park system (designed by Frederick Law Olmsted, creator of New York City's Central Park) and miles of secluded walking and bicycling paths add to one's appreciation of its surroundings.

At the same time, the climate fosters an easygoing, indoor lifestyle as well. Overcast days and long winter nights help make Seattle a haven for movie-goers and book-readers—the city is often used by Hollywood as a testing ground for new films and, according to independent bookstore sales and per-capita book purchases, the city ranks in the highest category.

Shedding its sleepy-town image, Seattle is one of the fastest-growing cities in the United States. For years, giant aerospace manufacturer Boeing was the only major factor in the area's economy besides lumber and fishing—the staples of the Northwest. But as the 1962 World's Fair (and its enduring symbol, the Space Needle) signaled a change from small town to medium-size city, so the 1990 Goodwill Games announced the city's new role as a respected international hub. Seattle is now a major seaport and a vital link in Pacific Rim trade, and the evidence of internationalism is everywhere, from the discreet Japanese script identifying downtown department stores (i.e., "Nordstrom" written as "Katakana") to the multilingual recorded messages at Seattle-Tacoma International Airport.

The town that Sir Thomas Beacham once described as a "cultural wasteland" now has all the artistic trappings of a full-blown big city, with ad agencies and artists' co-ops, symphonies and ballet companies. Several magazines compete with the two daily newspapers. There's an innovative new convention center, a covered dome for professional sports, a world-renowned theater scene, an excellent opera company, and a strong music community.

As the city grows, though, it is also beginning to display full-blown big-city problems. Increases in crime, drug abuse, homelessness, and poverty are coupled with a decline in the quality of the public schools. Suburban growth is also rampant; nearby Bellevue, the largest suburb, has swollen in just a few years from a quiet farming community to the second-largest city in the state. Further, the area is plagued with one of the worst traffic problems in the country. But Seattleites are an active political bunch with a great love for their city and a firm commitment to maintaining its reputation as one of the most liveable in the country.

Essential Information

Arriving and Departing by Plane

Seattle-Tacoma International Airport is 20 miles from downtown Seattle and is served by Air BC (tel. 206/467–7928 or 800/663–8868), Air Canada (tel. 206/467–7928), Alaska (tel. 206/433–3100), American (tel. 800/433–7300), America West (tel. 800/247–5692), British Airways (tel. 206/433–6714), Continental (tel. 206/624–1740 or 800/525–0280), Delta (tel. 206/433–4711), EVA Airways (tel. 206/687–2833 or 800/695–2833), Hawaiian (tel. 800/367–5320), Horizon (tel. 800/547–9308), Japan (tel. 206/624–4737 or 800/225–2525), Northwest (tel. 206/433–3500 or 800/221–2000), TWA (tel. 206/447–9400), Thai Airways (tel. 800/426–5204), United (tel. 206/441–3700 or 800/241–6522), United Express (tel. 206/441–3700), and USAir (tel. 206/587–6229 or 800/428–4322).

Between the Airport and Center City

By Bus

Gray Line Airport Express (tel. 206/626–6088) operates buses from major downtown hotels from 6:10 AM to 11:45, with departures every 20–30 minutes, depending on the hotel. The fare is $7 one-way, $12 round-trip.

Shuttle Express (tel. 206/622–1424) offers service to and from the airport. Fares are $16 for singles one-way or $22 for two one-way tickets.

By Taxi

Taxis to the airport take 30–45 minutes; the fare is about $25.

Arriving and Departing by Car, Bus, and Train

By Car

I–5 enters Seattle from the north and south, I–90 from the east.

Washington law requires all passengers to be buckled into seat belts. Children under age five should use car seats. Cars are allowed to turn right at a red light after stopping to check for oncoming traffic.

By Bus

Seattle is served by **Greyhound** (8th Ave. and Stewart St., tel. 800/231–2222), a nationwide bus line.

By Train

Amtrak (303 S. Jackson St., tel. 800/USA–RAIL) provides rail transportation from Seattle.

Getting Around Seattle

By Car Many downtown streets are one-way, so a map with arrows is especially helpful. Main thoroughfares into downtown are Aurora Avenue (the part through downtown is called the Alaskan Way Viaduct) and I-5.

By Bus **Metropolitan Transit** (821 2nd Ave., tel. 206/553-3000) provides a free-ride service in the downtown waterfront area. Fares to other destinations range from 85¢ to $1.60, depending on the zone and time of day.

By Ferry The **Washington State Ferry System** (tel. 206/464-6400 or 206/464-2000, ext. 5500) is the largest in the U.S., (*see* Getting There, by Ferry, Bainbridge Island, in Excursions from Seattle, *below*). Ferries leave from downtown Seattle for Bainbridge Island and Bremerton (Kitsap Peninsula) several times daily. Ferries for pedestrians travel to Vashon Island and Southworth (Kitsap Peninsula). Car and passenger ferries leave from Fauntleroy, in West Seattle, to Vashon Island and Southworth; from Edmonds, north of Seattle, to Kingston; and from Mukilteo, farther north, to Clinton (Whidbey Island). In Anacortes, about 90 minutes north of Seattle, ferries depart for the San Juan Islands and Vancouver Island, British Columbia. Fares range from as low as $1.10 for children 5-11 and senior citizens traveling the Mukilteo to Clinton route, to $31.25 for a car and driver going one-way from Anacortes to Sydney.

Clipper Navigation, Inc.'s (tel. 206/448-5000) passenger catamarans leave from Pier 69. They make the trip to Victoria in under three hours and depart four times daily in the summer, two times daily in the spring and fall, and once daily in winter. The fares are $74-$85 round-trip. The ships offer summer sunset cruises. Clipper Navigation also makes runs to Port Townsend and Friday Harbor on San Juan Island in the summer. Reservations are necessary.

By Monorail The **Monorail** (tel. 206/684-7200), built for the 1962 World's Fair, runs direct from Westlake Center to the Seattle Center every 15 minutes. Hours are Sunday to Thursday 9-9 and Friday and Saturday 9 AM-midnight. The fare is 85¢ each way; free for children under 6.

By Trolley **Waterfront trolleys** (tel. 206/553-3000) run from Pier 70 into Pioneer Square. The fares (85¢ nonpeak and $1.60 for travel during peak hours) are the same as bus fares.

By Taxi Taxis can be hailed on the street, and the fare is $1.20 at the flag drop and $1.40 per mile. Major companies are **Farwest** (tel. 206/622-1717) and **Yellow Cab** (tel. 206/622-6500).

Important Addresses and Numbers

Tourist Information The **Seattle/King County Convention and Visitors Bureau** (800 Convention Pl., tel. 206/461-5840), at the I-5 end of Pike Street, can provide you with maps and information about lodging, restaurants, and attractions throughout the city.

Emergencies For **police, ambulance,** or **other emergencies,** dial 911.

Hospitals Area hospitals with emergency rooms include **Harborview Medical Center** (325 9th Ave., tel. 206/223-3074) and **Virginia Mason Hospital** (925 Seneca St., tel. 206/583-6433).

Pharmacies **Fred Meyer** (417 Broadway Ave. E, tel. 206/323–6586) is open until 10 PM.

Guided Tours

Orientation Several guided tours of Seattle's waterfront and nearby areas are available, primarily during summer months. From Pier 55, **Seattle Harbor Tours** offers one-hour tours exploring Elliott Bay and the Port of Seattle. Some seven vessels take visitors on trips through the Hiram Chittendan Locks and Lake Washington. Sailings vary according to season. *Pier 55, Suite 201, 98101, tel. 206/623–1445. Cost: $9.50 adults, $8.50 senior citizens, $7 youths 12–17, $5 children 5–12.*

Gray Line offers some 20 guided bus tours of the city and environs ranging in scope from a daily 2½-hour spin to a six-hour "Grand City Tour." The company also offers various specialized tours, including the Boeing 747-767 plants, Mt. Rainier, and Seattle's waterways by boat. From May to October, Gray Line also offers tours via Seattle Trolleys through downtown. *All departures from the downtown Sheraton, 1400 6th Ave., tel. 206/626–5208 (except Seattle Trolley tours and the* Victoria Star *service between Bellingham and Victoria that operates June 1–Oct. 15). Free transfer service from major downtown hotels. Reservations required.*

For an off-beat introduction to the Emerald City, try the ***Name Dropper's Tour,*** a Trivial Pursuits–style guided bus tour. Book dealers Jim and Carol Norman offer insider's insight, bits of juicy gossip, and orientation information and historical data about Seattle. The three-hour tour covers 36 miles of town. *Box 12918, Seattle 98111, tel. 206/625–1317. Cost: $25 per person.*

Special-Interest **Emerald City Charters** offers a unique look at Seattle's waterfront from beneath the sails of a refurbished 64-foot 1939 yawl. There are 90-minute harbor sails and a 2½-hour sunset sail. *Pier 56, tel. 206/624–3931. May–Oct. Cost: harbor sail $20, sunset sail $37.*

The ***Spirit of Washington*** is a diesel-powered dinner train that takes passengers on a 3½-hour, 44-mile round-trip excursion along the eastern shore of Lake Washington from the depot in Renton to the Chateau Ste. Michelle winery in Woodenville. Passengers ride in regular or domed dining cars and are served dinner on the first leg of the trip, then disembark for a self-guided tour and tasting, or a stroll through the gardens at the winery. Dessert and coffee are served on the return trip. The route offers views of Lake Washington, the Bellevue skyline, and Mt. Rainier. The menu includes prime rib, baked cherry-smoked salmon with pineapple chutney and a seafood fettuccine. Desserts are flavorful and usually decadent, and bar offerings include Washington wines, beers and ales. There are also Saturday lunch and Sunday brunch trips. *Renton Depot, tel. 800/876–7245. Reservations required. No runs Mon. mid-Sept.–mid-May. Cost: $55; $65 for dome-car seating.*

The ***Spirit of Puget Sound*** runs dinner cruises in Elliott Bay evenings 7–10 on a sleek, 175-foot yacht. The cruise includes beef, salmon, and chicken buffet dinner; a 30-minute Broadway revue; and one hour of dancing to a five-piece band. Summer moonlight cocktail cruises set sail at about 11:30 and return at 2 AM, and feature a nightclub atmosphere. *2819 Elliot Ave., Suite*

204, Seattle 98121, tel. 206/443–1439. Cost for dinner cruise is about $50, depending on weekends or weeknight travel; for moonlight cruises, $15.95 per person. Call for schedules.

From Pier 56, **Tillicum Village Tours** sails across Puget Sound to Blake Island, south of Bainbridge Island, for a four-hour examination of traditional Native American life. A dinner including steamed clams and salmon is served, and Native American dancers perform a new production, *Dance on the Wind. Pier 56, tel. 206/443–1244. Tour schedule varies during the year, with up to 3 tours leaving daily during peak months. Cost: $43.23 adults, $39.98 senior citizens, $28.08 youths 13–19, $17.26 children 6–12, $8.60 children 4–5; children 3 and under free.*

The ***Victoria Clipper*** offers two-hour sunset cruises with two itineraries. One sails down the east coast of Vashon Island and returns along areas of Greater Seattle, including Alki Point, in West Seattle. The other goes northwest to Agate Passage, then south along the western shore of Bainbridge Island through Rich Passage. *Pier 69, tel. 206/448–5000. Cost: $16 adults, $8.50 children.*

Gray Line (*see above*).

Seattle's Chinatown, known as the International District, reflecting its multicultural flavor, is one of the largest Asian-American enclaves in North America. **Chinatown Discovery Tours** offers groups (and individuals on a space-available basis) a three-hour tour of the area that includes such sights as a fortune cookie factory, a Chinese market, and an herb dispensary. Tours end with a traditional dim sum or dinner banquet. *Box 3406, 98114, tel. 206/236–0657. $27.50 for the tour, including dim sum lunch. Tours offered several times during the day and evening.*

One of the most beloved of Seattle's tours is the **Underground Tour,** begun in 1965 by feisty entrepreneur/historian Bill Speidel as an effort to help preserve the then-derelict Pioneer Square area. This 90-minute walking tour explores (with tongue-in-cheek narration) the rough-and-tumble history of early Seattle; the Great Fire of 1889, which destroyed most of downtown; and the fascinating below-ground sections of Pioneer Square that have been abandoned (and built on top of) since 1907. This tour, however, is not wheelchair- or stroller-accessible, as six flights of stairs are involved. *Departure from Doc Maynard's Public House, 610 1st Ave., tel. for reservations, 206/682–4646; tel. for schedules, 206/682–1511. Cost: $5.50 adults, $4.50 senior citizens, $4 youths 13–17 or with valid student ID, $2.25 children 6–12, children under 6 free. Reservations recommended. Tours run daily except Easter, Thanksgiving, Christmas Eve, Christmas Day, and New Year's Day. Tour schedule varies with season, with up to 7 tours daily in summer.*

Self-Guided

Also worth exploring are the unusual self-guided tours found in "Steps to Enjoying Seattle's Public Art," an illustrated brochure published by the Seattle Arts Commission. It describes walks and drives to see more than 1,000 innovative works of **art in public places.** Among these treasures are brass dance-steps inlaid on the sidewalks of Broadway, whirligigs festooning a neighborhood electric power substation, an "ark" of animals at Woodland Park Zoo, murals on downtown high rises, and a "sound garden" of acoustical sculptures in a lakeside park.

"Steps to Enjoying Seattle's Public Art" is free from the Seattle Arts Commission (305 Harrison St., 98109, tel. 206/684–7171).

Ballooning **Balloon Depot** (16138 N.E. 87th St., Redmond 98052, tel. 206/881–9699) offers 60- to 90-minute balloon flights for $99–$145 per person depending on the length of flight and whether it's a weekday or weekend. **Lighter Than Air Adventures** (21808 N.E. 175th St., Woodinville 98072, tel. 206/788–2454) has evening flights that last 30 minutes–one hour for $125 per person, as well as morning flights that last one–two hours and feature a champagne brunch for $145 per person. The **Great Northwest Aerial Navigation Company** (7616 79th Ave. SE, Mercer Island 98040, tel. 206/232–2023) specializes in longer flights and gourmet picnics, lasting about four hours, surveying the Snohomish Valley north and east of Seattle. Morning and evening picnic flights, $145 on weekends, $120 weekdays; flights only, $105.

Highlights for First-Time Visitors

Kingdome (*see* Exploring Seattle, *below*)
Seattle Center (*see* Exploring Seattle, *below*)
Space Needle (*see* Exploring Seattle, *below*)
Seattle's waterfront (*see* Exploring Seattle, *below*)

Exploring Seattle

Numbers in the margin correspond to points of interest on the Downtown Seattle map.

Downtown Downtown Seattle is bounded by the Kingdome to the south, the Seattle Center to the north, I–5 to the east, and the waterfront to the west. You can reach most points of interest by foot, bus, or the monorail. Bear in mind that Seattle is a city of hills, so comfortable walking shoes are a must.

(1) Start at the **Seattle Visitor Information Center** to pick up maps, brochures, and listings of events. *666 Stewart St., tel. 206/461–5840. Open weekdays 8:30–5. Other location at the Seattle Center, adjacent to the Space Needle. Open Memorial Day–Labor Day.*

From the Information Center, you can proceed either north or south. If you choose the latter, take Westlake Avenue to
(2) **Westlake Center** (*see* Shopping, *below*), a complex completed in 1989 in spite of the controversy surrounding its construction. The conflict was between city residents—some of whom objected to the 27-story office tower and three-story shopping structure with enclosed walkways—and favored, instead, the large grassy park without commercial buildings. In any case, the center is a major terminus for buses and the monorail, which goes north to Seattle Center. *1601 5th Ave., tel. 206/467–1600. Open weekdays 9:30–9.*

Make your way from 5th Avenue west to 2nd Avenue. The
(3) doors to the new **Seattle Art Museum** opened in 1991, and the five-story building, designed by postmodern theorist Robert Venturi, is a work of art in itself. The building features a limestone exterior with large-scale vertical fluting, accented by terra-cotta, cut granite, and marble. The museum has a café and gift shop, and displays an extensive collection of Asian, Native American, African, Oceanic, and pre-Columbian art. *1320*

2nd Ave., tel. 206/625–8900. Admission: $5 adults, $3 senior citizens and students, children under 12 free; admission free first Tues. of the month; free tours daily at 2. Open Tues.–Sat. 10–5, Thurs. 10–9, Sun. noon–5. Closed Mon., Thanksgiving, Christmas, and New Year's Day.

4 Go west one block to 1st Avenue and one block north to the **Pike Place Market,** a Seattle institution. It began in 1907 when the city issued permits to farmers allowing them to sell produce from their wagons parked at Pike Place. Later the city built stalls that were allotted to the farmers on a daily basis. At one time the market was a madhouse of vendors hawking their produce, haggling over prices; some of the fishmongers still carry on this kind of frenzied banter, but chances are you won't get them to waver on their prices. Urban renewal almost killed the market, but just as planners were about to do away with it, city voters, led by the late architect Victor Steinbreuck (for whom the park near the market was named), rallied and voted it a historical asset. Many of the buildings have been restored, and the project is now connected to the waterfront by stairs and elevators. You can still find fresh seafood (which can be packed in dry ice for your flight home), produce, cheese, Northwest wines, bulk spices, tea, coffee, and arts and crafts here. *1st Ave. at Pike St., tel. 206/682–7453. Open Mon.–Sat. 9–6, Sun. 11–5.*

From the market, take the stairs or elevator down to the waterfront. In the early days, the waterfront was the center of activity in Seattle; today it stretches some 19 blocks, from Pier 70 and Myrtle Edwards Park in the north, where there is a bicycle and jogging trail, down to Pier 51 in Pioneer Square.

Pier 70, to the south of the park, is a large warehouse that has been converted into shops, galleries, restaurants, and bars.

5 At the base of the Pike Street Hillclimb at Pier 59 is the **Seattle Aquarium,** showcasing Northwest marine life. The Discovery Lab offers visitors a chance to see baby barnacles, minute jelly fish, and other "invisible" creatures through high-resolution video microscopes. The Tide Pool Exhibit re-creates Washington's rocky coast and sandy beaches at low tide with a 6,000-gallon wave that sweeps over the underwater life—spectators standing close by may get damp from the simulated sea spray. Sea otters and seals swim and dive in their pools, and the "State of the Sound" exhibit shows the aquatic life and ecology of Puget Sound. *Pier 59, tel. 206/386–4320. Admission: $6.50 adults, $5 senior citizens, $4 youngsters 6–18, $1.50 children 3–5, children under 2 free. Call for group rates. Open daily 10–5, 10–7 in summer.*

6 Next to the aquarium is the **Omnidome Film Experience,** which includes short films on such subjects as the eruption of Mt. St. Helens, mountain gorillas, and the Great Barrier Reef. *Pier 59, tel. 206/622–1868. Admission: $5.95 adults, $4.95 youths 13–18 and senior citizens, $3.95 children 3–12, children under 3 free; phone for special combination ticket prices for the Omnidome and aquarium. Open daily 10–5.*

North of the aquarium, at Pier 66 along Alaskan Way, is the site of the **Odyssey Contemporary Maritime Museum,** scheduled to open in 1995. This new center will feature cultural and educational maritime exhibits on Puget Sound and ocean trade, and offer visitors tours of ships and boats docked nearby. The development will also include a conference center, short-stay

Historical Marker, **7**
Omnidome Film Experience, **6**
Pike Place Market, **4**
Pioneer Square, **8**
Seattle Aquarium, **5**
Seattle Art Museum, **3**
Seattle Visitor Information Center, **1**
Westlake Center, **2**

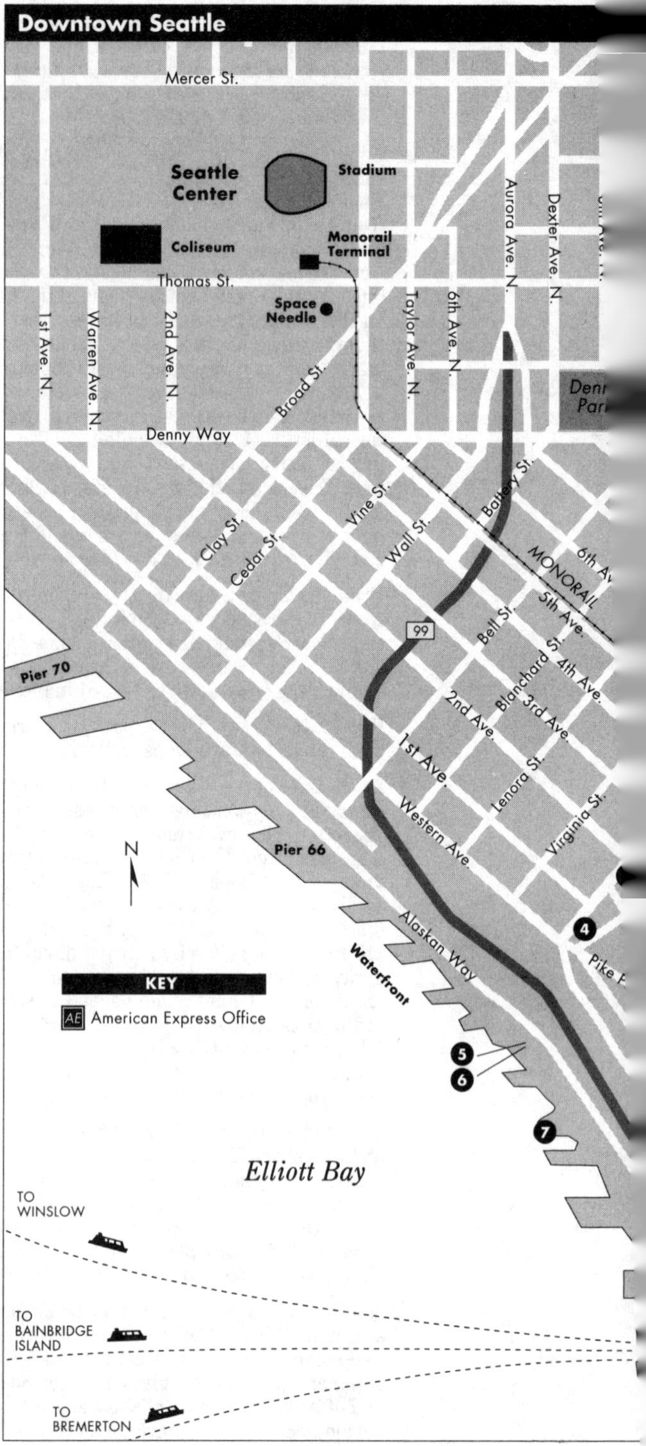

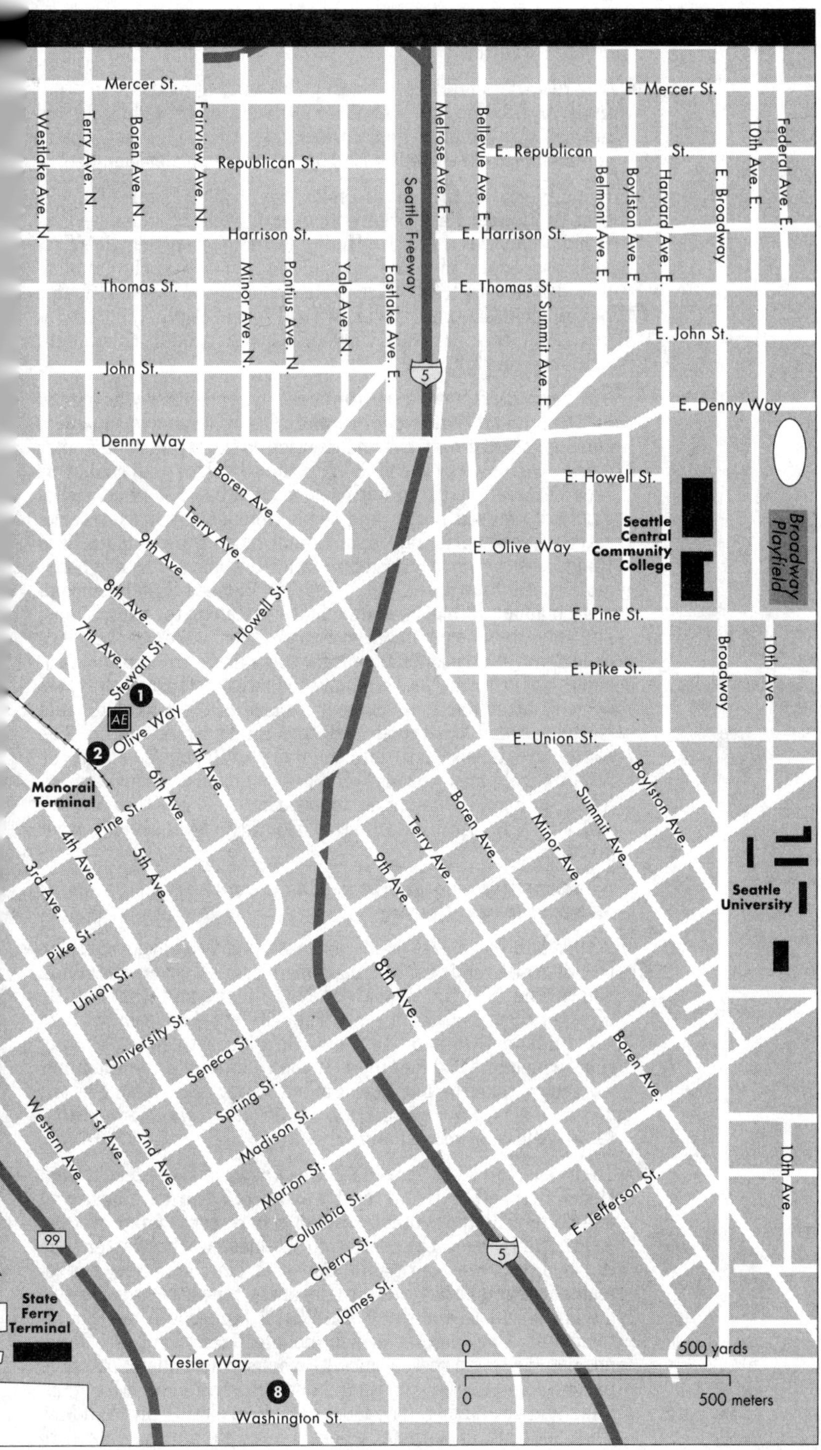

Mercer St.
E. Mercer St.
Westlake Ave. N.
Terry Ave. N.
Boren Ave. N.
Fairview Ave. N.
Republican St.
Melrose Ave. E.
Bellevue Ave. E.
E. Republican St.
Belmont Ave. E.
Boylston Ave. E.
Harvard Ave. E.
E. Broadway
10th Ave. E.
Federal Ave. E.
Seattle Freeway
Harrison St.
E. Harrison St.
Thomas St.
Minor Ave. N.
Pontius Ave. N.
Yale Ave. N.
Eastlake Ave. E.
E. Thomas St.
Summit Ave. E.
E. John St.
John St.
5
E. Denny Way
Denny Way
Boren Ave.
Terry Ave.
9th Ave.
8th Ave.
7th Ave.
Stewart St.
Howell St.
E. Howell St.
E. Olive Way
Seattle Central Community College
Broadway Playfield
E. Pine St.
E. Pike St.
Broadway
10th Ave.
1
AE
Olive Way
2
E. Union St.
Monorail Terminal
7th Ave.
6th Ave.
Pine St.
4th Ave.
5th Ave.
3rd Ave.
Boren Ave.
Terry Ave.
Minor Ave.
Summit Ave.
Boylston Ave.
9th Ave.
Seattle University
Pike St.
Union St.
8th Ave.
University St.
Seneca St.
Boren Ave.
Spring St.
Western Ave.
1st Ave.
2nd Ave.
Madison St.
Marion St.
Columbia St.
E. Jefferson St.
10th Ave.
99
Cherry St.
5
James St.
State Ferry Terminal
0
500 yards
Yesler Way
0
500 meters
8
Washington St.

boat basin, fish-processing and fisheries support terminals, and a restaurant.

7 The **historical marker** indicating the landing of the ship *Portland*, on July 17, 1897, is at Pier 58. The ship brought gold and news of the Klondike gold rush; shops at this pier continue to commemorate the event with gold-rush theme merchandise.

From Pier 51 at the foot of Yesler Way, walk a couple of blocks east to **Pioneer Park,** where an ornate iron-and-glass pergola stands. This was the site of Henry Yesler's (one of Seattle's first businesspeople) pier and sawmill, and Seattle's original business district. In 1889, a fire destroyed many of the wood-frame
8 buildings in the area now known as **Pioneer Square,** but the industrious residents and businesspeople rebuilt them with brick and mortar.

The term Skid Row originated here, when timber was logged off the hill and sent to the sawmill. The skid road was made of small logs laid crossways and greased so the freshly cut timber could slide down to the mill. With the Klondike gold rush, this area became populated with saloons and brothels; businesses gradually moved north, and the old pioneering area deteriorated. Eventually, only drunks and bums hung out on Skid Road, and the term changed to Skid Row and became synonymous with "down and out." Today's Pioneer Square encompasses about 18 blocks and includes restaurants, bars, shops, and the city's largest concentration of art galleries, but it is once again known as a hangout for those down on their luck. Incidents of crime in the neighborhood have increased lately, especially after dark. In Pioneer Square is the **Klondike Gold Rush National Historical Park** and interpretive center. The center provides insight into the story of Seattle's role in the 1897–98 gold rush through film presentations, permanent exhibits, and gold-panning demonstrations. *117 S. Main St., tel. 206/442–7220. Admission free. Open daily 9–5, except major holidays.*

Numbers in the margin correspond to points of interest on the Metropolitan Seattle map.

Walk a half block east on Main Street, and two blocks south on
9 Occidental Avenue to the **Kingdome,** Seattle's covered stadium where the Seattle Seahawks NFL team and the Seattle Mariners baseball team play. The 650-feet-diameter stadium was built in 1976 and has the world's largest self-supporting roof, which sits 250 feet high. If you're interested in the inner workings, take the one-hour guided tour. *201 S. King St., tel. 206/296–3111 for information. Tour admission: $3 adults, $1.50 children and senior citizens.*

10 To the east is a 40-square-block area known as the **International District** (the ID). Inhabited by about one-third Chinese and one-third Filipinos, other residents here come from all over Asia. The ID began as a haven for Chinese workers after they finished the Transcontinental Railroad. The community has remained largely intact, despite the anti-Chinese riots in Seattle during the 1880s and the World War II Japanese-American internment. The district, which includes many Chinese, Japanese, and Korean restaurants, also houses herbalists, massage parlors, acupuncturists, and about 30 private clubs for gambling and socializing. The most notorious club is the **Wah Mee Club,** on Canton Avenue, where a multiple murder linked to

Boeing Field, **21**
Henry Art Gallery, **18**
International District, **10**
Kingdome, **9**
Museum of History and Industry, **19**
Nippon Kan Theater, **11**
Seattle Center, **13**
Space Needle, **14**
Thomas Burke Memorial Washington State Museum, **17**
University of Washington, **16**
Washington Park Arboretum, **20**
Wing Luke Museum, **12**
Woodland Park Zoo, **15**

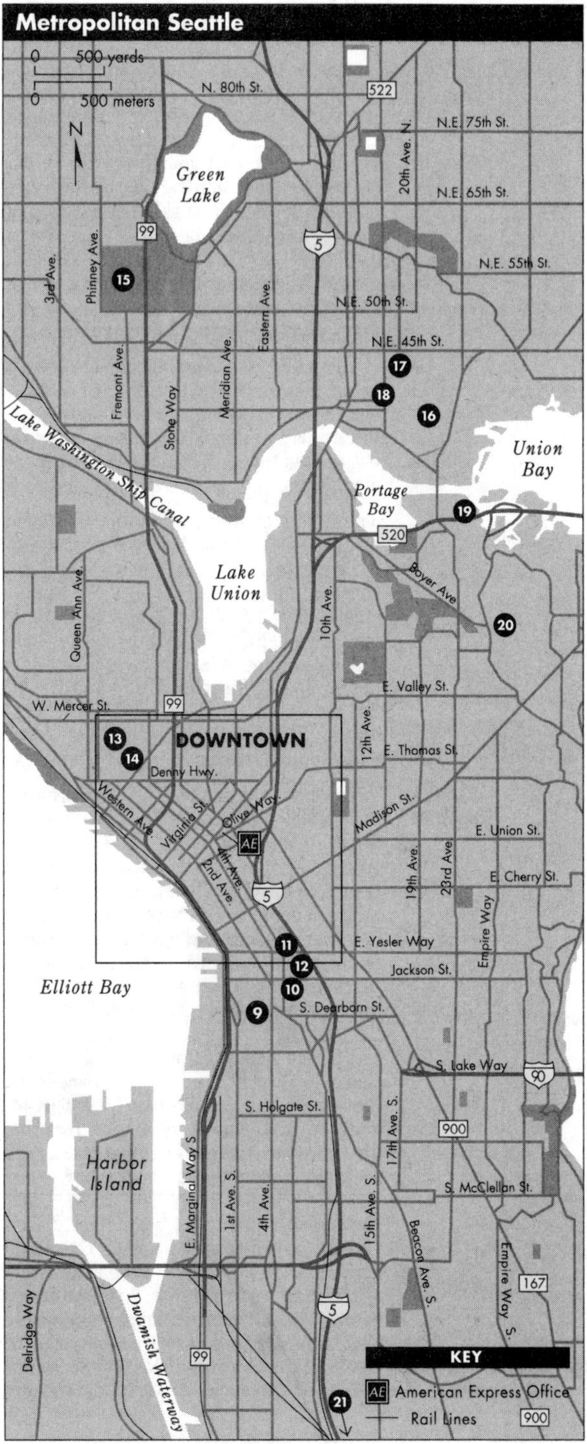

gangs and gambling occurred in 1983. **Uwajimaya** (519 6th Ave. S, tel. 206/624–6248), one of the—if not *the*—largest Japanese stores on the West Coast, is in this district as well. Here you will find china, gifts, fabrics, housewares, and a complete supermarket with an array of Asian foods.

Time Out If you need to rest your feet a bit by now, stop in at **Okazuya,** the Asian snack bar (tel. 206/624–6248) in Uwajimaya. You can get noodle dishes, sushi, tempura, *humbow,* and other Asian dishes for carryout or to eat in.

From Uwajimaya, continue north on 6th Street to Washington Street. In summer, as you walk up the hill, you can see the many gardens tended by residents of the ID.

11 Historically, the **Nippon Kan Theater** (628 S. Washington St., tel. 206/467–6807) was the focal point for Japanese-American activities, including Kabuki theater. Renovated and reopened in 1981 as a national historic site, it presents many Asian-interest productions, including the Japanese Performing Arts series, which runs from October through May.

The final stop on the southbound Downtown Seattle tour will
12 be at the **Wing Luke Museum,** named for the first Asian person to be elected to a Seattle city office, where exhibits emphasize Oriental history and culture. An acupuncture exhibit demonstrates how needles are inserted into parts of the body to release blocked energy and promote healing. Other elements of the permanent collection include costumes, fabrics, crafts, basketry, and Chinese traditional medicines. *407 7th Ave. S, tel. 206/623–5124. Admission: $2.50 adults, $1.50 senior citizens and students, 75¢ children. Open Tues.–Fri. 11–4:30, weekends noon–4; closed Mon.*

North of Downtown To explore outside the downtown area, take the 4th Avenue bus to Westlake Center, where you can pick up the Monorail to
13 **Seattle Center,** a 74-acre complex built for the 1962 Seattle World's Fair. It includes an amusement park, theaters, the Coliseum, exhibition halls, museums, shops, and the popular Space Needle with its restaurant and observation deck. The
14 landmark **Space Needle** can easily be seen from almost any spot in the downtown area, and looks like something from the old "Jetsons" cartoon show. The glass elevator to the observation deck offers an expansive view of the city.

Time Out The **Space Needle Lounge** (tel. 206/443–2100), on the observation deck (one floor above the Space Needle Restaurant), offers fabulous views of Elliott Bay and Queen Anne Hill. The black-and-gray exterior decor emphasizes the '60s style of the Needle. Ask the bartender for the special "Spirit of the Needle" cocktail or choose from the full bar.

From downtown or from the Seattle Center, take Highway 99 (Aurora Ave. N) north across the Aurora Bridge to the 50th
15 Street exit; follow signs to the **Woodland Park Zoo,** where many of the animals are free to roam their section of the total of 92 acres. The African savanna, the new elephant house, and the new tropical rain forest are popular features. Wheelchairs and strollers can be rented. *N. 59th St. and Fremont Ave., tel. 206/684–4800. Admission: $4.50 adults, $2.25 children 6–17 and*

senior citizens, children under 5 free. Open summer, daily 9:30–6; winter, daily 10–4.

From the Woodland Park Zoo, take the 50th Street exit to 15th Avenue NE, then drive south to 45th Street. Turn east for a
16 few blocks to the entrance of the 33,500-student **University of Washington.** The U-Dub, as locals call it, was founded in 1861. On the northwestern corner of the beautifully landscaped cam-
17 pus is the **Thomas Burke Memorial Washington State Museum,** Washington's natural-history and anthropological museum. The museum has been renovated recently and features exhibits on cultures of the Pacific region and the state's 35 Native American tribes. *17th Ave. NE and N.E. 45th St., tel. 206/543–5590. Admission: $2.50 adults, $1.50 youth and senior citizens; children 5 and under free. Open daily 10–5, Thurs. 10–8.*

18 Going south, on the west side of the campus is the **Henry Art Gallery,** which displays paintings from the 19th and 20th centuries, textiles, and traveling exhibits. *15th Ave. NE and N.E. 41st St., tel. 206/543–2280. Admission: $3 adults, $1.50 senior citizens; students and children 12 and under free; free Thurs. Open daily 10–5, Thurs. 10–9; closed Mon.*

Close to the university's Husky Stadium, off Montlake and
19 Lake Washington boulevards, is the **Museum of History and Industry.** An 1880s-era room and a Seattle time-line depict the city's earlier days. Other displays from the permanent collection are shown on a rotating basis, along with traveling exhibits. *2700 24th Ave. E, tel. 206/324–1125. Admission: $3 adults, $1.50 children 6–12 and senior citizens, children under 6 free. Open daily 10–4:30.*

At the museum pick up a brochure of self-guided walking tours
20 of the nearby **Washington Park Arboretum.** The arboretum's Rhododendron Glen and Azalea Way are in full bloom from March through June. During the rest of the year, other plants and wildlife flourish. A new visitor center at the north end of the park is open to instruct you on the species of flora and fauna you'll see here. *2300 Arboretum Dr. E, tel. 206/325–4510. Admission free. Park open daily 7 AM–sunset; visitor center open weekdays 10–3:45, weekends noon–3:45.*

21 If you have your own plane, you can land at **Boeing Field** to see the **Museum of Flight.** The earthbound can get there by metro bus No. 174 that follows 2nd Avenue from downtown Seattle. The **Red Barn,** Boeing's original airplane factory, houses an exhibit on the history of aviation. The **Great Gallery,** a dramatic structure designed by Seattle architect Ibsen Nelson, contains more than 20 vintage airplanes—suspended from the ceiling and on the ground—dating from the Wright brothers. For a complete lesson, take the free hour-long Boeing tour. *9404 E. Marginal Way S, tel. 206/764–5720. Admission: $5 adults and senior citizens, $3 children 6–16, children under 6 free. Open Fri.–Wed. 10–5, Thurs. 10–9; closed Christmas.*

Seattle for Free

Rainier Brewery, located 2 miles south of the Kingdome on I–5, offers 30-minute tours of the premises that conclude with free samples of the locally made beer for adults. If you don't want to drive, take Bus 130 bus from downtown. *3100 Airport Way S, tel. 206/622–2600. Tours weekdays 1–6. No children under 3.*

Gallery Walk (begin at any gallery in Pioneer Square, tel. 206/587–0260), an open house hosted by Seattle's art galleries, explores new local exhibits the first Thursday of every month, starting at 5.

The **Charles and Emma Frye Art Museum** features a large collection of Munich School and American School paintings. *704 Terry Ave., tel. 206/622–9250. Open Mon.–Sat. 10–5, Sun. noon–5.*

The **Elliott Bay Book Company** (101 S. Main St., tel. 206/ 624–6600) hosts lectures and readings by authors of local and international acclaim. Most are free, but phone ahead to be sure.

Recreational Equipment, Inc. (REI, tel. 206/323–8333), the largest consumer co-op in the United States, hosts free programs on travel, adventure, and outdoor activities in Seattle (1525 11th Ave.), Bellevue (15400 N.E. 20th St.), and Federal Way (2565 Gateway Center Blvd. S) locations, starting at 7 PM every Thursday, and at Lynnwood (4200 194th St. SW) at 7 PM on Tuesday.

Seattle's summer concerts, the **Out to Lunch Series** (tel. 206/623–0340), runs from mid-June to early September every weekday at noon in various parks, plazas, and atriums in downtown. Concerts feature local and national musicians and dancers. Call ahead for schedules and locations.

What to See and Do with Children

Burke-Gilman Trail (*see* Sports and the Outdoors, *below*) offers good bike trails for children.

Elliott Bay Book Company (*see* Seattle for Free, *above*) hosts a children's story hour at 11 AM on the first Saturday of the month.

Green Lake (*see* Sports and the Outdoors, *below*).

Museum of Flight (*see* Exploring Seattle, *above*).

Myrtle Edwards Park (*see* Sports and the Outdoors, *below*).

Seattle Aquarium (*see* Exploring Seattle, *above*).

Seattle Children's Museum is a colorful, spacious facility at the Seattle Center's Center House. An infant-toddler area features a giant, soft ferryboat for climbing and sliding. A bubble area helps children learn about shapes and gravity. The pretend neighborhood allows children to play in a post office, café, fire station, grocery store, and more. Intergenerational programs, special exhibits, and workshops are offered. *Fountain level of Seattle Center House, 305 Harrison St., tel. 206/441–1768. Admission: $3.50 adults and children, children under 1 free. Open Tues.–Sun. 10–5.*

The $10 million **Charlotte Martin Theatre,** which opened in the fall of 1993, is the new home of Seattle Children's Theatre. The space includes carpeted seating tiers and a curved, 485-seat auditorium, classrooms, and offices. SCT, the second-largest professional resident children's theater company in the United States, has developed a national reputation for its high-quality and innovative productions and has commissioned more than 55 new plays, adaptations and musicals, many of which have gone on to be produced by theater companies across the nation. Their season runs September–June. *Charlotte Martin Theatre* *at Seattle Center, Box 9640, 2nd Ave. N and Thomas St., tel 206/441–3322.*

Thomas Burke Memorial Washington State Museum (*see* Exploring Seattle, *above*).

Off the Beaten Track

Touring **brew pubs**—drinking establishments attached to actual breweries—is a congenial and educational alternative to usual city attractions. Seattle, as well as a good portion of the Pacific Northwest, has become a hotbed for **microbrews** (high-quality beers made for local distribution). All of the pubs listed below also serve food and nonalcoholic beverages. If live music is performed, a cover charge may be required; otherwise admission is free.

The **Pacific Northwest Brewing Co.,** located in the heart of Pioneer Square, offers six mild beers that reflect the taste of its British owner. The elegantly decorated interior—smooth high-tech design, blended with antiques and brewing equipment in full view—fits not only the personality of proprietor Richard Wrigley, but the downtown location as well. *322 Occidental Ave. S, tel. 206/621–7002. Open Tues.–Sat. 11:30 AM–midnight.*

Near the north end of the Fremont Bridge, just 8 miles from downtown, is the **Trolleyman,** birthplace of the local-favorites Ballard Bitter and Red Hook Ale. The premises mix Northwest style—whitewashed walls and a no-smoking policy—with a cozy British pub atmosphere that includes a fireplace and ample armchairs. *3400 Phinney Ave. N, tel. 206/548–8000. Open weekdays 8:30 AM–11 PM, Sat. 11–11, Sun. noon–6. Tours given weekdays at 3, weekends at 1:30, 2:30, 3:30, and 4:30.*

Catering to the nearby university crowd, the **Big Time Brewery** resembles an archetypal college-town pub, with a moose head on the wall and co-ed decor. Pale ale, amber, and porter are always on tap; specialty brews change monthly. *4133 University Way NE, tel. 206/545–4509. Open daily 11:30 AM–1 AM.*

Technically not a brew pub, **Cooper's Northwest Alehouse,** located north of the University District, nonetheless deserves mention for featuring the products of so many regional microbreweries. Its more than 20 brews are specialties from all over the West Coast, and the staff is awesomely knowledgeable about the subtle distinctions between each brew. If you don't come for the drink, come for the dart tournaments that are played on a regular basis. *8065 Lake City Way NE, tel. 206/522–2923. Open weekdays 3 PM–2 AM, Sat. 1 PM–2 AM, Sun. 1 PM–midnight.*

If your preference is viticulture, visit **Ste. Michelle Winery,** one of the oldest wineries in the state. It's located 15 miles northeast of Seattle, nestled on 87 wooded acres that were once part of the estate of lumber baron Fred Stimson. Some of the original 1912 buildings are still on the property, including the family home—the manor house—which is on the National Register of Historic Places. Trout ponds, a carriage house, a caretaker's cottage, and formal gardens are part of the original estate. The landscaping, created by New York's Olmsted family (designers of New York City's Central Park), has been restored, and the gardens feature hundreds of trees, shrubs, and plants. Visitors are invited to picnic and explore the grounds. Delicatessen items, wines, and wine-related gifts are available at the winery shop. In the summer, the company hosts a series of nationally known performers and arts events in the amphitheater. *14111 N.E. 145th St., Woodinville, tel. 206/488–1133. From downtown Seattle take I–90 east, then go north on I–405. Take Exit 23 east (S.R. 522) to the Woodinville exit. Complimentary wine tastings and cellar tours are available daily 10–4:30, except holidays.*

Another option if you're looking to go off the beaten track is to visit the Hiram M. Chittenden Locks, more commonly called the **Ballard Locks,** part of the 8-mile Lake Washington Ship Canal linking lakes Washington and Union with the salt water of Shilshole Bay and Puget Sound. Completed in 1917, the locks currently service some 100,000 boats yearly by raising and lowering water levels anywhere from 6 to 26 feet.

The locks themselves are fascinating to watch as a variety of commercial fishing boats and pleasure craft go through them, but there are several other sights nearby that are well worth seeing. The **Fish Ladder** has 21 levels that allow fish to swim upstream on a gradual incline. A series of seaquariumlike viewing rooms that runs alongside the ladder below the waterline allows visitors to watch several varieties of salmon and trout—an estimated half-million fish yearly—struggle against the current as they migrate upstream. (This, by the way, is where various attempts are being carried out to prevent sea lions, including the locally notorious Herschel, from depleting the salmon population.)

On the north side of the locks is a fine 7-acre **ornamental garden** of native and exotic plants, shrubs, and trees. Also on the north side is a staffed visitor center with displays on the history and operation of the locks, and several fanciful sculptures by local artists. Along the south side is a lovely 1,200-foot promenade with a footbridge, fishing pier, and an observation deck. *North entrance, 3015 N.W. 54th St., west of the Ballard Bridge. Locks tel. 206/783–7001; visitor center tel. 206/783–7059. Visitor center open daily 10–7; closed in winter, Tues., Wed.; locks open year-round, except for maintenance.*

Two legendary performers—rock guitarist Jimi Hendrix and kung-fu movie star Bruce Lee—are buried in the Seattle area; their graves are popular sites for fans who wish to pay their respects. In addition, there is a memorial to Hendrix, a Seattle native, overlooking the African Savannah exhibit at Woodland Park Zoo; appropriately enough, it's a big rock.

Jimi Hendrix's grave site is at the Greenwood Cemetery, in Renton. *From Seattle, take I–5 south to the Renton exit, then I–405 past Southcenter to Exit 4B. Bear right under the freeway, take a right along Sunset Blvd. 1 block and right again up 3rd St. Continue 1 mi and go right at the 3rd light; the cemetery is on the corner of 3rd and Monroe Sts., tel. 206/255–1511. Open daily until dusk. Inquire at the office; a counselor will direct you to the site.*

Bruce Lee's grave site is at the Lakeview Cemetery on the north slope of Capitol Hill. *1554 15th Ave. E, directly north of Volunteer Park, tel. 206/322–1582. Open weekdays 9–4:30. Inquire at the office for a map.*

Shopping

Shopping Districts

Westlake Center (1601 5th Ave., tel. 206/467–1600) lies in the middle of downtown Seattle. The three-story steel-and-glass building contains 80 upscale shops, as well as covered walkways to Seattle's two major department stores, **Nordstrom's** and **The Bon.**

Pike Place Market (*see* Exploring Seattle, *above*).

The **University District** (University Ave., north and south of 45th St., tel. 206/527–2567) has an eclectic mixture of such student-oriented imports as ethnic jewelry and South American sweaters; a few upscale shops; and many bookstores.

Seattle's **Fremont area** (N. 35th St. and Fremont Ave. N, north of the ship canal and the Fremont Bridge), a remnant from hippie days, offers products of a different variety—namely funky and used. There's the **Daily Planet** (3416 Fremont Ave. N, tel. 206/633–0895), and **Guess Where** (615 N. 35th St., tel. 206/547–3793) for vintage clothing. At **Armadillo & Co.** (3510 Fremont Pl. N, tel. 206/633–4241), you'll find jewelry, T-shirts, and other armadillo-theme accessories and gifts. The **Frank & Dunya Gallery** (3418 Fremont Ave. N, tel. 206/547–6760) features unique art pieces, from furniture to jewelry. You'll also find **Dusty Strings** (3406 Fremont Ave. N, tel. 206/634–1656), a hammered dulcimer shop.

Capitol Hill's **Broadway Avenue** features clothing stores, high-design housewares shops, espresso bars, and restaurants. An unusual boutique is the **Bead Works** (233 Broadway Ave. E, tel. 206/323–4998).

Northgate Mall, located 10 miles north of downtown, encompasses 118 shops, including **Nordstrom's, The Bon, Lamonts,** and **J.C. Penney.** *I–5 and Northgate Way, tel. 206/362–4777. Open Mon.–Sat. 9:30–9:30, Sun. 11–6.*

Southcenter Mall contains 140 shops and is anchored by major department stores. *I–5 and I–405 in Tukwila, tel. 206/246–7400. Open Mon.–Sat. 9:30–9:30, Sun. 11–6.*

Bellevue Square, an upscale shopping center about 8 miles east of Seattle, houses more than 200 shops and includes a children's play area, the Bellevue Art Museum, and covered parking. *N.E. 8th St. and Bellevue Way, tel. 206/454–8096. Open Mon.–Sat. 9:30–9:30, Sun. 11–6.*

Specialty Stores

Antiques — **Antique Importers** (640 Alaskan Way, tel. 206/628–8905) carries mostly English oak antiques.

Art Dealers — **Michael Pierce Gallery** (600 Pine St., tel. 206/447–9166) specializes in limited-edition prints and paintings on paper.

Art Glass — The **Glass House** (311 Occidental Ave. S, tel. 206/682–9939), Seattle's only working glass studio open for public viewing, features one of the largest displays of glass artwork in the city.

Chocolates — **Cafe Dilettante** (416 Broadway Ave. E, tel. 206/329–6463) is well-known for its mouth-watering dark chocolates. Recipes come via Julius Rudolf Franzen, who obtained them from the kitchen of the imperial court of Russia when he was commissioned by Czar Nicholas II as master pastry chef. Franzen emigrated to the United States where he passed his recipes on to the grandfather of Cafe Dilettante's owner.

Crafts **Pike Place Market** (*see* Exploring Seattle, *above*).
Flying Shuttle Ltd. (607 1st Ave., tel. 206/343–9762) displays handcrafted jewelry, whimsical folk art, handknits, and handwoven garments.

Jewelry **Fireworks Gallery** (210 1st Ave. S, tel. 206/682–8707; 400 Pine St., tel. 206/682–6462) features whimsical earrings and pins.
Turgeon-Raine Jewelers (1407 5th Ave., tel. 206/447–9488) is an exceptional store with a sophisticated but friendly staff.

Leather and Luggage **Bergman Luggage Co.** (1930 3rd Ave., tel. 206/448–3000) features luggage in a variety of prices and materials.

Men's Apparel **Joseph Abboud** (1335 5th Ave., tel. 206/682–4485) features his own sophisticated designer wear, as well as casual clothing predominantly for men.
Jeffrey-Michael (1318 4th Ave., tel. 206/625–9891) provides a fine line of traditional, business, and casual men's clothing.
Mario's (1513 6th Ave., tel. 206/223–1461) offers a wide selection of contemporary menswear.

Outdoor Wear and Equipment **REI** (1525 11th Ave., tel. 206/323–8333) sells clothing as well as outdoor equipment, including water bottles, tents, bikes, and freeze-dried food in a creaky, funky building on Capitol Hill.
Eddie Bauer (5th Ave. and Union St., tel. 206/622–2766) features sports and outdoor apparel.

Toys **Magic Mouse Toys** (603 1st Ave., tel. 206/682–8097) carries two floors of toys, from small windups to giant stuffed animals.
Great Windup (Pike Place Market, tel. 206/621–9370) carries all sorts of windup action toys.

Wine **Delaurenti Wine Shop** (1435 1st Ave., tel. 206/340–1498) has a knowledgeable staff and a large selection of Northwest Italian wines.
Pike & Western Wine Merchants (Pike Pl. and Virginia St., tel. 206/441–1307 or 206/441–1308) carries a wide selection of Northwest wines from small wineries.

Women's Apparel **Boutique Europa** (1015 1st Ave., tel. 206/624–5582) features sophisticated clothing from Europe.
Littler's (Rainier Sq., tel. 206/223–1331) offers classic fashions for women.
Local Brilliance (1535 1st Ave., tel. 206/343–5864) showcases fashions from local designers.

Sports and the Outdoors

Participant Sports

"The best things in life are free" is a homily that holds true, at least in part, when it comes to keeping fit in this most health-oriented of cities. Walking, bicycling, hiking, and jogging require little money; pay-as-you-go alternatives such as golf, kayak, sailboat, or sailboard rentals require only marginally more.

Bicycling Although much of Seattle is so hilly that recreational bicycling is strenuous, many residents nonetheless commute by bike. The trail circling **Green Lake** and the **Burke-Gilman Trail** are popular among recreational bicyclists, although at Green Lake the crowds of joggers and walkers tend to impede fast travel. The Burke-Gilman Trail is a city-maintained trail extending 12.1 miles along Seattle's waterfront from Lake Washington nearly to Salmon Bay along an abandoned railroad line; it is a much less congested path. **Myrtle Edwards Park,** north of Pier 70, has a two-lane path for jogging and bicycling. For general information about Seattle's parks and trails, call the Seattle Parks Department (tel. 206/684–4075).

A number of shops around Seattle rent mountain bikes as well as standard touring or racing bikes and equipment. Among them are **Greg's Greenlake Cycle** (7007 Woodlawn Ave. NE, tel. 206/523–1822) and **Mountain Bike Specialists** (5625 University Way NE, tel. 206/527–4310).

Fishing There are plenty of good spots for fishing on **Lake Washington, Green Lake,** and **Lake Union,** and there are several fishing piers along the **Elliott Bay** waterfront. A number of companies operating from **Shilshole Bay** also offer charter trips for catching salmon, rock cod, flounder, and sea bass. A couple of the many Seattle-based charter companies are **Ballard Salmon Charter** (tel. 206/789–6202) and **Sport Fishing of Seattle** (tel. 206/623–4253). A two-day fishing license costs $3.50, and some charter companies include it in their charges.

Golf There are almost 50 public golf courses in the Seattle area. Among the most popular municipally run courses are **Jackson Park** (1000 N.E. 135th St., tel. 206/363–4747) and **Jefferson Park** (4101 Beacon Ave. S, tel. 206/762–4513). For more information, contact the Seattle Parks and Recreation Department (tel. 206/684–4075).

Jogging, Skating, Walking **Green Lake** is far and away Seattle's most popular spot for jogging, and the 3-mile circumference of this picturesque lake is custom-made for it. Walking, bicycling, roller skating, fishing, and lounging on the grass and feeding the plentiful waterfowl are also popular pastimes here. In summer, a large children's wading pool on the northeast side of the lake is a popular gathering spot. Several outlets clustered along the east side of the lake offer skate and cycle rentals.

Other good jogging locales are along the **Burke-Gilman Trail,** around the reservoir at **Volunteer Park,** and at **Myrtle Edwards Park,** north of the waterfront.

Skiing Snoqualmie Pass in the Cascade Mountains, about an hour's drive east of Seattle on I–90, has a number of fine resorts offering both day and night downhill skiing. Among them: **Alpental, Ski Acres, Snoqualmie Summit** (for all areas: 3010 77th St. SE, Mercer Island 98040, tel. 206/232–8182). All of these areas rent equipment and have full restaurant/lodge facilities.

For ski reports for these areas and the more distant White Pass, Crystal Mountain, and Stevens Pass, call 206/634–0200 or 206/634–2754. For recorded messages about road conditions in the passes, call 206/455–7900.

Tennis There are public tennis courts in many parks around the Seattle area. For information, contact the King County Parks and Recreation Department (tel. 206/296–4258).

Water Sports

Boating

It stands to reason that sailboating and powerboating are popular in Seattle. **Sailboat Rentals & Yachts** (301 N. Northlake Way, tel. 206/632–3302), on the north side of Lake Union near the Fremont area, rents sailboats, with or without skippers, 14–38 feet in length, by the hour or the day. **Wind Works Rentals** (7001 Seaview Ave. NW, tel. 206/784–9386), on Shilshole Bay, rents sailboats ranging from 25 to 40 feet on the more challenging waters of Puget Sound, with or without skippers and by the half-day, day, or week. **Seacrest Boat House** (1660 Harbor Ave. SW, tel. 206/932–1050), in West Seattle, rents 18-foot aluminum fishing boats, with or without motors, by the hour or the day.

Kayaking

Kayaking—around both the inner waterways (Lake Union, Lake Washington, the Ship Canal) and open water (Elliott Bay)—is a terrific and easy way to get an unusual view of Seattle's busy waterfront. **The Northwest Outdoor Center** (2100 Westlake Ave. N, tel. 206/281–9694), on the west side of Lake Union, rents one- or two-person kayaks and equipment by the hour or week and provides both basic and advanced instruction. Canoes and rowing shells are also available.

Sailboarding

Lake Union and Green Lake are Seattle's prime sailboarding spots. Sailboards can be rented year-round at the **Bavarian Surf Shop** (711 N. Northlake Way, tel. 206/545–9463) on Lake Union. Lessons are available.

Spectator Sports

Baseball

The **Seattle Mariners,** an American-league team, play April through early October at the Kingdome (201 S. King St., tel. 206/628–3555).

Basketball

The **Seattle SuperSonics,** an NBA team, play October through April at the Seattle Center Coliseum (1st Ave. N, tel. 206/281–5850).

Boat Racing

The **unlimited hydroplane** (tel. 206/628–0888) races cap Seattle's Seafair festivities from mid-July through the first Sunday in August. The races are held on Lake Washington near Seward Park, and tickets cost $10–$20. Weekly **sailing regattas** are held in the summer on Lakes Union and Washington. Call the Seattle Yacht Club (tel. 206/325–1000) for schedules.

Football

Seattle's NFL team, the **Seahawks,** play August through December in the Kingdome (201 S. King St., tel. 206/827–9777).

Dining

By John Doerper

John Doerper is a local food critic and travel writer whose pieces have appeared in Travel & Leisure *and* Pacific Northwest Magazine.

Highly recommended restaurants are indicated by a star ★.

Category	Cost*
Very Expensive	over $35
Expensive	$25–$35
Moderate	$15–$25
Inexpensive	under $15

**per person, excluding drinks, service, and sales tax (about 7.9%, varies slightly by community)*

American/ Continental ★

Canlis. This sumptuous restaurant is almost more of a Seattle institution than a place of fine dining, dating from a time when steak served by kimono-clad waitresses was the pinnacle of high living in the city by the sound. Little has changed here since the '50s. The restaurant is still very expensive, very good at what it does, and very popular; and the view across Lake Union is as good as ever (though curtained off by a forest of recently built high rises on the far shore). Besides the famous steaks, there are equally famous oysters from Quilcene Bay and fresh fish in season, cooked to a turn. *2576 Aurora Ave. N, tel. 206/283-3313. Reservations advised. Jacket required. AE, DC, MC, V. Closed lunch and Sun. Very Expensive.*

Metropolitan Grill. This favorite lunch spot of the executive crowd serves custom-aged, mesquite-broiled steaks in a classic steakhouse atmosphere. The steaks—the best in Seattle—are huge and come with baked potatoes or pasta. This is not food for timid eaters: Even the veal chop is extra thick, and the hamburger ("Western Ground Sirloin Steak") is so big that one person may have problems finishing it. Among the accompaniments, the onion rings and sautéed mushrooms are tops. Don't be surprised if you hear more Japanese than English as you eat here: The place is so popular with visiting businessmen that there's a menu in Japanese, too. *818 2nd Ave., tel. 206/624-3287. Reservations advised. Dress: casual but neat. AE, DC, MC, V. Closed Sun. lunch. Moderate.*

Place Pigalle. Despite its French name, this is a very American restaurant and a popular place with locals. Large windows look out over Elliott Bay and, in nice weather, are open to admit the salt breeze. Bright flower bouquets lighten up the café tables, and the friendly staff makes you feel right at home in this small, intimate restaurant located behind a meat market in the Pike Place Market's main arcade. Seasonal meals feature seafood and local ingredients. Go for the rich oyster stew, the fresh Dungeness crab (available only when it is truly fresh), or the fresh fish of the day baked in hazelnuts. *Pike Place Market, tel. 206/624-1756. Reservations advised. Dress: casual but neat. MC, V. Closed Sun. Moderate.*

Asian ★

Wild Ginger. This restaurant near the Pike Place Market specializes in seafood and Southeast Asian fare, ranging from mild Cantonese to spicier Vietnamese, Thai, and Korean dishes. The *satay* (chunks of beef, chicken, or vegetables skewered and grilled, and usually served with a spicy peanut sauce) bar, where you can sit to sip local brews and eat tangy, elegantly seasoned skewered seafood or meat until 2 AM, has quickly become a favorite local hangout. The dining room has an old-fashioned club-like decor of high ceilings, lots of mahogany, and Asian art. House specialties include satay, live crab, sweetly flavored duck, and a variety of wonderful soups. A number of vegetarian dishes also are offered. *1400 Western Ave., tel. 206/623-4450. Reservations advised. Dress: casual but neat. AE, CB, DC, MC, V. Closed Sun. lunch. Moderate.*

Chinese

Linyen. This comfortable restaurant comes into its own late at night, when Seattle celebrities mingle here with chefs from Chinatown restaurants. The standard fare is light-style Cantonese, but you're best off sticking with the blackboard specials: clams in black-bean sauce, geoduck, spicy chicken, and fish dishes. The dart games in the bar are a popular—and heated—diversion. *424 7th Ave. S, tel. 206/622-8181. Reserva-*

Campagne, **6**
Casa-U-Betcha, **3**
Chau's Chinese, **16**
El Puerco Lloron, **7**
Emmet Watson's Oyster Bar, **5**
Fuller's, **1**
Hunt Club, **19**
Il Terazzo Carmine, **15**
Kells, **4**
Linyen, **18**
Metropolitan Grill, **13**
Nikko, **2**
The Painted Table, **12**
Place Pigalle, **10**
Siam Gourmet, **17**
Takara, **8**
Three Girls Bakery, **9**
Trattoria Mitchelli, **14**
Wild Ginger, **11**

Downtown Seattle Dining

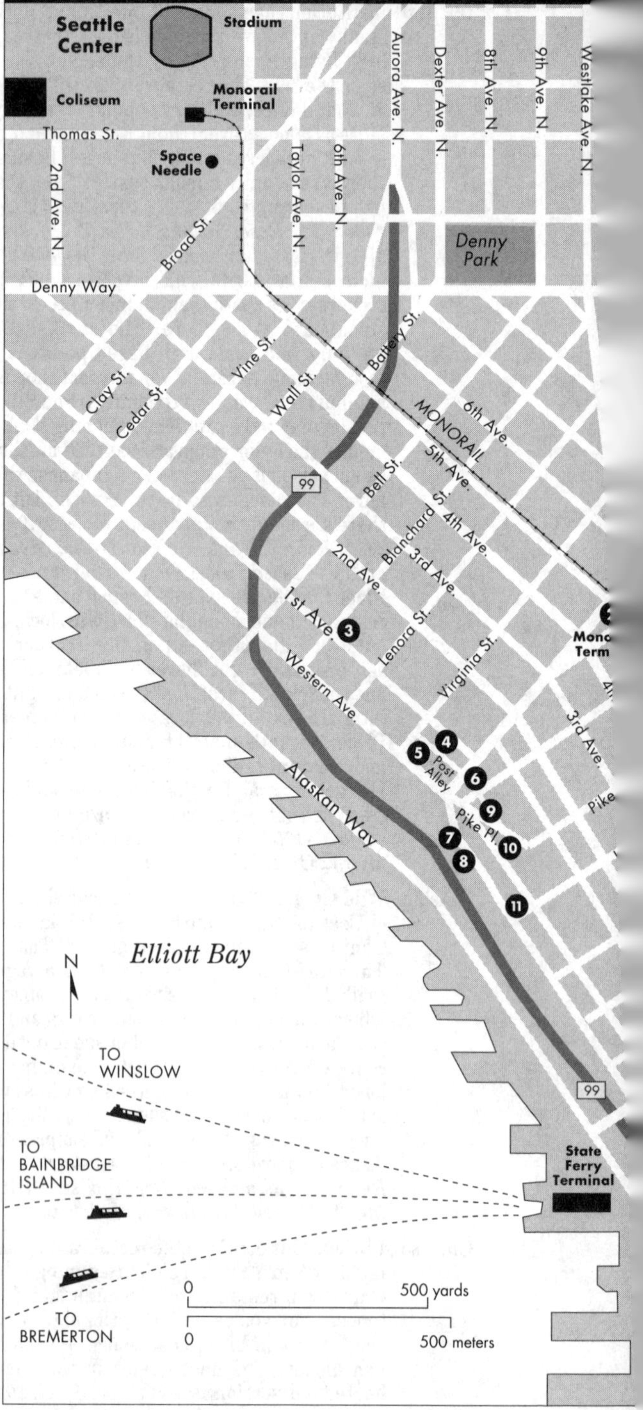

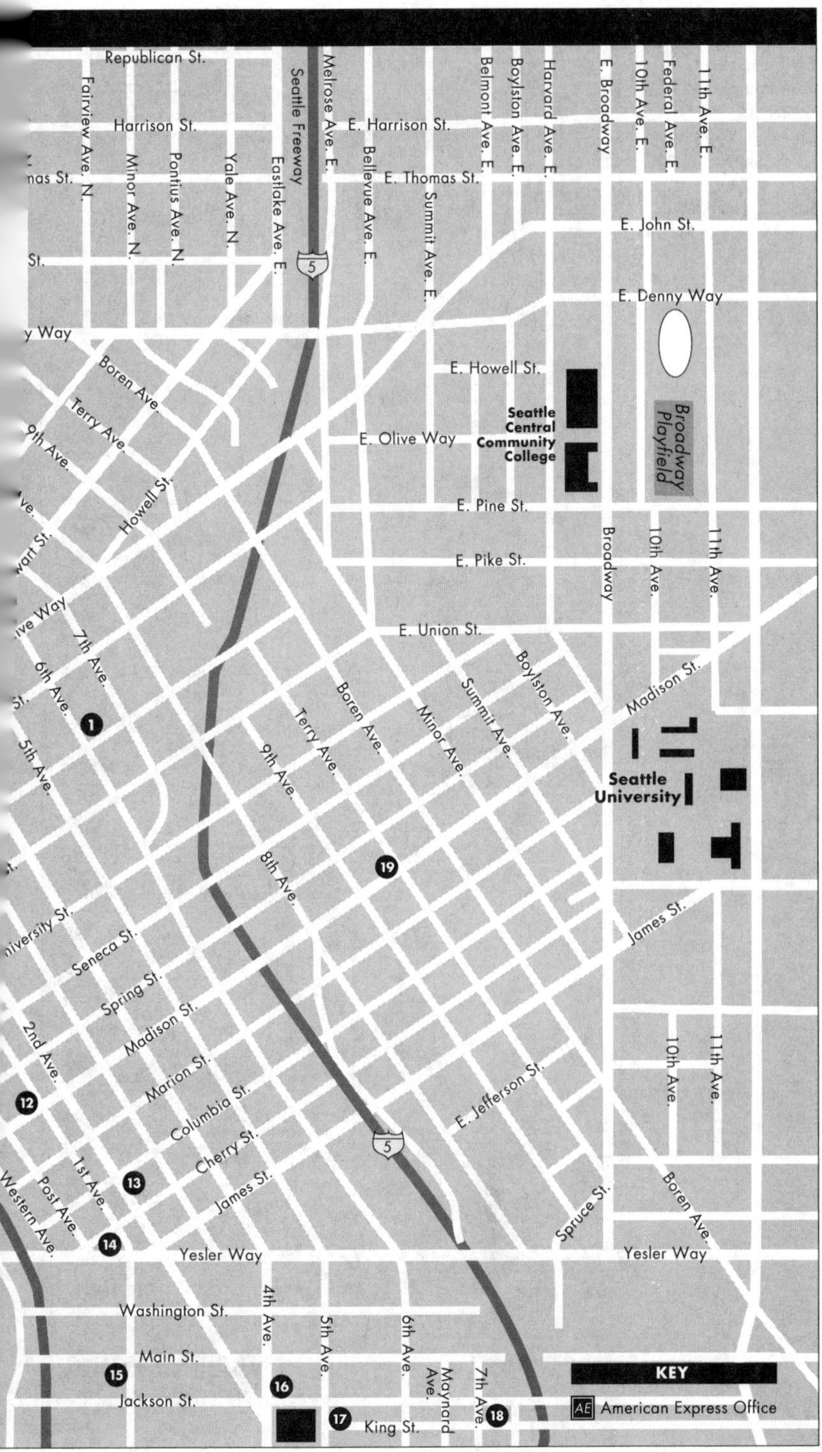
Republican St.
Harrison St.
Fairview Ave. N.
Minor Ave. N.
Pontius Ave. N.
Yale Ave. N.
Eastlake Ave. E.
Seattle Freeway
Melrose Ave. E.
E. Harrison St.
Bellevue Ave. E.
E. Thomas St.
Summit Ave. E.
Belmont Ave. E.
Boylston Ave. E.
Harvard Ave. E.
E. Broadway
10th Ave. E.
Federal Ave. E.
11th Ave. E.
E. John St.
E. Denny Way
5
Boren Ave.
Terry Ave.
9th Ave.
Howell St.
E. Howell St.
E. Olive Way
Seattle Central Community College
Broadway Playfield
E. Pine St.
E. Pike St.
Broadway
10th Ave.
11th Ave.
E. Union St.
7th Ave.
6th Ave.
5th Ave.
Boren Ave.
Terry Ave.
9th Ave.
Minor Ave.
Summit Ave.
Boylston Ave.
Madison St.
Seattle University
8th Ave.
James St.
Seneca St.
Spring St.
Madison St.
Marion St.
Columbia St.
Cherry St.
James St.
2nd Ave.
1st Ave.
Post Ave.
Western Ave.
E. Jefferson St.
Spruce St.
Boren Ave.
Yesler Way
Yesler Way
Washington St.
Main St.
Jackson St.
King St.
4th Ave.
5th Ave.
6th Ave.
Maynard Ave.
7th Ave.
10th Ave.
11th Ave.
1
12
13
14
15
16
17
18
19
KEY
AE American Express Office

A. Jay's, **30**
Adriatica, **26**
Bahn Thai, **28**
Cafe Juanita, **27**
Canlis, **25**
Le Tastevin, **29**
Ray's Boathouse, **22**
Rover's, **31**
Saleh Al Lago, **20**
Santa Fe Cafe, **21, 24**

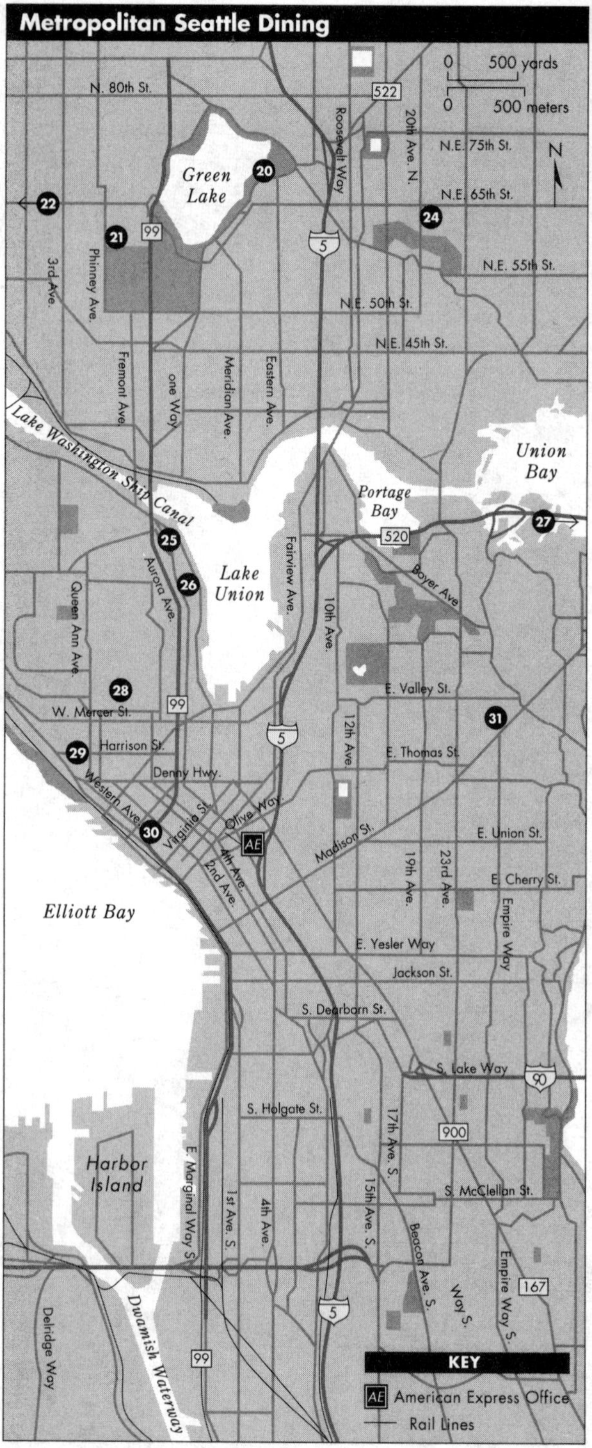

tions advised. Dress: casual but neat. AE, DC, MC, V. Closed lunch. Moderate.

Chau's Chinese Restaurant. This small, very plain place on the outer limits of Seattle's Chinatown serves great seafood, such as steamed oysters in garlic sauce, Dungeness crab with ginger and onion, and geoduck. Avoid the standard dishes of the Cantonese repertoire that dominate much of the menu, and stick to the seafood and specials. *310 4th Ave. S, tel. 206/621–0006. Reservations advised. Dress: casual. MC, V. Closed weekend lunch. Inexpensive.*

Deli

A. Jay's. This little deli has done so well that it's now open for dinner Tuesday–Saturday, serving eclectic bistro-style fare, but breakfast is still the big draw. Especially on weekends, people flock here for the eggs Benedict, blintzes, whitefish, and bagels piled high with cream cheese and lox. Service is friendly. You can sit and talk without being rushed. At lunch there are large sandwiches (good pastrami), pasta, burgers, and soup. *2619 1st Ave., tel. 206/441–1511. Reservations advised. Dress: casual. AE, MC, V. Closed Sun. night. Inexpensive.*

Three Girls Bakery. It's a 13-seat glassed-in lunch counter behind a bakery outlet, serving sandwiches and soups to hungry folks in a hurry. Go for the chili and a hunk of Sicilian sourdough. Another idea is to buy a loaf at the takeout counter, get smoked salmon at the fish place next door, and head for a picnic table in Waterfront Park. *Pike Place Market, 1514 Pike Pl., tel. 206/622–1045. No reservations. Dress: casual. No credit cards. No alcohol. Closed dinner and Sun. Inexpensive.*

French

Campagne. Overlooking Pike Place Market and Elliott Bay, Campagne is intimate and urbane. The white walls, picture windows, white linens, candles, and fresh flowers evoke southern France. Start out with fresh oysters on the half-shell, calamari fillets with ground almonds, or Campagne's own seafood sausage. The restaurant's unique French country fare replaces the traditional cream and butter sauces with oils, light stocks, and vegetable essences to create such flavorful treats as apricot-cider and green peppercorn sauce that accompanies the Oregon rabbit, or the carrot and orange essence served with the cinnamon-roasted quail. Seafood entrées include pan-fried scallops with a green peppercorn tarragon sauce. *Inn at the Market, 86 Pine St., tel. 206/728–2800. Reservations advised. Jacket required. AE, MC, V. Expensive.*

Le Tastevin. This restaurant set a new tone for Seattle's French restaurants when it opened. Instead of dark wood and subdued lighting, you'll find a sunny, trellised dining room, bright with light wood and green plants, and racks of wine bottles along the far walls. The windows face west, toward the Olympic Mountains and colorful sunsets. Le Tastevin serves a combination of classic French and Northwest nouvelle cuisine. The house specialty is fresh salmon with herbs baked in a puff pastry and served with a chardonney-pomegranate sauce. The wide variety of dishes featuring this ubiquitous fish also includes salmon with plum tomatoes, garlic, and basil. Cream, the staple of traditional French cookery, is almost absent except for the Coquilles St. Jacques, with a champagne-cream sauce. For dessert, you should not miss the fresh fruit ices—made daily from scratch—or the wine sorbets. As an alternative to the expensive regular lunch menu, try the bar lunch, which is just as good. In the late afternoon, during happy hour, inexpensive dishes and great snack food are served. The wine list is vast, spanning many countries and vintages, and quite reasonably priced. *19 W. Harrison St., tel. 206/283–0991. Reservations advised. Jacket required. AE, DC, MC, V. Closed Sat. lunch and Sun. Expensive.*

Rover's. This is French cooking at its best, with a daily menu based on what is locally available. Specialties include salmon, pheasant, quail, venison, and rabbit in elegant yet surprisingly light sauces. The enormous pasta dishes are among Seattle's best. Each of the dishes carries chef/owner Thierry Rautureau's Northwest-French stylings. The setting is highly romantic, in a small house with a garden. Herbs and flowers grow in flower beds just outside the windows. Service is excellent—friendly but unobtrusive. *2808 E. Madison St., tel. 206/325–7442. Reservations advised. Dress: casual but neat. AE, MC, V. Closed lunch and Mon. Moderate.*

Irish

Kells. Tucked into an old brick building along the Pike Place Market's most romantic thoroughfare, you'll forget you're in America when you step through the door of this pub. The accoutrements look like they've been brought over from the old country: bar, taps, wood paneling, sporting prints are all very Irish, down to the accents and politics. The food is simple but tasty: Irish stew, leg of lamb, meat pies, but there's also seafood and beef dishes. Fresh Guinness and Harp are on tap, as are hearty Northwest brews. The place rings with live Irish music Wednesday through Saturday nights. Kells is very friendly and feels an instant home away from home. In summer there's limited outdoor seating in the alley. *Pike Place Market, 1916 Post Alley, tel. 206/728–1916. Reservations advised. Dress: casual but neat. MC, V. Closed Sun. Moderate.*

Italian

Il Terrazo Carmine. On the ground floor of a Pioneer Square office building, this restaurant surrounds diners with a comfortable, but refined atmosphere from the ceiling-to-floor draperies to the genteel service and quiet music. Chef-owner Carmine Smeraldo prepares flavorful chicken dishes with procuitto and fontina, and his veal baked with spinach and scallops is simply excellent. The pasta dishes, too, are superb. In the summer, you can choose to eat outdoors on the patio that faces a large fountain. *411 1st Ave. S, tel. 206/467–7797. Reservations advised. Dress: casual but neat. AE, D, DC, MC, V. Expensive.*

Saleh Al Lago. This restaurant north of downtown with a view of Green Lake and the park serves up some of the best Italian fare in the city. The well-lit dining room of soft colors invites simple, well-paced evening dining and choices such as the antipasti, fresh pasta, and veal dishes are always excellent. Be sure to try the *ravioli al mondo mio*, the chef's special ravioli (filling and sauce vary), or the *tagliatelle* (flat, ribboned egg pasta) with champagne and caviar. Even deceptively plain fare, like grilled breast of chicken with olive oil and fresh herbs, is superb here, with just the right—and a very light—touch. *6804 E. Greenlake Way N, tel. 206/522–7943. Reservations advised. Jacket required. AE, MC, V. Closed Sat. lunch and Sun. Expensive.*

Cafe Juanita. This comfortable, casual place—with wonderful views from the windows—is more than just a restaurant. There's a winery in the basement, and the vintages made there—bottled under owner/chef/winemaker Peter Dow's Cavatappi label—are available upstairs. The veal scaloppine and chicken dishes can be a bit on the rich and buttery side, but there's plenty of inexpensive Italian wine on the lengthy wine list to dilute the cream. Other entrées include lamb, salmon, fresh pastas, and veal. *9702 N.E. 120th Pl., Kirkland, tel. 206/823–1505. Reservations advised. Dress: casual but neat. MC, V. Closed lunch. Moderate.*

Trattoria Mitchelli. This archetypal Seattle storefront café is usually noisy and crowded, especially in the wee hours of the morning (the place stays open till 4 AM); and has an urban Bohemian atmosphere that's fast-paced and friendly, though you're never rushed. The food isn't haute cuisine, but it's tasty, moderately priced, and comes in generous portions: heaping servings of Italian pasta, sandwiches, and antipasti. *84 Yesler Way, tel. 206/623–3885. No reservations. Dress: casual. AE, DC, MC, V. Moderate.*

Japanese

Nikko. Although Nikko has moved uptown from the International District into stylish quarters in the Westin Hotel, it continues to serve some of the best sushi and sashimi in town under the able direction of owner Shiro Kashiba. The sushi bar is the architectural centerpiece of the restaurant's sophisticated Japanese decor of low lighting and black lacquer-painted wood. The Kasuzuke cod and teriyaki salmon are both highly recommended. *Westin Hotel, 1900 5th Ave., tel. 206/322–4641. Reservations advised. Dress: casual but neat. AE, D, DC, MC, V. Closed lunch Sat., Sun. Moderate–Expensive.*

Takara. Sushi chef Kuma-san in full action can look like a character from a Japanese wood-block print: a master samurai swordsman preparing to fight heaven and earth. But there's nothing combative about the ever-smiling Kuma-san—except for his determination to serve only the freshest seafood for sushi and sashimi. It's the freshness of the raw materials and the quality of the knife handling (swordsmanship is more like it, actually) that's making him the hottest sushi chef in town. He's been known to create a perfect rose from translucent slices of raw tuna, and he can form a phoenix in full flight from a lump of rice (for the body), golden salmon caviar (to simulate the iridescent back feathers), and sparkling *nori* seaweed (for the head, beak, and wings). No wonder Japanese businessmen flock here for lunch. The dining room serves classic Japanese dishes using Northwest ingredients. The salmon teriyaki is superb, and so is the steamed black cod. *Pike Place Market Hillclimb, 1501 Western Ave., tel. 206/682–8609. Reservations advised for dining room, no reservations for sushi bar. Dress: casual but neat. AE, MC, V. Beer and sake. Closed Sun., except May–Labor Day. Moderate.*

Mediterranean

Adriatica. This place gathered a loyal local following, becoming a virtual Seattle institution along the way, and was then discovered by visitors who spread the word. Located in a hillside Craftsman-style house, the dining room and upstairs bar offer views of Lake Union. Over several years, the fare here has evolved into a unique Pacific Northwest–influenced Greek and Italian cuisine. Regular offerings include daily fresh fish, a pasta, a risotto, and seafood souvlaki. Phyllo pastries with honey and nuts are among the tasty and interesting dessert choices. *1107 Dexter Ave. N., tel. 206/285–5000. Reservations advised. Dress: casual but neat. AE, DC, MC, V. Moderate–Expensive.*

Mexican **Casa-U-Betcha.** Colorful neon signs and faux granite sculptures standing in for room dividers create a fittingly lively atmosphere for the upscale crowd and cuisine at this trendy south of the border-themed spot. Familiar Mexican dishes are served using less grease, less cheese, and black beans rather than refried. But the menu isn't too strict, and it injects the influence of Caribbean, Central and South American cooking (south of the border here seems to mean anywhere between Texas and the equator) into such inventive offerings as Coyote Moon Carnitas—lean pork seasoned with herbs and marinated in lime juice, then grilled. *2212 1st Ave., tel. 206/441–1989. Reservations advised. Dress: casual but neat. AE, DC, MC, V. Moderate.*

El Puerco Lloron. Don't be put off by the cafeteria line and the studied "sleazy-south-of-the-border" bar look. The fresh, handmade tortillas have great texture, and the fillings are endowed with all the right flavors. The chili relleno is tops. But it almost doesn't matter what you order—tacos, *taquitos*, tamales—they're all good. The salsas are zesty and the beer is cold. *Pike Place Market Hillclimb, 1501 Western Ave., tel. 206/624–0541. No reservations. Dress: casual. AE, MC, V. Inexpensive.*

Northwest ★ **Fuller's.** The works of northwest artists hang over the booths in this dining room favored by locals for special occasions. Starter dishes include a sesame-crusted tuna pizza or a vegetable strudel with sun-dried tomatoes and goat cheese, and spinach salad with smoked duck and honey-mustard dressing. Entrées include pork loin with an apple-brandy bleu cheese sauce and monk fish with a wild mushroom-tomato ragu. All the dishes are enhanced by the elegant china and crystal settings atop linen tablecloths. Chef Monique Andree Barbeau specializes in low-fat sauces made from vegetable purées and natural reductions, but you'll forget all about that when you see the wonderfully decadent desserts. *1400 6th Ave. (in the Seattle Sheraton, at Pike St.), tel. 206/447–5544 or 800/325–3535. Reservations advised. Jacket required. AE, D, DC, MC, V. Closed Sat. lunch and Sun. Expensive.*

Hunt Club. This restaurant has gained tremendous popularity over the past few years. Located in the elegant Sorrento Hotel, the Hunt Club's traditional decor of dark wood and plush seats provides a comfortable if unlikely looking setting for the innovative and exciting cuisine. Chef Christine Cass uses fresh northwest produce in such Asian-inspired dishes as Thai-style crab cakes or Dungeness crab bisque. Entrées include tuna with a Szechuan-peppercorn sauce served with rice paper sushi. For the less adventurous, there is also rack of lamb, beef tenderloin, and salmon. The enticing desserts include gingersnap cannoli and lemon-pistachio cake. *Sorrento Hotel, 900 Madison St., tel. 206/622–6400. Reservations advised. Jacket required. AE, DC, MC, V. Expensive.*

★ **The Painted Table.** This sophisticated dining room in the Alexis Hotel opened in 1992 and is currently the only four-star restaurant in Seattle. Sand-colored walls and warm mahogany paneling and columns provide an elegant backdrop for the room's displays of works by local artists. Under the direction of French-trained executive chef Emily Moore, otherwise ordinary meats and vegetables are transformed into works of art, framed by the hand-painted plates. The northwest cuisine offers seasonal selections made from the freshest regional produce available from nearby small vendors, farms, and the Pike Place Market. Although you'll be tempted to order another bowl of the tasty crab and corn chowder and skip the entrées, make yourself try the crab cakes with aioli or the lightly smoked duck breast in ginger sauce. The wonderful and chewy walnut-onion bread is baked on the premises, and Moore, a former pastry chef, personally designed the desserts here, as well. *Alexis Hotel, 1007 1st Ave., tel. 206/624–3646. Reservations advised. Dress: casual but neat. AE, D, DC, MC, V. Closed weekend lunch. Moderate–Expensive.*

Seafood
★ **Ray's Boathouse.** The view of Puget Sound may be the drawing card here, but the seafood is impeccably fresh and well prepared. Perennial favorites include broiled salmon, sake kasu cod, teriyaki salmon fillets, blackened cod, and oysters prepared almost any way you could want them. Ray's has a split personality: a fancy dining room downstairs; a casual café and bar upstairs. Go for the café; the prices are lower and the food is just as good as it is downstairs. In warm weather, sit on the deck outside the café and watch a continuous parade of pilot boats, tugs, fishing boats, and pleasure yachts floating past almost below your table. You won't get bored. *6049 Seaview Ave. NE, tel. 206/789–3770. Reservations advised for window seats in dining room; no reservations for café. Dress: casual but neat. AE, DC, MC, V. Moderate.*

Emmet Watson's Oyster Bar. This small oyster bar may be a bit hard to find: It's in the back of the Pike Place Market's Soames-Dunn Building and fronts a small flower-bedecked (from spring through fall) courtyard. The decor is unpretentious, the inside booths are cramped, and a seat at the bar (in rainy weather) or in the courtyard (when the sun shines) is hard to find. But Seattleites know their oysters, and they know that this is where they'll find them. The place is worth the special effort, for the oysters are very fresh (and come in a great number of varieties) and the beer list is ample (50 or more selections, from local microbrews to fancy imports). Both oysters and beer are inexpensive. If you don't like oysters, try the salmon soup or the fish-and-chips (large flaky pieces of fish with very little grease). *Pike Place Market, 1916 Pike Pl., tel. 206/448–7721. No reservations. Dress: casual. No credit cards. Closed dinner and Sun. Inexpensive.*

Southwest
★ **Santa Fe Cafe.** The delicious, authentic southwestern fare here includes such spicy New Mexican dishes as green-chili burritos made with blue-corn tortillas. Interesting brews on tap help mitigate the heat of such fiery fare as the red-chili burrito (it's so hot, the waiter warns you as you order). Other choices are less *picante,* but still flavorful: the green-chili stew, the blue-corn crepes, the red or green enchiladas. Specialties are artichoke ramekin, chile relleno torte, and roasted garlic appetizer. Sauces are made from red and green chilis brought in from New Mexico. The 65th Street location offers a cozier, homey appeal, with its woven rugs and dried flowers, and is popular with graduate students and professors. The Phinney Avenue restaurant is slicker and more chic; skylights fill the place with light that brightens the soft pink-and-mauve color scheme. Visitors from Santa Fe admit that this is about as authentic as it gets. *Two locations: 2255 N.E. 65th St., tel. 206/524–7736; 5910 Phinney Ave. N, tel. 206/783–9755. Reservations advised. Dress: casual but neat. MC, V. Closed weekend lunch and Mon. Moderate.*

Thai **Bahn Thai.** Thai cooking is ubiquitous in Seattle—it can almost be considered a mainstream cuisine. Because of the variety of dishes and the quality of the preparations, the Bahn Thai, one of the pioneers of local Thai food, is still one of the best and most popular. Start your meal with a skewer of tangy chicken or pork satay, or with the *tod mun goong* (spicy fish cake), and continue with hot-and-sour soup and one of the many prawn or fish dishes. The deep-fried fish with garlic sauce is particularly good—and you can order it very hot. This restaurant promises a relaxed—particularly romantic—atmosphere in the evenings. *409 Roy St., tel. 206/283–0444. Reservations advised. Dress: casual but neat. AE, DC, MC, V. Closed weekend lunch. Inexpensive.*

Vietnamese ★ **Saigon Gourmet.** Talk about unpretentious: This small café, set in the International District, is about as plain as it gets in Seattle, but the food is superb. Aficionados make special trips for the Cambodian soup and the shrimp rolls. The peanut dipping sauce is more flavorful than usual. Do try the papaya with beef jerky—it's unusual but enjoyable. The prices are incredibly low, just one reason why this is one of the best lunch places in town. Parking, however, can be a problem. *502 S. King St., tel. 206/624–2611. No reservations. Dress: casual. No credit cards. No alcohol. Closed Tues. Inexpensive.*

Lodging

There is no shortage of lodging in Seattle. The variety ranges from the elegant deluxe hotels of downtown to the smaller, less expensive hotels in the University District; from a number of budget motels along Aurora Avenue North (Hwy. 99), many of which are legacies of the 1962 World's Fair, to the large, standard hotels strung along Pacific Highway South (Hwy. 99) that accommodate travelers near Seattle-Tacoma International Airport. Always inquire about special rates based on occupancy, weekend stays, or special packages. Also available are a number of bed-and-breakfast accommodations: For more information, contact the **Washington State Bed-and-Breakfast Guild** (2442 N.W. Market St., Seattle, WA 98107, tel. 509/548–7171) or the **Pacific Bed & Breakfast Agency** (701 N.W. 60th St., Seattle, WA 98107, tel. 206/784–0539).

Highly recommended hotels are indicated by a star ★.

Category	Cost*
Very Expensive	$180 and over
Expensive	$120–$179
Moderate	$70–$119
Inexpensive	under $70

**per room, double occupancy, not including 14.1% combined hotel and state sales tax*

Downtown Seattle *Very Expensive* ★ **Alexis.** The Alexis is an intimate four-story, European-style hotel in an artfully restored historic 1901 building on 1st Avenue near the waterfront, the Public Market, and the Seattle Art Museum. Guests are greeted with complimentary sherry at this understated and elegant hotel. The rooms are decorated in subdued colors, with at least one piece of antique furniture in each. Some suites feature Jacuzzis, wood-burning fireplaces, and some have marble fixtures. Unfortunately, none of the rooms have any kind of view, and those facing the avenue can be noisy. Amenities include complimentary Continental breakfast, shoe shines, morning newspaper, and access to workout facilities and private steam room. The Painted Table restaurant is on the hotel's ground floor (*see* Dining, *above*). *1007 1st Ave., 98104, tel. 206/624–4844 or 800/426–7033; fax 206/621–9009. 54 rooms. Facilities: restaurant, café/bar, access to health club, steam room. AE, MC, V.*

★ **Four Seasons Olympic Hotel.** The Olympic is Seattle's most elegant hotel. In 1982, Four Seasons restored it to its 1920s Renaissance Revival–style grandeur, with the public rooms appointed with marble, wood paneling, potted plants, and thick rugs, and furnished with plush armchairs. Palms and skylights in the Garden Court provide a relaxing background for lunch, afternoon tea, or dancing to a live swing band on the weekends. The Georgian Room, the hotel's premier dining room, exudes Italian Renaissance elegance, while Shuckers oyster bar is more casual. Guest rooms are less luxurious than the public rooms and have a homey feel. They are furnished with sofas, comfortable reading chairs, and desks and decorated with period reproductions and floral print fabrics. Amenities include valet parking, 24-hour room service, stocked bar, chocolates on your pillow, complimentary shoe shines, and a bathrobe in the room for each guest. Locals drop in occasionally to pamper themselves with a massage and swim at the health club. *411 University St., 98101, tel. 206/621–1700 or 800/223–8772; fax 206/682–9633. 450 rooms. Facilities: 3 restaurants, health club, indoor pool. AE, DC, MC, V.*

Hotel Vintage Park. As tribute to the state's growing wine industry, each guest room in this small hotel is named for a Washington winery or vineyard. The theme is extended to complimentary servings of local wines each evening in the elegant lobby, where guests can relax on richly upholstered sofas and chairs arranged around the ornate marble fireplace. The rooms, which are decorated in rich color schemes of dark green, plum, deep reds, taupe and gold, are furnished with custom-made cherrywood pieces. Each room also contains original works by San Francisco artist Chris Kidd. For literary-minded guests, hotel staff will check out and deliver your choice of books from the nearby Seattle Public Library. *1100 5th Ave., 98101, tel. 206/624–8000 or 800/624–4433; fax, 206/623–0568. 129 rooms. No-smoking floors. Facilities: restaurant, health club access, secretarial services, room service. AE, DC, MC, V.*

Westin Hotel. This large high-rise hotel, located just north and east of the Pike Place Market and renovated in 1992, is easily recognizable by its twin-tower cylindrical shape. With this design, all rooms, equipped with balconies, make the most of the terrific views of the waterfront and Lake Union. The rooms themselves are airy and bright, though furnished in a plain but high-quality style. The informal Market Cafe, the more formal Palm Court, and Nikko, a stylish Japanese restaurant, as well as three lounges, are located in-house. *1900 5th Ave., 98101, tel. 206/728–1000 or 800/228–3000; fax 206/728–2259. 865 rooms, including 47 suites; no-smoking and handicapped rooms available. Facilities: 3 restaurants, 3 lounges, indoor*

Alexis, **13**
Doubletree, **22**
Edgewater, **2**
Four Seasons Olympic Hotel, **11**
Holiday Inn Sea-Tac, **25**
Hotel Vintage Park, **16**
Hyatt Regency Bellevue, **28**
Inn at the Market, **5**
Mayflower Park, **6**
Meany Tower, **19**
Pacific Plaza, **14**
Park Inn Club & Breakfast, **1**
Red Lion Bellevue, **26**
Red Lion/Sea-Tac, **21**
Seattle Airport Hilton, **23**
Seattle Hilton, **12**
Seattle International Youth Hotel, **10**
Seattle Marriott, **24**
Seattle Sheraton Hotel and Towers, **9**
Seattle YMCA, **15**
Sixth Avenue Inn, **4**
Sorrento, **18**
Stouffer Madison, **17**
University Plaza, **20**
Warwick, **3**
West Coast Bellevue Hotel, **29**
WestCoast Camlin, **8**
Westin, **7**
Woodmark, **27**

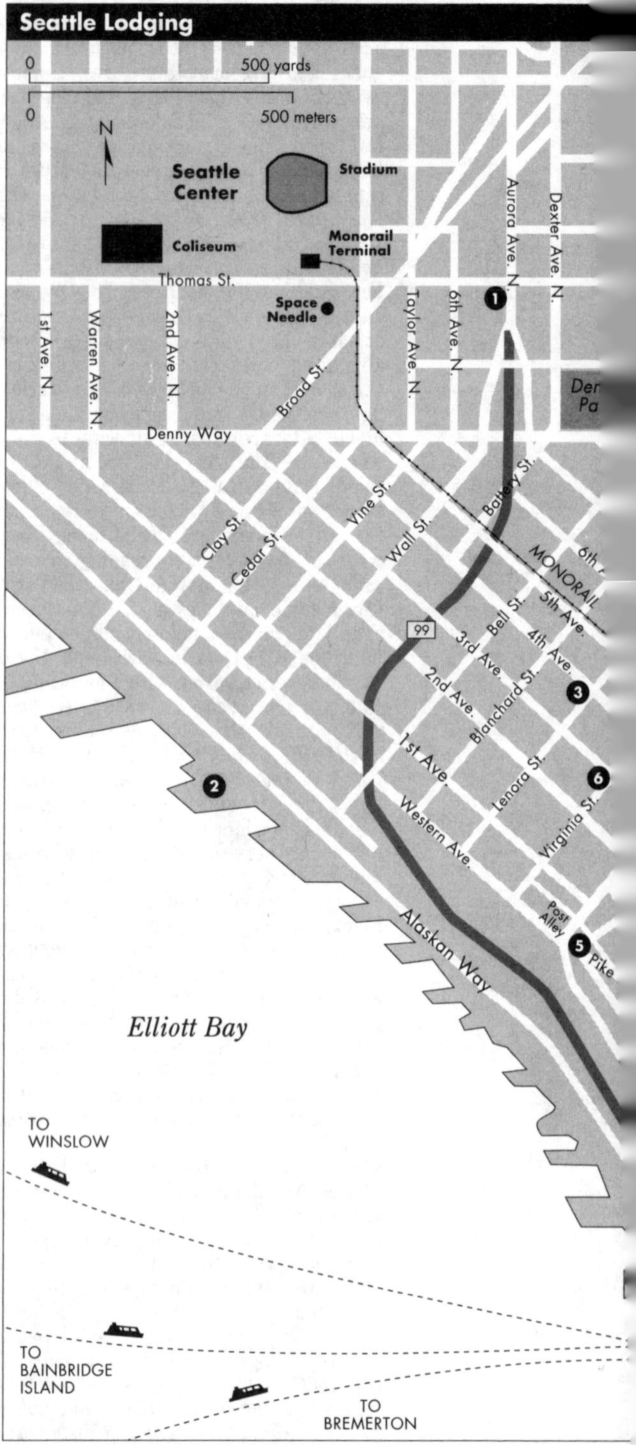

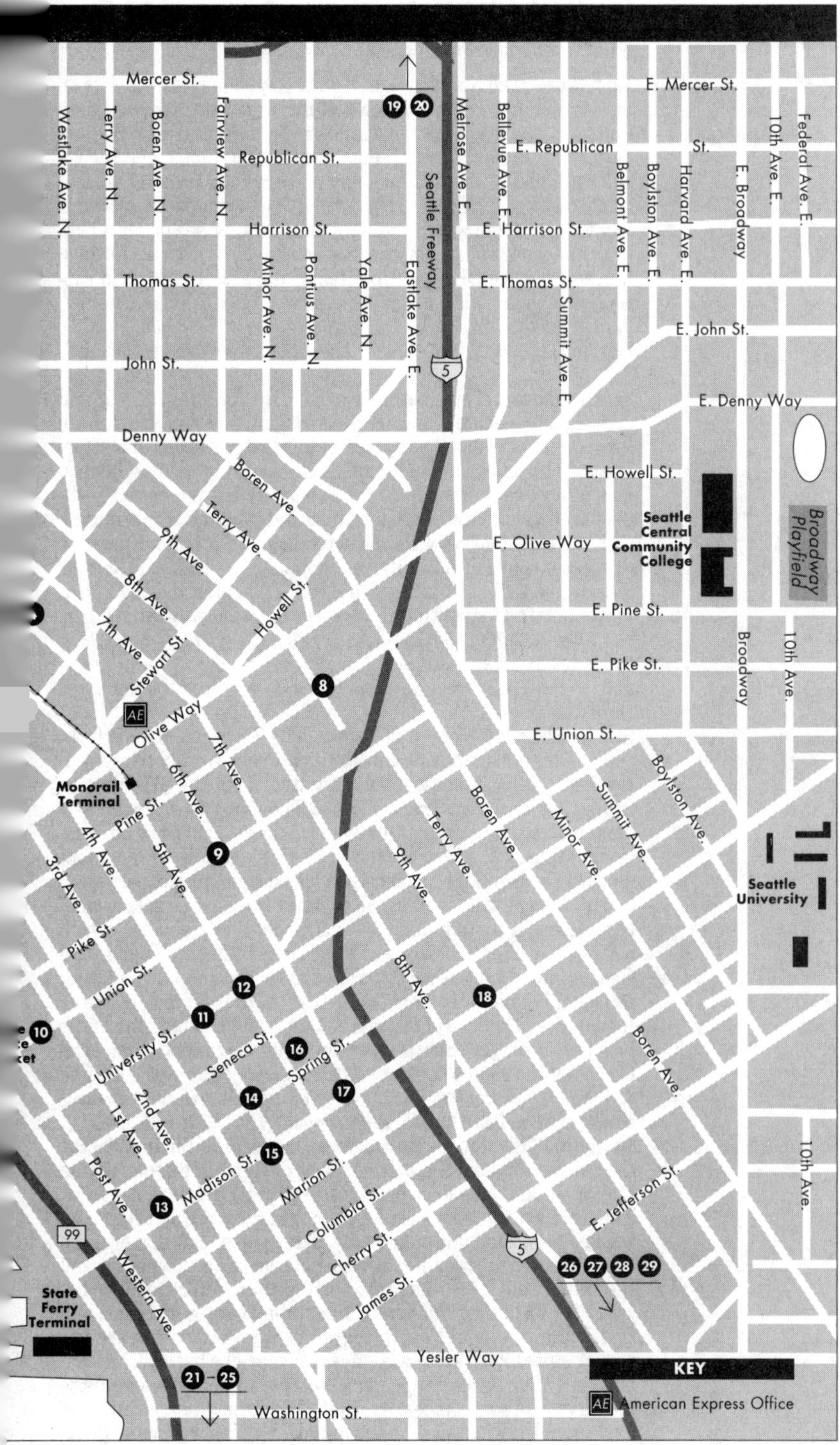
Mercer St.
E. Mercer St.
Republican St.
E. Republican St.
Harrison St.
E. Harrison St.
Thomas St.
E. Thomas St.
John St.
E. John St.
Denny Way
E. Denny Way
E. Howell St.
E. Olive Way
E. Pine St.
E. Pike St.
E. Union St.
Westlake Ave. N.
Terry Ave. N.
Boren Ave. N.
Fairview Ave. N.
Minor Ave. N.
Pontius Ave. N.
Yale Ave. N.
Eastlake Ave. E.
Seattle Freeway
Melrose Ave. E.
Bellevue Ave. E.
Summit Ave. E.
Belmont Ave. E.
Boylston Ave. E.
Harvard Ave. E.
E. Broadway
10th Ave. E.
Federal Ave. E.
Seattle Central Community College
Broadway Playfield
Broadway
10th Ave.
Boren Ave.
Terry Ave.
9th Ave.
8th Ave.
7th Ave.
Stewart St.
Howell St.
Olive Way
Monorail Terminal
Pine St.
6th Ave.
5th Ave.
4th Ave.
3rd Ave.
Pike St.
Union St.
University St.
Seneca St.
Spring St.
2nd Ave.
1st Ave.
Madison St.
Marion St.
Columbia St.
Cherry St.
James St.
Post Ave.
Western Ave.
Boylston Ave.
Summit Ave.
Minor Ave.
Seattle University
E. Jefferson St.
State Ferry Terminal
Yesler Way
Washington St.
KEY
American Express Office

pool, Jacuzzi, sauna, exercise and weight rooms, voice mail for guests, concierge service. AE, D, DC, MC, V.

Expensive **Edgewater.** The only hotel on Elliott Bay, the Edgewater is an institution, known for the now-defunct tradition of guests' fishing from their waterside windows. In 1988 the new owners banned hotel fishing and remodeled the 238 rooms, and the results are magnificent. The lobby features oak furnishings and comfortable chairs and sofas, with a fireplace and a panoramic bay window from which you can sometimes see sea lions frolicking. Spacious rooms on the water provide views of ferries, barges, and the Olympic Mountains, and are decorated in rustic Northwest plaids and unfinished wood furnishings. *Pier 67, 2411 Alaskan Way, 98121, tel. 206/728–7000 or 800/624–0670; fax 206/441–4119. 238 rooms. Facilities: restaurant, bar. AE, DC, MC, V.*

Seattle Hilton. This Hilton is a favorite for conventions and meetings, especially because of its central location. Rooms are furnished in the same nondescript but tasteful style characteristic of Hiltons worldwide, and have soothing color schemes. One of its two restaurants, the Top of the Hilton, serves well-prepared variations of salmon steak and other local specialties, and has excellent views of the city. An underground passage connects the Hilton with a shopping concourse, Rainier Square, as well as with the 5th Avenue Theater and the Washington State Convention Center. *1301 University St., 98101, tel. 206/624–0500, 800/542–7700, or 800/426–0535; fax 206/682–9029. 237 rooms, including 6 suites; no-smoking floors available. Facilities: 2 restaurants, lobby, top-floor piano bar, gift shop. AE, D, DC, MC, V.*

Seattle Sheraton Hotel and Towers. The Sheraton is a modern, 840-room hotel (renovated in 1991) catering largely to conventioneers, as it is conveniently located near the Washington State Convention & Trade Center. The lobby features an art-glass collection by Dale Chihuly, a Northwest artist of international repute. The Towers (top five floors) feature larger, more elegant rooms with concierge service, and complimentary Continental breakfast. Within the complex is a diverse selection of restaurant entertainment options, including Banners, which offers an authentic Japanese breakfast, buffet luncheon, and Continental menu; Gooey's (named after the geoduck, a large, sausagelike northwestern clam that is the subject of many jokes), the bar/disco nighttime hot spot; and Fullers, one of the best restaurants in Seattle, serving nouvelle cuisine using local ingredients. *1400 6th Ave., 98101, tel. 206/621–9000 or 800/325–3535; fax 206/621–8441. 840 rooms. Facilities: 2 restaurants, 2 bars, health club, indoor pool. AE, D, DC, MC, V.*

★ **Sorrento.** This deluxe European-style hotel, built in 1909 for the Alaska-Yukon Exposition, was designed to look like an Italian villa. It has since been restored to its original elegance. The dramatic entrance is along a circular driveway around an Italian fountain, and ringed by palm trees. Sitting high on First Hill, it has wonderful views overlooking downtown and the waterfront. The rooms are smaller than a more modern hotel's, but are quiet and very comfortable; they're decorated in understated, elegant earth tones. The largest rooms are the corner suites with some antiques and spacious baths. The stylish Hunt Club (*see* Dining, *above*) restaurant features exquisite Northwest-Asian dishes by chef Christine Cass, while the dark-paneled Fireside Lounge in the lobby is a warm and inviting spot for sipping coffee, tea, or a cocktail. Other amenities include a complimentary limousine service within the downtown area, concierge, and guest privileges at a nearby athletic club. *900 Madison St., 98104, tel. 206/622–6400; fax 206/625–1059. 76 rooms, 42 suites. Facilities: restaurant, lounge, access to health club. AE, DC, MC.*

Stouffer Madison Hotel. This high-rise hotel, located between downtown and I–5, was built in 1983. Rooms are decorated in peach and green tones, and come equipped with wood cabinets and marble countertops, and those on the 10th floor and up have good views of downtown, Elliott Bay, and the Cascade Mountains. Views above the 20th floor are excellent. Club-level floors (25 and 26) feature their own concierge, complimentary Continental breakfast, and a library. Amenities on other floors include complimentary coffee, morning newspaper and shoe shines. The health club includes a 40-foot rooftop pool and a Jacuzzi. *515 Madison St., 98104, tel. 206/583–0300 or 800/468–3571; fax 206/622–8635. 554 rooms. Facilities: 2 restaurants, lounge, indoor pool, Jacuzzi, health club, indoor parking. AE, D, DC, MC, V.*

Warwick Hotel. The Warwick manages to combine its somewhat large size with intimate European-style charm. Service is friendly and leisurely (but not slow), and the rooms, renovated in 1991, are understated without being bland. All rooms have small balconies and good views of downtown. The lobby was renovated in 1993. There is live entertainment in the Liaison restaurant and lounge. *401 Lenora St., 98121, tel. 206/443–4300; fax 206/448–1662. 230 units, including 4 suites; no-smoking and handicapped rooms available. Facilities: 24-hr courtesy transportation within downtown, pool, Jacuzzi, exercise room, sauna. AE, D, DC, MC, V.*

Moderate–Expensive

★ **Inn at the Market.** This is a sophisticated but unpretentious hotel which opened in 1985 adjacent to the Pike Place Market. It combines the best aspects of a small, French country inn with the informality of the Pacific Northwest, offering a lively setting that's perfect for travelers who prefer originality, personality, and coziness to big-hotel amenities. The rooms are spacious and tastefully decorated with comfortable modern furniture and small touches such as fresh flowers and ceramic sculptures. Ask for a room with views of the Market and Elliott Bay. An added plus is a 2,000-square-foot deck, furnished with Adirondack chairs and overlooking the water and the market. There are three restaurants that are not part of the hotel but share the building: Campagne (*see* Dining, *above*); the Gravity Bar, an ultratrendy hangout with a variety of juices and coffees; and Cafe Dilettante for light meals, fine chocolates, and coffees. *86 Pine St., 98109, tel. 206/443–3600; fax 206/448–0631. 65 rooms; no-smoking rooms available. Facilities: 3 restaurants, access to health club and spa, room service, TV. AE, D, DC, MC, V.*

Mayflower Park Hotel. This pleasant older hotel, built in 1927, is conveniently connected with Westlake Center and the Monorail terminal to Seattle Center. Brass fixtures and antiques give both the public and private spaces a muted Oriental feel, and the service is similarly unobtrusive and smooth. The rooms are somewhat smallish, but the Mayflower Park is so sturdily constructed that it is much quieter than many modern downtown hotels. *405 Olive Way, 98101, tel. 206/623–8700; fax 206/382–6997. 182 units, including 14 suites; no-smoking rooms* *available. Facilities: restaurant, lounge, access to health club. AE, DC, MC, V.*

Moderate **Pacific Plaza.** Built in 1929 and refurbished in 1992, this hotel reflects its original character. The rooms and furnishings, reminiscent of the '20s and '30s, are appropriate for singles or couples but are too small to comfortably accommodate a family. Because of its downtown location and modest rates, the Plaza is a good choice for anyone who is not seeking contemporary luxury. *400 Spring St., 98104, tel. 206/623–3900 or 800/426–1165; fax 206/623–2059. 160 rooms. Facilities: 2 restaurants, complimentary Continental breakfast. AE, DC, MC, V.*

WestCoast Camlin Hotel. This 1926 Seattle apartment/hotel was remodeled in 1987 and resulted in a gracious lobby featuring Oriental carpets, large mirrors, and lots of marble. Located on the edge of the downtown office area, but close to the convention center, this reasonably priced hotel is popular with business travelers. Rooms ending with 10 are best because they feature windows on three sides, and all have working spaces with a chair and a table, along with cushioned chairs for relaxing. One drawback here, though, is the noisy heating, air-conditioning, and ventilation system. *1619 9th Ave., 98101, tel. 206/682–0100 or 800/426–0670; fax 206/682–7415. Facilities: restaurant, lounge, outdoor pool. AE, D, DC, MC, V.*

Inexpensive **Seattle YMCA.** This accommodation has 198 units and is a member of the American Youth Hostels Association. Rooms are clean and plainly furnished with a bed, phone, desk, and lamp. Rooms cost about $40; bunk units, designed to accommodate four people each, cost about $20. *909 4th Ave., 98104, tel. 206/382–5000. 198 units. Facilities: pool, health club. No credit cards.*

Youth Hostel: Seattle International. Situated near the Pike Place Market is a bright, clean youth hostel with 128 dormitory-style beds, kitchen, dining room, lounge, and small library for about $20 a night. It's closed between 11 and 4 daily for cleaning and has a 2 AM curfew. *84 Union St., 98101, tel. 206/622–5443. 128 units. No credit cards.*

Seattle Center
Moderate
★ **Meany Tower Hotel.** This pleasant hotel is just a few blocks from the University of Washington's campus. Built in 1931 and remodeled many times since, it has managed to retain much of its old-fashioned charm, with a muted-peach color scheme throughout, brass fixtures, and careful, attentive service. The rooms, especially those on the higher floors, have good views of the college grounds with glimpses of Green Lake and Lake Union. Other amenities include room service and a complimentary morning paper. The Meany Grill on the ground floor serves breakfast, lunch, and dinner; there is a large street-level lounge as well. *4507 Brooklyn Ave. NE, 98105, tel. 206/634–2000; fax 206/634–2000. 55 rooms; no-smoking rooms available. Facilities: restaurant, lounge. AE, DC, MC, V.*

Sixth Avenue Inn. This small but comfortable motor hotel a few blocks north of downtown is a suitable location for families and business travelers. Rooms are pleasant, with wicker furnishings and standard-issue but well-maintained decor and color schemes; the service is cheerful. This is the hotel of choice for musicians playing at Dimitriou's Jazz Alley, the highly regarded club across the street. *2000 6th Ave., 98121, tel. 206/441–8300; fax 206/441–9903. 166 rooms; no-smoking rooms available. Facilities: restaurant, lounge. AE, DC, MC, V.*

University Plaza Hotel. This is a full-service motor hotel, just across I–5 from the University of Washington's campus, making it popular with families and others who have business in the area. The mock-Tudor decor gives its lobby and other public areas a slightly outdated feel, but the service is cheerful and the rooms are spacious and pleasantly decorated in teak furniture, with pale pinks and grays being the predominant colors. The rooms on the freeway side, however, can be noisy. *400 N.E. 45th St., 98105, tel. 206/634–0100; fax 206/633–2743. 135 rooms; no-smoking rooms available. Facilities: restaurant, lounge, outside heated pool, beauty parlor, fitness room. AE, D, DC, MC, V.*

Inexpensive

Park Inn Club & Breakfast. This '60s-vintage motel, set off Aurora Avenue (Hwy. 99), is relatively close to Seattle Center. The decor is comfortable but not fancy, featuring nondescript contemporary furnishings and color schemes of beige and brown or pastels. Service is friendly and brisk. Continental breakfast, a cafeteria, weight room, and play area for children make this lodging a good value. *225 Aurora Ave. N, 98107, tel. 206/728–7666. 160 rooms, no-smoking rooms available. Facilities: complimentary Continental breakfast, indoor pool, Jacuzzi, parking. AE, MC, V.*

Seattle-Tacoma Airport

Expensive

Red Lion/Sea-Tac. The Red Lion is a popular, hospitable 850-room, full-service convention hotel. Built in about 1970, it has since been remodeled in mauve, teal, and gray. Rooms are spacious and bright, with large panoramic balconies; the corner "King Rooms" feature wraparound balconies and have the best views. Furnishings include chests of drawers, comfortable chairs, a dining table, and a desk; this is the perfect accommodation for the business traveler who plans on doing some work between meetings. *18740 Pacific Hwy. S, 98168, tel. 206/246–8600; fax 206/242–9727. 850 rooms. Facilities: 2 restaurants, coffee shop, 2 lounges, 24-hr workout facility with outdoor pool. AE, D, DC, MC, V.*

Seattle Airport Hilton. This relatively small hotel (for a Hilton) has an intimate, original feel accentuated by the lobby's oak furnishings, cozy fireplace, and paintings of Northwest scenery. The large rooms, renovated in 1993, are bright and decorated in pastel colors. This is also conveniently located: only a half-hour drive from downtown and a 10-minute drive from Southcenter shopping mall. *17620 Pacific Hwy. S, 98188, tel. 206/244–4800; fax 206/439–7439. 173 rooms. Facilities: restaurant, sports bar, health facilities, outdoor pool, complimentary shuttle to airport. AE, D, DC, MC, V.*

Moderate–Expensive

Doubletree Inn and **Doubletree Suites.** These two hotels, situated across the street from each other, are adjacent to Southcenter shopping mall and convenient to the myriad of business-park offices there. The inn is a classic Pacific Northwest–style lodge. Rooms are smaller and less lavish than those at the Suites, but otherwise perfectly nice and cost at least $25 less. Suites, decorated in neutrals, mauves, and pinks, feature a sofa, table and chairs, and a wet bar in the living room. The vanity area includes a full-size closet with mirrored doors. *Doubletree Inn, 205 Strander Blvd., Tukwila 98188, tel. 206/246–8220. 198 rooms. Facilities: dining room, coffee shop, lounge, outdoor pool. Doubletree Suites, 16500 Southcenter Pkwy., Tukwila 98188, tel. 206/575–8220; fax 206/575–4743. 221 suites. Facilities: restaurant, lounge, health club, indoor* *pool, Jacuzzi, sauna, 2 racquetball courts. Doubletree Inn: Moderate; Doubletree Suites: Moderate–Expensive. AE, D, DC, MC, V (for both).*

★ **Seattle Marriott.** A surprisingly luxurious and substantial hotel considering its non-downtown location, this Marriott, built in 1981, features a five-story-high, 20,000-square-foot tropical atrium that's complete with waterfall, dining area, indoor pool, and lounge. The rooms are decorated in greens and mauve with dark wood and brass furnishings. *3201 S. 176th St., 98188, tel. 206/241–2000, international reservations tel. 800/228–9290; fax 206/248–0789. 459 rooms; no-smoking rooms available. Facilities: restaurant, 2 whirlpools, health club, games room, airport shuttle, concierge service. AE, D, DC, MC, V. Special rates available to AAA and AARP members; package rates available for weekends.*

Moderate

Holiday Inn Sea-Tac. This 260-room hotel, built in 1970, was remodeled in 1991, and a more private garden room, convenient for meeting people, was added to the atrium lobby. The Top of the Inn revolving-view restaurant features singing waiters. *17338 Pacific Hwy. S, 98188, tel. 206/248–1000 or 800/HOLIDAY; fax 206/242–7089. 260 rooms. Facilities: restaurant, coffee shop, gift shop, lounge, health club, indoor pool, Jacuzzi. AE, DC, MC, V.*

Bellevue/ Kirkland

Expensive

Hyatt Regency Bellevue. This deluxe high-rise complex in the heart of downtown Bellevue, within a few blocks of Bellevue Square and other fine shopping locales, opened in 1989. The exterior looks pretty much like any other sleek high rise, but the interior has such Oriental touches as antique Japanese *tansu* (wood chests of drawers) and huge displays of fresh flowers. The rooms are decorated in similarly understated ways, with floor-to-ceiling windows and dark wood and earth tones predominating the color scheme. The service is impeccable. Some rooms have been specially designed for Japanese travelers. Deluxe suites include two bedrooms, bar facilities, and meeting rooms with desks and full-length tables. The Eques restaurant serves excellent and reasonably priced breakfast, lunch, and dinner; an English-style pub serves a variety of drinks as well as lunch and dinner. *900 Bellevue Way NE, 98004, tel. 206/462–2626; fax 206/646–7567. 382 units, including 30 suites and deluxe suites; no-smoking rooms available. Facilities: restaurant, pub, 24-hr room service, access to health club and pool. AE, D, DC, MC, V.*

Red Lion Bellevue. This 10-story hotel was built in 1982 and has a large, airy atrium filled with trees, shrubs, and flowering plants. The property also has a formal dining room, a lounge with two dance floors, and 353 oversize rooms, many decorated in mauve and sea-foam green. Rooms have either king- or queen-size beds, and two-room suites feature wet bars and spas or Jacuzzis. A new Italian restaurant, Velato's, opened here in 1993. *300 112th Ave. SE, Bellevue 98004, tel. 206/455–1300 or 800/274–1415; fax 206/454–0466. 353 rooms. Facilities: 2 restaurants, lounge, health club, outdoor pool. AE, D, DC, MC, V.*

★ **Woodmark Hotel.** This hotel, built in 1989, is the only one on the shores of Lake Washington; downtown Kirkland is only a few steps away from the hotel. Its 100 contemporary-style rooms face the water, courtyard, or street and are tastefully furnished in European-style luxury, with earth tones, heavy comforters, and numerous amenities such as terry-cloth bathrobes and fragrant soaps. Comfortable chairs surround the fireplace in the large, open lobby; and a circular staircase descends to the lounge, passing a huge bay window and vast view of Lake Washington. The Carillon Room restaurant offers pasta and fresh fish dishes and excellent waterviews. *1200 Carillon Point, Kirkland 98033, tel. 206/822–3700 or 800/822–3700; fax 206/822–3699. 100 rooms. Facilities: restaurant, access to health club. AE, MC, V.*

Inexpensive **West Coast Bellevue Hotel.** This hotel/motor inn features 176 rooms, 16 of which are town-house suites, suitable for two to four people, with sleeping lofts and wood-burning fireplaces. Rooms are clean; those in the corporate wing face the courtyard and are larger and quieter than the others. The hotel is about eight blocks or a 20-minute walk from Bellevue Square. A complimentary appetizer buffet, offered in the lounge weekdays between 5 and 7 PM, is substantial and includes seafood and roast beef, and is sometimes built around a theme, such as Mexican or Scandinavian cuisine. *625 116th Ave. NE, Bellevue 98004, tel. 206/455–9444, fax 206/455–2154. 176 rooms. Facilities: restaurant, coffee shop, lounge, outdoor pool. AE, D, DC, MC, V.*

The Arts and Nightlife

The Arts

Seattle has gained a world-class reputation as a theater town, and it also has a strong music and dance scene for local, national, and international artists. A good handle on what's happening in town can be found in any of several periodicals. Both the *Seattle Times* and *Post-Intelligencer* have pull-out sections on Friday detailing most of the coming week's events. The *Seattle Weekly*, which hits most newsstands on Wednesday, has even more detailed coverage and arts reviews. *The Rocket*, a lively free monthly, covers music news, reviews, and concert information, with an emphasis on rock and roll.

Ticketmaster (tel. 206/628–0888) provides (for an added fee) tickets to most productions in the Seattle area through charge-by-phone. **Ticket/Ticket** (401 Broadway E, tel. 206/324–2744) or **Pike Place Market Information Booth** (1st Ave. and Pike St., tel. 206/682–7453 ext. 26) sell half-price tickets for most events on the day of the performance or the day before for matinees. Cash only, and in-person only.

Part of the legacy left by the 1962 World's Fair is a series of performance halls at **Seattle Center** (305 Harrison St., tel. 206/684–8582). Seattle also boasts two fine classic (and beautifully renovated) early 20th-century music halls—the **Fifth Avenue** (1308 5th Ave., tel. 206/625–1900) and the **Paramount** (907 Pine St., tel. 206/682–1414). Other prominent venues are the **Moore Theater** (1932 2nd Ave., tel. 206/443–1744), the small but acoustically outstanding **Broadway Performance Hall** (1625 Broadway, tel. 206/323–2623) at Seattle Central Community College, and **Kane** and **Meany halls** on the University of Washington campus (tel. 206/543–4880).

The **Cornish College of the Arts** (710 E. Roy St., tel. 206/323–1400) is an internationally recognized school that also serves as home to a number of distinguished professional performing groups. These groups stage productions September–May, ranging from dance and jazz to art lectures and multimedia performances. Of particular note are the Professional Acting Conservatory and the renowned Cornish New Performance Group, which often premieres important new pieces of music.

Theater **The Annex Theatre** (1916 4th Ave., Way, tel. 206/728–0933) is a cabaret-style, avant-garde, nonEquity theater specializing in new works and is run by a collective of 35 artists.

A Contemporary Theater (100 W. Roy St., tel. 206/285–5110) specializes in developing works by emerging playwrights, including at least one world premiere every year. The season runs May–November, and every December ACT mounts a popular production of Dickens's *A Christmas Carol*. There are tentative plans for a move in 1995 to the Eagles Auditorium site near the Convention Center.

The **Bathhouse Theater** (7312 W. Greenlake Dr. N, tel. 206/524–9108) produces six productions on a year-round schedule, specializing in innovative updates on classics. In addition, it mounts numerous free public shows in various Seattle parks.

Crêpe de Paris (1333 5th Ave., tel. 206/623–4111), a restaurant in the Rainier Tower building downtown, offers some side-splitting cabaret theater and musical revues, such as The Bouffants, an all-girl group complete with tall beehive hairdos and cat's-eye glasses.

The **Empty Space Theater** (3509 Fremont Ave., tel. 206/547–7500) has a reputation for introducing Seattle to new playwrights. The season generally runs Nov.–June, with five or six main-stage productions and several smaller shows throughout the season.

The **Fifth Avenue Musical Theater Company** (Fifth Avenue Theater, 1308 5th Ave., tel. 206/625–1468) is a resident professional troupe that mounts four lavish musicals between October and May each year, with each run lasting about two weeks. (During the rest of the year, this chinoiserie-style historical landmark, carefully restored to its original 1926 condition, hosts a variety of other traveling musical as well as theatrical performances.)

The **Group Theater** (305 Harrison St., on the fountain level of the Center House in Seattle Center, tel. 206/441–1299) is a multicultural troupe that prides itself on presenting socially provocative works—old and new—by artists of varied cultures and colors. The season runs September–June, and the Group also mounts a special summertime playwrights' festival. Of the regular season's six productions, one is always the popular *Voices of Christmas*, a study of the holidays with consideration to cultural differences and ethnic and emotional barriers.

The **Intiman Theater** (Playhouse at Seattle Center, 2nd and Mercer Sts., tel. 206/624–4541) presents the great plays with enduring themes of world drama in an intimate, high-quality setting. The season generally runs May–November.

The **New City Theater and Arts Center** (1634 11th Ave., tel. 206/323–6800) is home to a wide range of experimental performances, produced by a resident company as well as in conjunction with major national and international artists. Its yearly output includes six plays, a director's festival and a playwright's festival, three dance concerts, a monthly film showing, and a lively, late-night monthly cabaret.

The **Seattle Repertory Theater** (Bagley Wright Theater at Seattle Center, 155 Mercer St., tel. 206/443–2222) presents a variety of high-quality programming, from classics to new plays. During its October–May season, six main stage productions and three smaller shows (in the adjoining PONCHO Forum) are presented.

The **Village Theater** (120 Front St. N, Issaquah, tel. 206/392–2202) produces high-quality family musicals, comedies, and dramas September–May in Issaquah, a town east of Seattle.

Dance **Allegro Dance Company** (Broadway Performance Hall, 1625 Broadway, tel. 206/32–DANCE) presents the best in local and regional choreography, with some productions that include other elements of the performing arts. It schedules about 10 concerts a year between September and June.

Meany Hall for the Performing Arts (University of Washington campus, tel. 206/543–4880) presents important national and international companies, September–May, with an emphasis on modern and jazz dance.

On the Boards (Washington Performance Hall, 153 14th Ave., tel. 206/325–7901) presents and produces a wide variety of contemporary performances, including not only dance but also theater, music, and multimedia events by local, national, and international artists. Although the main subscription series runs October–May, OTB events happen nearly every weekend year-round.

Pacific Northwest Ballet (Opera House at Seattle Center, tel. 206/547–5920) is a resident company and school that presents 60–70 performances annually. Its Christmastime production of *The Nutcracker*, with choreography by Kent Stowell and sets by Maurice Sendak, has become a beloved Seattle tradition.

Music **Civic Light Opera** (11051 34th Ave. NE, tel. 206/363–2809) is a non-Equity, semipro company that offers three or four high-quality productions of large-scale American musical theater per season. The season runs roughly October–May.

Northwest Chamber Orchestra (tel. 206/343–0445) is the Northwest's only professional chamber-music orchestra. At the Moore Theater, the Nippon Kan, and other venues, it presents a full spectrum of music, from Baroque to modern. The season, generally September–May, includes a Bach festival every fall, a spring subscription series, and special holiday performances in December.

Seattle Symphony (Opera House at Seattle Center and other locations, tel. 206/443–4747) presents some 120 concerts September–June in Seattle and around the world and—under the musical direction of Gerard Schwartz—continues its long tradition of excellence.

A number of other organizations sponsor classical series throughout the year. An integral part of Seattle's strong early music scene is the **Early Music Guild** (tel. 206/325–7066), which presents regional, national, and international artists in various intimate settings during a season running roughly September–May. The 100-year-old **Ladies Musical Club** (tel. 206/328–7153), composed of professional or retired musicians, sponsors four or five recitals each year by internationally known artists.

For live rock concerts, the **Moore Theater** (1932 2nd Ave., tel. 206/443–1744) and the **Paramount** (907 Pine St.; for tickets and information, Ticketmaster, tel. 206/628–0888) are elegant former movie/music halls that now host visiting and national rock acts.

Opera **Seattle Opera** (Opera House at Seattle Center, Mercer St. at 3rd Ave., tel. 206/389–7676) is a world-class opera company, generally considered to be one of the top organizations in the United States. During the August–May season, it presents six performances of six productions.

Nightlife

For a city its size, Seattle has a remarkably strong and diverse music scene. On any given night, you can hear high-quality live sounds—ranging from traditional jazz and ethnic folk music to garage-punk rock—at a variety of venues. Jazz, blues, and R&B have long been Seattle favorites, and each year are showcased on major stages at the Labor Day Bumbershoot Festival at the Seattle Center. The Cornish School fosters a healthy jazz scene through its students and internationally known instructors. There is also a particularly strong blues circuit in and around town. Seattle is a center for grunge rock, as seen in the movie *Singles,* which was filmed on location here. Some of the better-known Seattle bands to spring from this scene include Nirvana, Screaming Trees, Pearl Jam, and Alice in Chains. Areas with high concentrations of clubs and taverns include Belltown, also known as the Denny Regrade, just north of the Pike Place Market, Ballard, Pioneer Square, and Capitol Hill. Many of these clubs feature a wide variety of live rock, including hard-rock, funk-rock, roots-rock, folk-rock, garage-punk, grunge, and probably whatever comes along next. (*see* Rock Clubs, *below*).

Bars and Lounges Bars with waterfront views are plentiful in Seattle. Among the best: on Elliott Bay, **Ernie's Bar & Grill** (2411 Alaskan Way, Pier 67, tel. 206/728–7000) in the Edgewater Hotel (the hotel's lobby offers great views of the bay and the Olympic Mountains); on the Ship Canal, **Hiram's at the Locks** (5300 34th Ave. NW, tel. 206/784–1733); on Lake Union, **Triple's Seafood Bistro** (1200 Westlake Ave. N, tel. 206/284–2535) and **Arnie's** (1900 N. Northlake Way, tel. 206/547–3242); and on Shilshole Bay, **Ray's Boathouse** (6049 Seaview Ave. NW, tel. 206/789–3770) and **Anthony's Home Port** (6135 Seaview Ave. NW, tel. 206/783–0780).

Panoramic views of the city can be found at **Salty's** (1396 Harbor Ave. SW, tel. 206/937–1600), a noisy sprawling restaurant and lounge in West Seattle with unparalleled views of downtown, and at the **Space Needle** (Seattle Center, tel. 206/443–2100), where the revolving restaurant provides a 360-degree view during the course of an hour.

Other fine places for a drink downtown are the **Garden Court** (411 University St., tel. 206/621–1700) at the Four Seasons Olympic, a rather formal and elegant locale; the **J&M Cafe** (201 1st Ave. S, tel. 206/624–1670), a lively and casual Pioneer Square joint; and, near the Kingdome, **F. X. McRory's** (419 Occidental Ave. S, tel. 206/623–4800), famous for its huge selection of single-malt whiskies and the equally huge singing bartender.

Folk Clubs

Backstage (2208 N.W. Market St., tel. 206/781–2805) is an often-packed basement venue in Ballard that has a lively mix of national and local acts with the emphasis on world music, offbeat rock, and new folk.

Kells (1916 Post Alley, tel. 206/728–1916), a snug Irish-style pub, is located near the Pike Place Market and plays live Celtic music Wednesday–Saturday starting at 9 PM.

Murphy's Pub (2110 45th St. NE, tel. 206/634–2110) features open-mike Wednesdays, with Irish and other folk music on Friday and Saturday in this cozy neighborhood bar.

Blues/R&B Clubs

The **Ballard Firehouse** (5429 Russell St. NW, tel. 206/784–3516) is the music mecca in the heart of Ballard, with an emphasis on local and national blues acts.

Chicago's (315 1st Ave. N, tel. 206/282–7791) features Chicago-style pizza and other kinds of good, reasonably priced Italian food in this restaurant just west of the Seattle Center. Live blues is played on weekends.

Larry's (209 1st Ave. S, tel. 206/624–7665) features live R&B and blues nightly in an unpretentious, friendly, and usually jam-packed tavern/restaurant in Pioneer Square.

Old Timer's Cafe (620 1st Ave., tel. 206/623–9800) is a popular Pioneer Square restaurant and bar with live music—mostly R&B—nightly.

The **Scarlet Tree** (6521 Roosevelt Way NE, tel. 206/523–7153), a neighborhood institution, is a restaurant and bar just north of the University District. Great burgers and live R&B are offered nightly.

Jazz Clubs

Dimitriou's Jazz Alley (2037 6th Ave., tel. 206/441–9729) is a downtown club with nationally known, consistently high-quality performers every night but Sunday. Excellent dinners are served before the first shows.

Latona Tavern (6423 Latona Ave. NE, tel. 206/525–2238) is a funky, friendly, often jazz-oriented, neighborhood bar at the south end of Green Lake that features a variety of local musicians playing folk, blues, and jazz nightly.

Lofurno's (2060 15th Ave., tel. 206/283–7980), located south of the Ballard Bridge, offers reasonably priced Italian food and jazz on Sunday nights.

New Orleans Creole Restaurant (114 1st Ave. S, tel. 206/622–2563) is a popular Pioneer Square restaurant with good food and live jazz nightly—mostly top local performers but occasionally national acts as well.

Rock Clubs

Central Tavern (207 1st Ave. S, tel. 206/622–0209) is a crowded Pioneer Square tavern with an ever-changing roster of local and national rock acts.

The **Crocodile Cafe** (2200 2nd Ave., tel. 206/441–5611) is described by a local music critic as Seattle's "hippest hangout," with its variety of folk-rock, acoustic-rock, hard-rock, and new-wave groups every night but Monday.

Doc Maynard's (610 1st Ave., tel. 206/682–4649) is a classic rock-and-roll-oriented tavern with a small and always jam-packed dance floor.

The **Off-Ramp Music Cafe** (109 Eastlake E, tel. 206/628–0232) features a rock nightly, often the heavy-metal kind.

OK Cafe/Gallery & Club (212 Alaskan Way S, tel. 206/621–7903) offers rock, folk, and jazz nightly in a small venue near Pioneer Square.

Parker's (17001 Aurora Ave. N, tel. 206/542–9491) was a venerable North Seattle teen palace of the '50s and '60s but has since become a more sophisticated dinner-and-show venue for a variety of more traditional popular rock artists, often nationally known acts.

The **Re-Bar** (1114 Howell St., tel. 206/233–9873) presents an eclectic mix of music nightly including acid-jazz and soul-rhythm.

Vogue (2018 1st Ave., tel. 206/443–0673), a club in Belltown, the artists' community just north of the Public Market, presents a variety of au courant local and national rock.

Comedy Clubs **Comedy Underground** (222 S. Main St., tel. 206/628–0303), a Pioneer Square club (literally underground, beneath Swannie's), presents stand-up comedy nightly, with Monday and Tuesday reserved as open-mike nights; the other nights are mixtures of nationally known and local comics.

Giggles (5220 Roosevelt Way NE, tel. 206/526–JOKE), in the University District, presents the best of local and nationally known comedians five nights a week, with late shows on weekend nights. Closed Sunday and Monday.

Dance Clubs Several of the rock clubs listed above offer dancing (*see* Rock Clubs, *above*). In Pioneer Square there are several popular, chic clubs featuring recorded dance music, including the **Celebrity** (313 2nd Ave. S, tel. 206/467–1111).

In the downtown area, **Fitzgerald's on Fifth** (1900 5th Ave., tel. 206/728–1000) in the Westin Hotel and **Pier 70 Bay Cafe** (2815 Alaskan Way at Broad St., tel. 206/728–7071) are dance clubs that feature Top-40 music.

Ballroom Dancing The U.S. Amateur Ballroom Dancing Association's local chapter (tel. 206/822–6686) sponsors regular classes and dances throughout the year. These are either at the **Avalon Ballroom** (1017 Stewart St.) or at **Carpenter's Hall** (2512 2nd Ave.). The **Washington Dance Club** (1017 Stewart St., tel. 206/628–8939) sponsors nightly workshops and dances on various styles, and the **All-City Dance Club** (2245 N.W. 57th St., tel. 206/747–2707) hosts regular Saturday-night get-togethers.

Excursions from Seattle

The heavily developed I–5 corridor runs through Seattle, north to Vancouver, British Columbia, or south to Portland, Oregon. But venturing off this ribbon of highway—either toward the mountains in the east or the water to the west—will quickly bring the traveler to some relatively isolated areas. Four of the many excellent trips that can be taken from Seattle are to Bainbridge Island, a short but delightful ferry ride from downtown across Puget Sound; the scenic Snoqualmie Falls, where snowcapped mountains meet lush farmland; Whidbey Island and the San Juan Islands, with scenic beaches, rolling countryside, and good fishing; or Leavenworth, a mock Bavarian village high in the Cascade Mountains.

Bainbridge Island

On a nice day, there's no better way to escape Seattle than on board a Washington State Ferry for a trip across Puget Sound.

It's a great way to watch sea gulls, sailboats, and massive container vessels in the sound—not to mention the surrounding scenery, which takes in the Kitsap Peninsula and Olympic Mountains, Mt. Rainier, the Cascade Mountains, and the Seattle skyline. Even when the weather isn't all that terrific, travelers can stay snug inside the ferry, have a snack, and listen to the folk musicians who entertain the cross-sound commuters. Bainbridge Island combines a small-town atmosphere with scenic country surroundings.

Tourist Information **Bainbridge Island Chamber of Commerce** (590 Winslow Way, tel. 206/842–3700), just two blocks from the ferry dock, has free maps that detail shops, restaurants, and sights.

Getting There

By Ferry Although there are several ferries that leave from the Seattle area (*see* Getting Around Seattle, *above*), probably the best one for a single-day excursion is the ferry to **Bainbridge Island.** The advantages of walking on board are obvious; it's cheap (only $3.30 for a round-trip ticket) and hassle-free (no long waits in lines of frustrated drivers during peak commute hours or on weekends).

The ferry leaves from Seattle's busy downtown terminal at Colman Dock (Pier 52, south of the Pike Place Market and just north of Pioneer Square), and the trip takes about a half-hour each way.

A word on ferries in general: The Washington State Ferry System, the biggest in the United States, includes vessels ranging from the 40-car *Hiyu* to jumbo ferries capable of carrying more than 200 cars and 2,000 passengers each. They connect points all around Puget Sound and the San Juan Islands. No smoking is allowed in public areas.

If you do take your car, there are several points to note: Passengers and bicycles always load first unless otherwise instructed. Prior to boarding, lower antennas. Only parking lights should be used at night, and it is considered bad form to start your engine before the ferry docks.

Sunny weekends are heavy traffic times all around the San Juan Islands, and weekday commuting hours for ferries headed into or out of Seattle are also crowded. Peak times on the Seattle runs are sunny weekends, eastbound in the morning and Sunday nights, as well as westbound Saturday morning and weekday afternoons. Since no reservations are accepted on Washington State Ferries (except for the Sidney–Anacortes run during summer), arriving at least a half hour before a scheduled departure is always advised. *Colman Dock, Pier 52, tel. 206/464–6400, 206/464–2000 (ext. 5500 for schedules), or 800/843–3779 and 800/542–7052 in WA. Cost: Bainbridge Island ferry auto and driver: $6.65; passenger (in car or as walk-on) $3.30; senior citizens and disabled persons half-fare; children under 5 free. Special rates for mobile homes and other oversize vehicles. Schedules vary according to season and time of day, but generally ferries leave daily every 30–40 min, early morning–2 AM.*

Once you reach the Bainbridge Island terminal, walk north up a short hill on Olympic Drive to Winslow Way; about ¼ mile farther north on Olympic is the Bainbridge Island Vineyard and Winery (682 S.R. 305, tel. 206/842–9463), which is open for tastings and tours Wednesday–Sunday noon–5.

Bloedel Reserve, the 150-acre estate of Vancouver, B.C. lumber baron Prentice Bloedel, was opened to the public in 1988. The grounds were designed to recapture the natural, untamed look of the island. Within the park are ponds with ducks and trumpeter swans, Bloedel's grand mansion, and 2 miles of trails. In spring the displays of blooming rhododendrons and azaleas are dazzling, and in fall the leaves of the Japanese maples and other trees colorfully signal the change of seasons. *7571 N.E. Dolphin Dr., Bainbridge Island 98110, tel. 206/842–7631. Admission: $4 adults, $2 senior citizens, children under 5 free. Reservations necessary. Open Sun.–Wed. 10–4.*

If you turn west on Winslow Way, you'll find yourself in town, with several square blocks of interesting antiques shops, clothing stores, gift shops, galleries, restaurants, and other services. Shopping in the town of Bainbridge Island is refreshingly slower than in downtown Seattle, but you will still find boutiques, designer housewares, and bookstores.

Whidbey Island

Whidbey Island, 30 miles northwest of Seattle, is one of the nearest "escapes" from the city. In fact, some folks escape to it from Seattle every night—they live on Whidbey and commute to work. The island is easily accessible via ferry from Mukilteo (pronounced muck-ill-TEE-oh) to Clinton on the southern part of the island or a drive across Deception Pass on the northern end of the island on Highway 20.

The first white settlers included Colonel Walter Crockett and Colonel Isaac Ebey, who came in the early 1850s. Their names are found on Crockett Lake and Ebey's Landing National Historic Reserve. On the west side of the island, visitors can watch container ships ply the waters of Puget Sound between Asia and ports in Seattle and Tacoma. Wildlife is plentiful. There are eagles and great blue herons; in the water, there are orcas, gray whales, dolphins, and otters.

At 60 miles long and 8 miles wide, Whidbey Island is the longest in the contiguous United States—the U.S. Supreme Court having decided that Long Island in New York was actually a peninsula. The island is a blend of bucolic rolling hills, forests, meadows, sandy beaches, and dramatic, high cliffs. It's a great place for country drives, bicycle touring, exploring the shoreline by boat or kayak, and viewing sunsets.

Tourist Information

For information, contact the **Langley Chamber of Commerce** (Box 403, Langley 98260, tel. 206/221–6765) or **Central Whidbey Chamber of Commerce** (Box 152, Coupeville 98239, tel. 206/678–5434).

Getting There

By Plane

Harbor Airlines (tel. 800/359–3220) flies to Whidbey Island from Friday Harbor and Sea-Tac Airport.

Kenmore Air (tel. 206/486–8400 or 800/543–9595) can arrange charter float plane flights to Whidbey Island.

By Car

Whidbey Island can be reached via the Mukilteo-to-Clinton ferry, or you can drive from Seattle north along I–5, then heading west on Hwy. 20; cross the dramatic Deception Pass via the bridge at the north end of the island.

Maps of the island, helpful to motorists and cyclists, are available at realty offices in Clinton.

By Ferry The **Washington State Ferry System** (tel. 206/464–6400 or 800/84-FERRY in WA) provides car and passenger service from Mukilteo to Clinton (Whidbey Island).

Exploring *Numbers in the margin correspond to points of interest on the Puget Sound map.*

This tour begins at the southern tip of Whidbey, a 50-mile, mostly rural island of undulating hills, gentle beaches, and little coves. Naturally, on an island such as Whidbey, wildlife is plentiful, and it's not unusual to see eagles, great blue herons, and oyster catchers, as well as orcas, gray whales, dolphins, and otters. Perhaps the best view of the sea creatures can be
1 had from **Langley,** the quaint town that sits atop a 50-foot-high bluff overlooking the southeastern shore. In the heart of town, along **First Street** and **Second Street,** there are boutiques that sell art, glass, antiques, jewelry, and clothing.

About halfway up this long, skinny island is Whidbey's town of
2 **Greenbank,** home to the historically recognized **Loganberry Farm.** The 125-acre site is now the place of production for the state's unique spirit, Whidbey's Liqueur. *657 Wonn Rd., tel. 206/678–7700. Admission free. Tours offered daily 10–4.*

While in Greenbank, you may want to see the 53-acre **Meerkerk Rhododendron Gardens,** with 1,500 native and hybrid species of rhododendrons, numerous walking trails, and ponds. The best time to view the flowers in full bloom is April and May. *Resort Rd., Greenbank, tel. 206/321–6682. Admission: $2.*

3 Farther north you'll come to **Keystone,** an important town because it is the port of call for the ferry bound for Port Townsend on the Olympic Peninsula.

4 **Ft. Casey State Park** (tel. 206/678–4519), just north of Keystone, is one of three forts built in 1890 to protect Puget Sound. Today it offers a small interpretive center, camping, picnic sites, fishing, and a boat launch.

5 About two-thirds of the way up this long island is **Coupeville,** home of many restored Victorian houses and one of the largest National Historic Districts in the state. The town was founded in 1852 by Captain Thomas Coupe; his house, built in 1853, is one of the state's oldest. The town is also the site of the new **Island County Historical Museum** (908 N.W. Alexander St., tel. 206/678–3310).

6 **Ebey's Landing National Historic Reserve** (tel. 206/678–4636), west of Coupeville, is a 22-acre area that include Keystone, Coupeville, and Penn Cove. Established by Congress in 1980, the reserve is the first and largest of its kind. It is dotted with some 91 nationally registered historical structures, farmland, parks, and trails.

7 About 11 miles farther north is **Oak Harbor,** which derived its name from the Garry oaks in the area. It was settled by Dutch and Irish immigrants in the mid-1800s, and several Dutch windmills are still in existence. Unfortunately, the island's largest city has not maintained the sleepy fishing-village pace that much of the rest of the island follows. Instead, Oak Harbor has the look of suburban sprawl, with strips of fast-food restaurants and service stations. Just north of Oak Harbor is **Whidbey Island Naval Air Station** (tel. 206/257–2286), at which group tours can be arranged. At **Deception Pass State Park,** 3 miles

Puget Sound

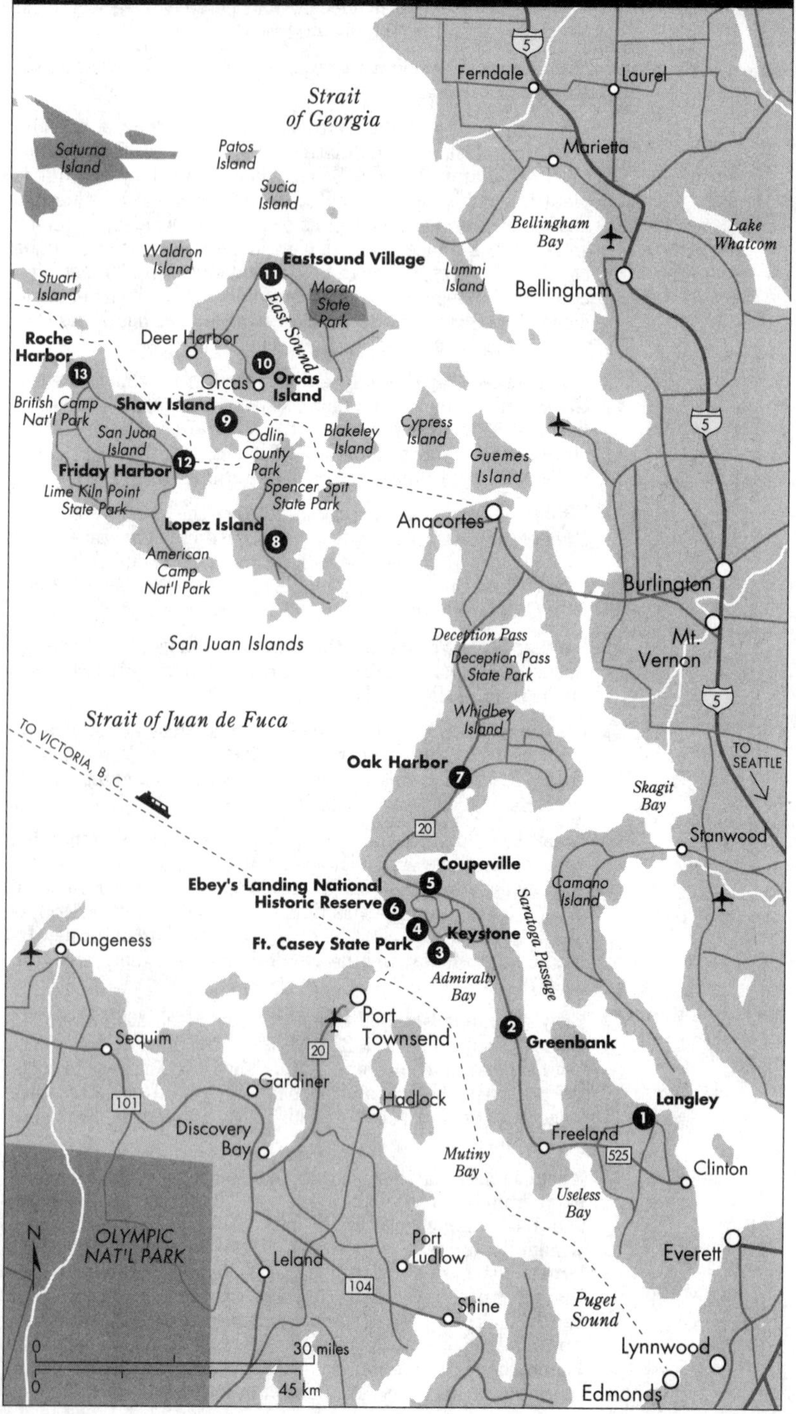
Strait of Georgia
Saturna Island
Patos Island
Sucia Island
Waldron Island
Stuart Island
Eastsound Village
11
Moran State Park
East Sound
Lummi Island
Roche Harbor
13
Deer Harbor
10
Orcas
Orcas Island
British Camp Nat'l Park
Shaw Island
9
San Juan Island
Odlin County Park
Blakeley Island
Cypress Island
Guemes Island
Friday Harbor
12
Lime Kiln Point State Park
Spencer Spit State Park
Lopez Island
8
American Camp Nat'l Park
San Juan Islands
Ferndale
Laurel
Marietta
Bellingham Bay
Lake Whatcom
Bellingham
5
Anacortes
Burlington
Mt. Vernon
Deception Pass
Deception Pass State Park
Whidbey Island
Strait of Juan de Fuca
TO VICTORIA, B. C.
Oak Harbor
7
20
TO SEATTLE
Skagit Bay
Stanwood
Coupeville
5
Ebey's Landing National Historic Reserve
6
4
Keystone
Ft. Casey State Park
3
Camano Island
Saratoga Passage
Admiralty Bay
Dungeness
Port Townsend
2
Greenbank
Sequim
Gardiner
Hadlock
Langley
1
101
Discovery Bay
Freeland
525
Mutiny Bay
Clinton
Useless Bay
OLYMPIC NAT'L PARK
N
Leland
Port Ludlow
Everett
104
Shine
Puget Sound
Lynnwood
Edmonds
0
30 miles
0
45 km

from the naval base, take some time to notice the spectacular view and stroll among the madrona trees with their reddish-brown peeling bark. While walking across the bridge, you won't be able to miss seeing the dramatic gorge below, well-known for its tidal currents. The Deception Pass bridge links Whidbey to Fidalgo Island and the mainland. From here it's just a short distance to Anacortes and ferries to the San Juan Islands.

Shopping On Whidbey Island, **Langley's First Street** and **Second Street** offer a number of unique items. **Annie Steffen's** (101 1st St., tel. 206/321–6535) specializes in hand-painted, handwoven, and hand-knit apparel and jewelry.

You can meet the artist and shop owner, Gwenn Knight, at **The Glass Knight** (214 1st St., Langley, tel. 206/321–6283), where her glass art and jewelry are for sale.

The **Childers/Proctor Gallery** (302 1st St., Langley, tel. 206/321–2978) exhibits and sells paintings, jewelry, pottery, and sculpture.

Just outside of Langley is the **Blackfish Studio** (5075 S. Langley Rd., tel. 206/321–1274), where you can see works in progress as well as finished pieces by artist Kathleen Miller, who produces enamel jewelry and hand-painted clothing and accessories, and photographer Donald Miller's depictions of the land and people of the Northwest.

Sports and the Outdoors

Bicycling In the Bayview area of Whidbey Island, just off Highway 20, southeast of Anacortes, **The Pedaler** (5603½ S. Bayview Rd., tel. 206/321–5040) bicycle sales and service shop also has 25-or-so mountain bikes and hybrids for rent year-round.

Boating **Langley's small boat harbor** (tel. 206/221–6765) offers moorage for 35 boats, utilities, and a 160-foot fishing pier, all protected by a 400-foot timber-pile breakwater. No reservations.

Fishing You can catch salmon, perch, cod, and bottomfish from the Langley dock. Supplies are available from the **Langley Marina** (202 Wharf St., tel. 206/321–1771).

Beaches Beaches are best on Whidbey Island's west side, where the sand stretches out to the sea and you have a view of the shipping lanes and the Olympic Mountains. **Maxwelton Beach** (Maxwelton Beach Rd.), popular with the locals, is on the west side of the island. **Possession Point** (west on Coltas Bay Rd.) includes a park, a beach, and a boat launch. **Forts Casey** and **Ebey** offer more hiking trails and bluff outlooks than wide, sandy beaches. **West Beach,** north of the forts, is a stormy beach with lots of driftwood.

Dining For prices, *see* the Dining chart in Seattle, *above*

Garibyan Brothers Café Langley. Terra-cotta tile floors, antique oak tables, Italian music, and the aromas of garlic, basil, and oregano set the tone for your lunch or dinner. Greek salads, vegetarian eggplant, fresh mussels, lamb loin chops, moussaka, and lamb shish kebabs are just a few of the offerings. *113 1st St., Langley, tel. 206/221–3090. Reservations suggested. Dress: neat but casual. MC, V. Moderate.*

Star Bistro. This black, white, and red bistro, atop the Star Store, serves up Caesar salads, shrimp-and-scallop linguine, and gourmet burgers. *201½ 1st St., Langley, tel. 206/221–2627. No reservations. Dress: casual. AE, MC, V. Moderate.*

Dog House Backdoor Restaurant. This extremely casual waterfront tavern and restaurant serves large, juicy burgers, has a great view of Saratoga Passage, and a pool table. *230 1st St., Langley, tel. 206/321–9996. No reservations. Dress: casual. No credit cards. Inexpensive.*

Lodging For prices, *see* the Lodging chart in Seattle, *above.*

Cliff House. This luxury house, situated near Freeland, sleeps one to two couples in a secluded setting overlooking Admiralty inlet. The three-story house, one side nearly all glass, affords romantic views to the couple enjoying the elegant bedroom loft. Rain and occasionally snow whisk through the open-air atrium in the middle of the house. Guests are pampered with fresh flowers, a huge stone fireplace, and miles of driftwood beach. *5440 Windmill Rd., Freeland 98249, tel. 206/321–1566. 1 room. Facilities: fireplace, spa, art collection. No credit cards. Very Expensive.*

Guest House Cottages. This B&B, just outside Greenbank, includes a luxurious log lodge for one couple, four private cottages, and a three-room suite in a farmhouse located on 25 acres of forest and pastureland. The accommodations are cozy, with fireplaces, stained-glass pieces, and country antique furnishings. *835 E. Christianson Rd., Greenbank 98253, tel. 206/678–3115. 6 units. Facilities: fireplaces, microwaves, some kitchens, swimming pool, exercise room, spa. Expensive.*

Fort Casey Inn. These restored, two-story, Georgian Revival officers' quarters were built in 1909. Each has two bedrooms, a living room and full country kitchen, and are perfect for families. Owners Gordon and Victoria Hoenig have restored the tin ceilings and decorated the units with rag rugs, old quilts, hand-painted furniture, and sundry Colonial touches. *1124 S. Engle Rd., Coupeville, 98239, tel. 206/678-8792. 9 units. Facilities: fireplaces in each, use of bicycles. Fixings for breakfast are provided. AE, MC, V. Moderate.*

Twickenham House. The weekend-in-the-country ambience of this new cedar-sided inn takes hold as soon as you catch sight of the sheep grazing and ducks wandering in the surrounding pasture. This inn makes for a quiet country retreat, and the rooms are decorated simply with trunks, pine armoires, and matching duvets and pillow shams. One of the highlights of a stay here is the gourmet breakfasts, made from fresh, local ingredients and reflecting the English and French Canadian heritage of the inn's owners. *5023 Langley Rd., Langley, WA 98260, tel. 800/874–5009. 2 suites, 4 double rooms. MC, V. Moderate.*

Dining and Lodging ★

Inn at Langley. This concrete-and-wood Frank Lloyd Wright–inspired structure perches on the side of a bluff that descends to the beach. Guest rooms feature Asian-style decor using neutral colors, wood and glass, and spectacular views of Saratoga Passage and the Cascade Mountains. Entering the inn's Country Kitchen restaurant you first see a fireplace, and what looks like a living room, until you notice the tables for two unobtrusively lining the walls. On the other side of the fireplace is the "great table," which seats 10. Dinner may include locally gathered mussels in a black-bean sauce, breast of duck in a loganberry sauce, or rich Columbia River salmon. Appetizers, side dishes, salad greens so fresh they've never seen the inside of a refrigerator, and desserts such as a bowl of island-grown strawberries with cream complement the entrées. Continental breakfast (for guests) is served Monday–Wednesday, 8–10. Dinner starts promptly at 7, with a glass of sherry and a tour of the wine cellar. *400 1st St., Langley, tel. 206/221–3033. 24 rooms. Facilities: restaurant. Reservations for restaurant necessary. Jacket and tie suggested. MC, V. Expensive.*

Captain Whidbey Inn. This inn offers a wide variety of accommodations, including the original madrona log inn (listed on the National Register of Historic Places), cottages, a duplex, and houses with views of Penn Cove. Inn rooms are rustic, though they feature a few antiques, but do have feather beds and shared baths. Lagoon rooms are large and have private baths. Cottages and the duplex have one or two bedrooms, sitting rooms, and some have kitchens, fireplaces, and private baths. The dining room, serving breakfast, lunch, and dinner, is cozy, with dark paneling, soft lighting, and several tables overlooking Penn Cove. *2072 W. Captain Whidbey Inn Rd., Coupeville 98239, tel. 206/678–4097. 33 units. Facilities: bicycles and rowboats available. Reservations for restaurant suggested. Dress: neat but casual. MC, V. Moderate.*

The San Juan Islands

The San Juan Islands are the jewels of the Northwest. Because the islands are reachable only by ferry or airplane, they beckon to souls longing for a quiet change of pace, whether it be kayaking in a cove, walking a deserted beach, or nestling by the fire in an old farmhouse.

Unfortunately, solitude becomes a precious commodity in summer when the San Juan's are overrun with tourists. On weekends and even some weekdays, expect to wait at least three hours in line once you arrive at the ferry terminal. You will face the same challenge or worse if you return on Sunday afternoon or evening.

Island residents enjoy their peace and quiet; while some of them rely on tourism, many do not, and they would just as soon not have their country roads and villages jammed with "summer people." So it should come as no surprise that tourism and development are hotly contested issues on the islands.

One way to avoid crowds and the possibility of a cantankerous island resident is to plan a trip in the spring, fall, or winter. Reservations are a must anytime in the summer and are advised for weekends in the off-season, too.

Tourist Information For information on the San Juan Islands, contact the **San Juan Islands Visitor Information Service** (Box 65, Lopez 98261, tel. 206/468–3663).

Getting There

By Plane **West Isle Air** (tel. 800/874–4434) flies to Friday Harbor on San Juan Island from Sea-Tac and Bellingham airports; **Harbor Airlines** (tel. 800/359–3220) also flies from Friday Harbor to Whidbey Island.

Kenmore Air (tel. 206/486–8400 or 800/543–9595) flies float planes from Lake Union in Seattle to the San Juan Islands.

By Car To reach the **San Juan Islands** from Seattle, drive north on I–5 to Mt. Vernon, Exit 230, go west and follow signs to Anacortes; pick up the Washington State Ferry (*see below*).

By Ferry The **Washington State Ferry System** (tel. 206/464–6400 or 800/84-FERRY in WA only) provides car and passenger service from Anacortes, about 90 miles north of Seattle, to the San Juan Islands.

Island Shuttle Express (tel. 206/671–1137) takes passengers from Bellingham to Orcas Island and Friday Harbor. The San Juan *Express* (tel. 800/888–2535) leaves from Seattle and travels routes to Friday Harbor and Port Townsend.

Getting Around It is convenient to have a car in the San Juan Islands, but taking your car with you may mean waiting in long lines at the ferry terminals. In addition to the car-passenger ferries, the **Washington State Ferry System** (tel. 206/464–6400 or 800/84–FERRY) provides passenger-only service among the various islands. With prior arrangement, most bed-and-breakfast owners can pick up walk-on guests at the ferry terminals.

Car rentals are available from the **Inn at Friday Harbor** (tel. 206/378–4351) on San Juan Island. **West Isle Air** (tel. 206/378–2440 or 800/874–4434) serves both Friday Harbor and the Orcas Island Airport. Rentals are about $30 per day.

Guided Tours **Gray Line Cruises** (355 Harris Ave., Bellingham, 98225, tel. 800/443–4552) operates 3½-hour nature cruises through the San Juan Islands.

The **Rosario Princess** (5 Harbor Esplanade, Bellingham 98225, tel. 206/734–8866) conducts whale-watching, nature, and island cruises on an 83-foot tour boat.

Western Prince Cruises (tel. 206/378–5315) charters boats for half-day whale-watching cruises during the summer; in the spring and fall, bird-watching and scuba-diving tours are offered. Cruises depart from Friday Harbor.

Exploring *Numbers in the margin correspond to points of interest on the Puget Sound map.*

There are 172 named islands in the San Juan archipelago, although at low tide the islands total 743 and at high tide, 428. Sixty are populated, and 10 are state marine parks. Ferries stop at Lopez, Shaw, Orcas, and San Juan; other islands, many privately owned, must be reached by private plane or boat. In any case, the San Juan Islands are a gold mine for naturalists, because they are home to more than 94 orcas, a few minke whales, seals, dolphins, otters, and more than 100 active pairs of breeding bald eagles.

8 The first ferry stop is **Lopez Island,** with old orchards, weathered barns, and pastures of sheep and cows. Because of the relatively flat terrain, this island is a favorite for bicyclists. Two popular parks to note are **Odlin County Park** and **Spencer Spit State Park.**

9 At the next stop, **Shaw Island,** Franciscan nuns wear their traditional habits while running the ferry dock. You may notice that few people get off here; the island is mostly residential, and tourists rarely stop.

10 **Orcas,** the next in line, is a large, mountainous, horseshoe-shape island. Roads sweep down through wide valleys and rise to marvelous hilltop views. A number of little shops featuring the island's cottage industries—jewelry, weaving, pottery—
11 are in **Eastsound Village,** the island's business and social center situated in the middle of the horseshoe. Walk along Prune Alley, where you'll find a handful of small shops and restaurants.

On the other side of the horseshoe from the ferry landing, following aptly named Horseshoe Highway, is **Moran State Park** (Star Rte., Box 22, Eastsound 98245, tel. 206/376–2326). The ranger station will supply information, but applications for camping permits within the park for Memorial Day through Labor Day must be received by mail at least two weeks prior to the requested date. From the summit of the 2,400-foot-tall **Mt. Constitution** are panoramic views of the San Juan Islands, the Cascades, the Olympics, and Vancouver Island.

12 The last ferry stop in the San Juan Islands is at **Friday Harbor** on San Juan Island, with a colorful, active waterfront that always conveys a holiday feeling. Friday Harbor—the islands' county seat and the only incorporated town on San Juan Island—is also the most convenient destination in the San Juans for visitors traveling on foot. The shops here cater to tourists, offering clever crafts, gifts, and whimsical toys. A short walk from the ferry dock, the **San Juan Historical Museum** displays a number of farm implements used by early settlers. *405 Price St., tel. 206/378–3949. Admission free. Open June–Aug., Wed.–Sat. 1–4:30.*

Standing at the ferry dock facing the bluff and downtown, you'll recognize the **Whale Museum** by the mural of the whale painted on the wall. To reach the entrance, walk up Spring Street and turn right on 1st Street. This modest museum doesn't attempt to woo you with expensive exhibits; models of whales, whale skeletons, baleen, recordings of whale sounds, and videos of whales are the attractions. There are also workshops on marine mammals and San Juan ecology. *62 1st St. N, tel. 206/378–4710. Admission: $2.50 adults, $2 senior citizens, $1 children 3–12. Open June–Sept., daily 10–5; Oct.–May, daily 11–4.*

For an opportunity to see whales cavorting in the Strait of San Juan de Fuca, go to **Lime Kiln Point State Park,** on San Juan's west side, just 6 miles from Friday Harbor. This viewpoint is America's first official whale-watching park. The best seasons to visit are late spring, summer, and fall. *6158 Lighthouse Rd., tel. 206/378–2044. Admission free. Open daily 6:30 AM–10 PM. Day-use only; no camping facilities.*

The **San Juan Island National Historic Park** is a remnant of the "Pig War," a prolonged scuffle between American and British troops who were brought in after a Yank killed a Brit's pig in 1859, setting off tempers on both sides. The mere presence of the soldiers was pretty much the extent of the hostilities (no gunfire was ever exchanged), although troops from both countries remained on the island until 1872. The park encompasses two separate areas: a British camp on the west side of the island, containing a blockhouse, commissary, and barracks; and an American camp with a laundry, fortifications, and a visitor's center. From June through August the park offers hikes and historic reenactments of 1860s-era military life. For information contact the **San Juan Island Chamber of Commerce Office** (125 Spring St., tel. 206/378–2240).

13 **Roche Harbor,** at the northern end of San Juan, is an elegant little town of well-manicured lawns, rose gardens, cobblestone waterfront, hanging flower baskets on the docks, and the Hotel de Haro, with its restaurant and lounge.

Shopping
Lopez Island

The **Chimera Gallery** (Lopez Village, tel. 206/468–3265) is a local artists' cooperative.

Grayling Gallery (3630 Hummel Lake Rd., tel. 206/468–2779) features the paintings, prints, sculptures, and pottery of about 10 artists from Lopez Island, some of whom live and work on the gallery's premises. The gallery is open Friday–Sunday 10–5.

Orcas Island

Darvill's Rare Print Shop (Eastsound, tel. 206/376–2351) specializes in antique and contemporary prints.

San Juan Island

Boardwalk Bookstore (5 Spring St., Friday Harbor, tel. 206/378–2787) is strong in classics and has a collection of good, popular literature selected by a most literate owner, Dorthea Augusztiny.

Ravenhouse Art (1 Spring St. W, Friday Harbor, tel. 206/378–2777) features watercolors, oil paintings, jewelry, and pottery.

Cabezon Gallery (60 1st St. W, tel. 206/378–3116) features the works of local artists.

Island Wools & Weaving (30 1st St. S, Friday Harbor, tel. 206/378–2148) carries wonderful yarns, some handspun and handdyed, imaginative buttons, and some handknit items.

Waterworks Gallery (315 Argyle St., Friday Harbor, tel. 206/378–3060) emphasizes marine art.

Sports and the Outdoors
Bicycling

Lopez Island: **The Bike Shop** (Rte. 1, Box 1162, Lopez, 98261, tel. 206/468–3497) provides bikes for rent year-round.

Orcas Island: **Key Moped Rental** (Box 279, Eastsound, tel. 206/376–2474) rents mopeds during the summer.

Wildlife Cycles (Box 1048, Eastsound, tel. 206/376–4708) has bikes for rent in Eastsound.

San Juan Island: **San Juan Island Bicycles** (380 Argyle St., Friday Harbor, tel. 206/378–4941) has a reputation for good service as well as equipment.

Susie's Mopeds (Box 1972, Friday Harbor, tel. 206/378–5244) offers mopeds for rent.

Boating

Lopez Island: **Islands Marine Center** (tel. 206/468–3377) has most standard marina amenities and repair facilities.

Orcas Island: **Deer Harbor Resort & Marina** (tel. 206/376–4420), **Lieber Haven Marina Resort** (tel. 206/376–4420), and **West Sound Marina** (tel. 206/376–2314) offer standard marina facilities and more. **Russell's Landing/Orcas Store** (tel. 206/376–4389) has gas, diesel, tackle, and groceries at the ferry landing.

San Juan Island: **Port of Friday Harbor** (tel. 206/378–2688), **San Juan Marina** (tel. 206/378–2841), and **Roche Harbor Resort** (tel. 206/378–2155) have standard marina facilities; Port of Friday and Roche harbors are also U.S. Customs ports of entry.

Marine State Parks (tel. 206/753–2027) are accessible by private boat only. No moorage or camping reservations are available, and fees are charged at some parks from May through Labor Day. Fresh water, where available, is limited. Island parks are **Blind, Clark, Doe, James, Jones, Matia, Patos, Posey, Stuart, Sucia,** and **Turn.** All have a few campsites; there are no docks at Blind, Clark, Patos, Posey, or Turn islands.

Skippered sailing charters are available through **Amante Sail Tours** (tel. 206/376–4231), **Custom Designed Charters** (tel. 206/376–5105), **Harmony Sailing Charters** (tel. 206/468–3310), **Kismet Sailing Charters** (tel. 206/468–2435), **Nor'wester Sailing Charters** (tel. 206/378–5478), and **Wind N' Sails** (tel. 206/378–5343).

Bare-boat sailing charters are available through **Wind N' Sails** (tel. 206/378–5343).

If you are kayaking on your own, beware of ever-changing conditions, ferry and shipping landings, and strong tides and currents. Go ashore only on known public property. Day trips and longer expeditions are available from **Shearwater Sea Kayak Tours** (tel. 206/376–4699), **Doe Bay Resort** (tel. 206/376–2291), **Black Fish Paddlers** (tel. 206/376–4041), **San Juan Kayak Expeditions** (tel. 206/378–4436), and **Seaquest** (tel. 206/378–5767).

Fishing You can fish year-round for bass and trout at **Hummel Lake** on Lopez Island, and at **Egg** and **Sportsman lakes** on San Juan Island. On Orcas, there are three lakes at **Moran State Park** that are open to fishing from late April through October.

You can go saltwater fishing through **Buffalo Works** (tel. 206/378–4612), **Captain Clyde's Charters** (tel. 206/378–5661), and **King Salmon Charters** (tel. 206/468–2314).

Beaches Lopez Island: The best beaches on this island include the low-bank beach at **Odlin County Park** (Rte. 2, Box 3216, tel. 206/468–2496) and a mile of waterfront at **Spencer Spit State Park** (Rte. 2, Box 3600, tel. 206/468–2251).

San Juan Island: You'll find 10 acres of beachfront at the **San Juan County Park** (380 Westside Rd. N, Friday Harbor, tel. 206/378–2992).

Dining For prices, *see* the Dining chart in Seattle, *above*.

Lopez Island **Bay Cafe.** A varied, seasonal menu of soups, salads, and entrées of seafood, pasta, chicken, and beef is served with an international flair. This restaurant is a special treat for the locals, who must otherwise choose between rather uninspired burgers and pizza. *Lopez Village, tel. 206/468–3700. Reservations accepted. Dress: casual. MC, V. Dinner only. Inexpensive–Moderate.*

Orcas Island **Christina's.** The atmosphere here is elegant whether you dine inside, on the enclosed porch, or on the rooftop terrace with views of East Sound. The emphasis is on fresh, local seafood, with some of the best salmon entrées in the Northwest. Other specialties include grilled breast of chicken with an eggplant-and-pepper stuffing and mouth-watering desserts. *North Beach Rd. and Horseshoe Hwy., tel. 206/376–4904. Reservations suggested. Dress: neat but casual. AE, DC, MC, V. Moderate–Expensive.*

Bilbo's Festivo. This house with a courtyard features stucco walls, Mexican tiles, wood benches, and weavings from New Mexico. The menu features burritos, enchiladas, and other Mexican favorites such as orange-sauce-marinated chicken grilled over mesquite and served with fresh asparagus, potatoes, and salad. *Northbeach Rd. and A St., Eastsound, tel. 206/376–4728. No reservations. Dress: casual. AE, MC, V. Closed Mon.; lunch Tues.–Wed. Inexpensive–Moderate.*

San Juan Island

Duck Soup Inn. This Mediterranean-inspired kitchen makes the most of fresh local fish in dishes such as squid sautéed in butter and olive oil and served in a fresh tomato sauce, Wescott Bay oysters from across the island, and mussels in a tomato-wine sauce. There is also a good list of Northwest, California, and European wines. *3090 Roche Harbor Rd., tel. 206/378-4878. Reservations suggested. Dress: casual. MC, V. Closed winter; rest of year, closed dinner Mon.–Tues. Expensive.*

Springtree Eating Establishment and Farm. Meals are prepared from organically grown produce on the farm, and entrées include such items as cod with a fresh citrus and garden mint sauce, seafood chowder, and meal-size salads. Lots of plants and chintz fabrics decorate the interior, patio dining is available, and the service has improved under new management. *Spring St., tel. 206/378-4848. Reservations suggested. Dress: casual. MC, V. Moderate.*

Front Street Ale House. This English-style pub features sandwiches, salads, as well as such traditional pub fare as lamb stew, meat pasties, steak-and-kidney pie, and trifle. For vegetarians, there's the Hooley Burger, a quarter-pound of vegetable patty lightly sautéed, then stacked with cheese, mushrooms, lettuce, tomato, and onions. The pub wouldn't be complete without local brews from the San Juan Brewing Company, and with names such as Pig War Stout, they don't get much more local. *1 Front St., Friday Harbor, WA 98250, tel. 206/378-2337. No reservations. Dress: casual. MC, V. Inexpensive.*

Lodging For prices, *see* the Lodging chart in Seattle, *above*.

Lopez Island

Edenwild. The imposing gray Victorian-style farmhouse, surrounded by rose gardens, looks as if it's a restored island building, but dates only from 1990, not 1890. Rooms feature whitewashed oak floors, a muted gray interior, and white painted woodwork, along with botanical prints, lace curtains from Scotland, leaded-glass windows, and some antiques. A three-course breakfast is served in the dining room. *Box 271, Lopez Island, WA 98261, tel. 206/468-3238. 7 double rooms with baths. MC, V. Expensive.*

Inn at Swifts Bay. Robert Herrman and Chris Brandmeir take guests into their sumptuously comfortable Tudor-style home as if they were welcoming old friends. Here you will find an English country ambience with electic furnishings, including antiques and well-stocked book and video libraries. Bay windows in the living and dining areas overlook well-kept gardens, and a crackling fire warms the living room on winter evenings. Thick terry robes, flip-flops, and flashlights are available for your walk down the garden path to the hot tub under the stars. The rooms and suites are all decorated tastefully and without fussiness. In the morning, Chris treats you to a gourmet breakfast, such as eggs Dungeness (poached eggs with hollandaise and fresh crab). *Rte. 2, Box 3402, Lopez Island, WA 98261, tel. 206/468-3636. 2 double rooms, 3 suites with bath. Facilities: hot tub. AE, D, MC, V. Moderate–Expensive.*

Mackaye Harbor Inn. At the south end of Lopez Island, across the road from MacKaye Harbor, is this inn, a two-story frame 1920s sea captain's house with ½ mile of beach. Rooms features golden oak and brass details and wicker furniture; three have views of the harbor. Owners Robin, who is Swedish, and Mike Bergstrom take turns cooking breakfast, which often includes Scandinavian specialties such as *aebleskiver* (apple pancake) and *panukakku* (Finnish pancake). *Box 1940, Lopez Island, WA 98261, tel. 206/468–2253. 5 rooms. Facilities: kayak tours, bikes, rowboat. MC, V. Moderate.*

Orcas Island

Rosario Spa & Resort. Originally built by shipbuilding magnate Robert Moran (who was told he had six months to live, and therefore went all-out on this, his last extravagance), this Mediterranean-style mansion cost $1.5 million in 1905 and holds up a roof made of six tons of copper. The interior of the mansion, now the dining room and spa, is of fine teak and mahogany. As it happened, Moran lived another 30 years, and now the mansion is on the National Register of Historic Places. Fire codes prohibit rental of guest rooms in the old structure, so villas and hotel units were added after Rosario was converted into a resort in 1960. These guest rooms are nowhere near as spectacular as the mansion, but they do have decent views of the water, and most have decks or patios. *Horseshoe Hwy., Eastsound 98245, tel. 206/376–2222 or 800/562–8820. 179 rooms. Facilities: dining room, indoor pool, 2 outdoor pools, health spa, sauna, whirlpool, games room, tennis courts, marina with boat rentals, fishing, hiking. AE, DC, MC, V. Expensive.*

Orcas Hotel. On the hill overlooking the Orcas Island ferry landing is this three-story, red-roofed Victorian hotel, complete with a wraparound porch and white picket fence. Construction first began in 1900, and the building is on the National Register of Historic Places. The dining room (open for dinner to nonguests as well) overlooks the ferry landing and gardens, and the parlor is decorated with Victorian antiques. Guest rooms feature wicker, brass, antique furnishings, and featherbeds, and some units have small sun decks. Breakfast is in the dining room and guests order from the restaurant's regular menu, which includes French toast, omelets, and other egg dishes. *Box 155, Orcas, WA 98280, tel. 206/376–4300; fax 206/376–4399. 12 rooms. Facilities: restaurant, lounge. AE, DC, MC, V. Moderate–Expensive.*

Turtleback Farm. Just 15 minutes from the ferry landing is this forest-green-with-white-trim inn, set on 80 acres of meadow, forest, and farmland in the shadow of Turtleback Mountain. The interior is spacious and airy, without frills. Guest rooms have easy chairs, good beds with woolen comforters made from the fleece of resident sheep, some antiques, cream-colored muslin curtains, and views of meadows and forest. Breakfast, cooked by Susan Fletcher and served by her husband, Bill, can be taken in the dining room or on the deck overlooking the valley. *R.R. 1, Box 650, Eastsound, WA 98245, tel. 206/376–3914. 7 rooms. MC, V. Moderate–Expensive.*

Doe Bay Village Resort. This is a rustic place that is a personal-growth center and retreat. The resort feels faintly countercultural: holdover from its earlier days as an artists' colony. Units vary from dormitory rooms to cottages, some with sleeping quarters only and access to shower house and community kitchen; other units feature kitchens and baths. The peaceful, scenic grounds are great for walks or for sitting and reading. *S.R. 86, Olga 98279, tel. 206/376–2291. 100 units. Facilities: natural-food café, general store, guided kayak trips, hot tub, massage therapist. AE, MC, V. Inexpensive–Moderate.*

San Juan Island

Roche Harbor Resort. Here you've got a choice between cottage, condominium, or rooms in the 1886 restored Hotel de Haro. The old hotel building is better to look at than to stay in; its guest rooms are fairly shabby or, at best, very rustic. *Box 1,*

Friday Harbor 98250, tel. 206/378–2155. 60 rooms. Facilities: restaurant, swimming pool, tennis court, boat moorage for 200 yachts, complete boating facilities, 4,000-ft airstrip. MC, V. Moderate–Expensive.

Blair House. Just four blocks uphill from the ferry landing in Friday Harbor on more than an acre of landscaped grounds is the Blair House bed-and-breakfast. The two-story gray Victorian house with dormer windows and a wide wraparound porch, now furnished with wicker chairs and table, was built in 1909 and has since been enlarged several times. The rooms are decorated with sophisticated wallpapers, color-coordinated linens, and ivory comforters on the beds. Guests can eat breakfast in the large dining room, on the front porch, or alongside the outdoor pool. *345 Blair Ave., Friday Harbor, WA 98250, tel. 206/378–5907. 7 rooms, 1 cottage. Facilities: cable TV, outdoor pool, hot tub. AE, MC, V. Moderate.*

Fridays. Since it was built in 1891 this house, within walking distance of the ferry terminal, has been a hotel, restaurant, private home, and a youth hostel. Debbie and Steve Demarest have converted it into a downtown bed-and-breakfast hideaway with Arts and Crafts–style furniture in the sitting room and several guestrooms that open onto decks flanked by roses, geraniums, and other flowers. All rooms are upstairs and are decorated with antiques, colorful floral print comforters on the beds, and art on the walls. Continental breakfast features fresh orange juice, scones baked daily, and gourmet coffee. *35 First St., Friday Harbor 98250, tel. 206/378–5848 or 800/352–2632. 4 rooms with bath, 4 rooms share 2 baths, 2 suites. MC, V. Moderate.*

Hillside House. Less than a mile outside of Friday Harbor, this contemporary house sits on a hill, providing stunning views of the harbor and Mt. Baker. The home features a large living room, kitchen, and 1,000 square feet of deck space. Each of the comfortable guest rooms has a sophisticated decor. The Eagle's Nest suite features several windows with expansive views, a king-size bed, and a sitting area. In the large, maroon-and-teal-green-tiled bathroom, guests can luxuriate in the whirlpool while gazing up at the moon through the large, high windows. Queen-size beds, oak chests, and one- or two-person window seats are in all rooms. Some rooms overlook the 10,000-square-foot full-flight aviary, filled with pheasants, ducks, and doves. The Robinsons, who own the inn, encourage guests to use the recycled books in the hallway—take one or leave one—and provide badminton, horseshoes, and a cable swing (a present from guests with fond memories of their stay) in the yard. Breakfast includes entrées made with resident hens' eggs, island jams, and fresh berries. *365 Carter Ave., Friday Harbor, WA 98250, tel. 206/378–4730 or 800/232–4730. 6 rooms, 1 suite. Facilities: access to health club in town. AE, MC, V. Moderate.*

San Juan Inn. This restored 1873 inn is comfortably furnished and within walking distance of the ferry terminal. Rooms, which are all on the second floor, are small but have brass, iron, or wicker beds, a few antiques, and decorative wallpaper. Some rooms have views of a lovely courtyard garden. A breakfast of muffins, coffee, and juice is served each morning in a parlor overlooking the harbor. *50 Spring St., Box 776, Friday Harbor 98250, tel. 206/378–2070 or 800/742–8210. 10 rooms. No facilities. Car rentals available. MC, V. Moderate.*

Dining and Lodging
Orcas Island

Deer Harbor Inn. The original log lodge—situated on a knoll overlooking Deer Harbor—was the first resort built on the island (1915) and is now the dining room of the inn. A newer log cabin features eight spacious, airy rooms with peeled log furniture; views; balconies; and breakfast delivered to your door in a picnic basket. Although large, the dining room, which specializes in fresh seafood, is cozy, with its natural wood and floral prints, and has an adjoining deck for outdoor dining. *Box 142, Eastsound 98243, tel. 206/376–4110. 8 units. Facilities: restaurant. Reservations for restaurant suggested. Dress: casual. AE, MC, V. Moderate.*

The Arts

On the San Juan Islands, check performance schedules at the **Orcas Performing Arts Center** (Box 567, Eastsound 98245, tel. 206/376–ARTS) and the **San Juan Community Theatre** (100 2nd Ave., Friday Harbor 98250, tel. 206/378–3210).

Snoqualmie Falls

Driving east out of Seattle, you'll travel through bucolic farmland with snowcapped mountains in the background. Spring and summer snowmelt turns the Snoqualmie River into a thundering torrent as it cascades through a 268-foot rock gorge (100 feet higher than Niagara Falls) to a 65-foot-deep pool below.

Tourist Information

For information on Snoqualmie, contact the **Upper Snoqualmie Valley Chamber of Commerce** (Box 356, North Bend, 98045, tel. 206/888–4440).

Getting There
By Car

Snoqualmie, Exit 27 off I–90, is about 30 miles east of Seattle.

Snoqualmie is the site of the first major electric plant in the Northwest to use falling water as a power source, and the world's first completely underground electric-generating facility. The power plant, started in 1889, is a National Historic Civil Engineering Landmark; plant No. 2 was added just downstream from the falls in 1910 and expanded in 1957. Electricity from the two power plants provides enough power to serve 16,000 homes.

A two-acre park, including an observation platform 300 feet above the Snoqualmie River, offers a view of the falls and surrounding area. Hike the **River Trail,** a 3-mile round-trip route through trees and open slopes, ending with a view from the base of the falls. (Note: Be prepared for an uphill workout on the return to the trailhead.)

Steam locomotives power vintage trains on **Puget Sound** and **Snoqualmie Valley Railway.** The 75-minute trip travels through woods and farmland. Railroad artifacts and memorabilia are displayed at both the Snoqualmie Depot (Hwy. 202, in downtown Snoqualmie) and Railroad Park Depot in downtown Northbend. For children, a special Santa train runs the first two weekends in December and a spook train runs the last two weekends in October; tickets for all special trips must be prepurchased. *Box 459, Snoqualmie, tel. 206/746–4025 in Seattle or 206/888–0373. Admission: $6 adults, $5 senior citizens, $4 children. Trains operate Sept., May, and June, weekends; Oct. and Apr., Sun.; July–Aug., Fri.–Sun. Call for departure times.*

Snoqualmie Falls Forest Theater produces three plays a summer (the Passion Play, a melodrama, and a well-known classic performed by acting students and community theater performers) in the 250-seat outdoor amphitheater near Fall City, usually on Friday and Saturday nights and Sunday afternoons. *From I–90 take Exit 22 and go 4 mi; take a right on David Powell Rd., follow signs, continue through gate to parking area. 36800 S.E. David Powell Rd., tel. 206/222–7044. Admission: $8.50; for another $9 per person, you can enjoy a salmon or steak barbecue after the matinee and before the evening performances. Reservations required for dinner.*

Snoqualmie Pass is the site of three ski areas—Alpental, Ski Acres, and Snoqualmie Summitt for downhill and cross-country skiing in winter and spring, and for hiking in the summer (*see* Sports and the Outdoors, *above*).

The **Snoqualmie Winery** (1000 Winery Rd., tel. 206/888–4000) offers daily tours, tastings, and great views.

Dining ★

The Herbfarm. If there is such a thing as Northwest cuisine, then The Herbfarm must rank as its temple. But the attraction here is more than the fine, fresh food: This restaurant offers intimate, elegant dining among wildflower bouquets, Victorian-style prints, and a friendly staff. Try such delicacies as goat's milk cheese and parsley biscuits, green pickled walnuts in the husk, fresh salmon with a sauce of fresh garden herbs, and sorbet of rose geranium and lemon verbena. There's only one drawback: The Herbfarm is commonly booked up months ahead of time, which means you should plan a meal long before you're getting to Seattle. Is all that effort worth it? Yes. Wine is the only alcohol served. *From I–90, Exit 22, go 3 mi. to 32804 Issaquah-Fall City Rd., Fall City, tel. 206/784–2222. Some 75% of the 24 seats for each lunch or special dinner are reserved in early Apr. The other 6 seats can be reserved by phoning at 1 PM the Fri. before you wish to go. Allow 2 hours for lunch ($45 per person) and the garden tour. Dinners, including 9 courses and 5 fine wines, are scheduled in the summer ($89–$115 per person). Dress: casual but neat. Restaurant closed Mon.–Thurs.; dinner, Jan.–early Apr. MC, V. Expensive.*

Dining and Lodging

Salish. This lodge at the top of the falls has been rebuilt and is operated by the Oregon-based Salishan Lodge. Eight of the 91 rooms look out over the falls, and others have a view upriver. All of the rooms have an airy feeling, wood furniture, and window seats or balconies. You can sit in the whirlpool bath and open a window to view the fire in the flagstone fireplace. The Salish restaurant, which serves three meals daily, also has a widespread reputation for its Sunday brunch, which includes course upon course of eggs, bacon, fish, fresh fruit, pancakes, and its renowned oatmeal. *37807 Snoqualmie-Fall City Rd., Fall City 37807, tel. 206/888–2556. 91 rooms. Facilities: 2 restaurants, lounge, health club, country store. Reservation for restaurant necessary. Dress for restaurant: casual; jacket and tie recommended for dinner. AE, DC, MC, V. Expensive.*

Leavenworth

On the way to Leavenworth, traveling northeast from Seattle along I–5 and U.S. 2, visitors will pass through the densely forested mountain country along the Skykomish River. At the summit, in the Stevens Pass/Leavenworth area, the main attractions are the towering Cascades. (Leavenworth itself is at an elevation of 1,170 feet; the surrounding mountains rise to

8,000 feet.) Some of the best skiing, hiking, rock climbing, rafting, canoeing, and snowshoeing in the Northwest start from Leavenworth, and the town itself is well worth exploring.

Although it was once a center for mining and railroading, by the early 1960s Leavenworth had become a moribund village. Civic leaders seeking ways to revitalize the area decided to capitalize on the town's spectacular alpine setting; the result is a charming (and only sometimes *too* cute) center for both winter and summer sports. Shopkeepers and hostelers, maintaining the town's buildings in gingerbread Tyrolean style and sponsoring events modeled after those found in a typical Bavarian village, keep a European spirit of simple elegance alive in a setting that is never short of spectacular.

Virtually all of the many specialty shops, restaurants, and hotels subscribe to the Bavarian theme. There are restaurants specializing in Bavarian food; candy shops with gourmet Swiss-style chocolate; shops featuring music boxes, nutcrackers, and other Bavarian specialties; and charming European-style pension hotels. (There's even a laundromat called Die Washerie.) Throughout the year the village engages in festivities that reflect the alpine theme.

Tourist Information **Leavenworth Chamber of Commerce** (894 Hwy. 2, Box 327, 98826, tel. 509/548–5807).

Getting There

By Plane Small airports in Wenatchee, Cashmere, and Lake Wenatchee serve the Leavenworth area.

By Car Leavenworth is about 120 miles from Seattle, north on I–5 to Everett and east on U.S. 2. To return, take the long scenic loop by continuing on U.S. 2 past Leavenworth, then south on Highway 97 to Cle Elum, and back to Seattle on I–90 across Snoqualmie Pass.

By Bus **Greyhound** (tel. 800/231–2222) serves Leavenworth with two westbound and two eastbound buses daily, year-round. The bus stop is in the Department of Highways parking lot at the east end of town.

Sports and the Outdoors Leavenworth's setting in the mountains can be appreciated from a car, of course, but the main attraction here is a variety of vigorous outdoor sports in the backcountry.

Cross-Country and Downhill Skiing Beginning and advanced skiers will find more than 20 miles of maintained cross-country ski trails in the Leavenworth area. Meanwhile, Stevens Pass has downhill slopes and lifts for skiers of every level. Several shops in Leavenworth rent and sell ski equipment. For more information, contact the **Leavenworth Winter Sports Club** (Box 573, 98826, tel. 509/548–5115).

Golf Those hankering for more placid, or at least warmer-weather, sports can try the **Leavenworth Golf Club** (Box 247, 98826, tel. 509/548–7267), an 18-hole, par-71 course with a pro shop and clubhouse.

Hiking and Rock Climbing Leavenworth also offers hiking trails that take in some of the most breathtaking vistas in the entire Cascades. There are more than 320 miles of scenic trails in the Leavenworth Ranger District alone, including **Hatchery Creek, Icicle Ridge,** the **Enchantments, Tumwater Canyon, Fourth of July Creek, Snow Lake, Stuart Lake,** and **Chatter Creek**. Contact the **Leavenworth Ranger District** (600 Sherburne St., 98826, tel. 509/782–1413) for more details, or consult one of the many fine books detailing backcountry hikes in the Northwest. Rock climbing is also popular because of the solid granite cliffs in the area.

Horseback Riding The hourly and daily horseback rides and pack trips at **Eagle Creek Ranch** (7951 Eagle Creek Rd., Leavenworth 98826, tel. 509/548–7798) may also be appealing to the less rugged.

White-Water Rafting Rafting is a popular sport during March–July, with the prime high-country runoff in May and June. The **Wenatchee River,** which runs through Leavenworth, is generally considered the best white-water river in the state—a Class 3 (out of six on a scale of difficulty) on the International Canoeing Association scale. Depending on the season and location, anything from a relatively calm scenic float to an invigorating white-water shoot is possible on the Wenatchee or on one of several other nearby rivers. Some rafting outfitters and guides in the Leavenworth area are **Northern Wilderness River Riders** (10645 Hwy. 209, Leavenworth 98826, tel. 509/548–4583), **Wenatchee Whitewater and Scenic Float Trips** (Box 12, Cashmere 98815, tel. 509/782–2254), and **Leavenworth Outfitters** (21588 S.R. 207, Leavenworth 98826, tel. 509/763–3733).

Dining For prices, *see* the Dining chart in Seattle, *above.*

Edelhaus. From its prime spot in downtown Leavenworth, the Edelhaus exudes quiet, European country–style ambience with white stucco walls, old wooden tables, and crisp white linens. The sophisticated menu is closer to that of the Asian-accented Northwest cuisine found in Seattle restaurants than it is to the German-themed restaurants hereabouts. *320 9th St., Leavenworth, tel. 206/548–4412. Reservations accepted. Dress: casual but neat. MC, V. Moderate–Expensive.*

Cougar Inn. This stylish family restaurant is on the shores of Lake Wenatchee, about 25 miles outside Leavenworth. Locals often come by boat and tie up at the restaurant's dock. The atmosphere is pleasant, with lots of natural wood, airy rooms, great views of the lake and, in summer, a big outdoor deck. Breakfast, lunch, and dinner are served daily, and the hearty American-style Sunday brunch is especially popular. The menu, featuring burgers, steaks, and prime rib, is not particularly adventurous, but the food is well prepared and the service friendly. *23379 S.R. 207, Lake Wenatchee, tel. 509/763–3354. Reservations advised, especially for Sun. brunch. Dress: casual. AE, MC, V. Moderate.*

The Pewter Pot. This intimate restaurant with lace curtains and fresh flowers in downtown Cashmere is some 10 miles from Leavenworth, but worth the drive. Owner Kristi Bjornstad focuses on comfort food and very personal service. Start with one of her great soups. Entrées include a stuffed breast of chicken with an apple-cider sauce, turkey and dressing, and sour cream beef pot pie. The deep-dish marionberry pie is memorable. Ms. Bjornstad serves lunch and afternoon tea, but stops serving dinner at 8 PM. *124 ½ Cottage Ave., Cashmere 98815, tel. 509/782–2036. Reservations advised. Dress: casual but neat. MC, V. Moderate.*

Reiner's Gasthaus. Authentic central European cuisine with a Hungarian/Austrian accent is presented in this small, cheerful restaurant. The decor is heavy on the pine furnishings and thick drapes, with lots of vintage photographs and knickknacks on the walls, and the service is bustling and friendly. Music is performed on weekend evenings: Usually a jolly accordion player is featured. Specialties include pork schnitzel and

Hungarian goulash; these two dishes, as well as all the reasonably priced and well-prepared dinners, come with hearty soups and salads. *829 Front St. (upstairs), Leavenworth, tel. 509/548–5111. No reservations. Dress: casual. MC, V. Moderate.*

Baren Haus. Hearty, unpretentious food is served in this spacious, noisy, and often crowded high-ceiling beer-hall-style room. The cuisine may not be haute, or even particularly interesting, but the generous servings and low prices will appeal to families and those traveling on a tight budget. Seating is at large booths with blue tablecloths. House specialties include German-style sandwiches (such as bratwurst on grilled whole-wheat bread with sauerkraut and hearty mustards) and pizzas. *208 9th St., tel. 509/548–4535. Reservations accepted, except during festival time (Aug. and late Sept.–early Oct.). Dress: casual. MC, V. Inexpensive.*

Danish Bakery. Tasty homemade pastries, good strong espresso drinks, and a self-serve coffee bar are the attractions in this small, pleasant shop. The decor is tastefully done with dark woods and mural paintings, and the service is fast and friendly. This is a perfect place to escape the crowds on the sidewalks. *731 Front St., tel. 509/548–7514. No reservations. Dress: casual. No credit cards. Inexpensive.*

Homefires Bakery. Locals come to this bakery when they want hearty, chewy bread baked in an old brick oven. Try the German sourdough black rye bread—it's great for sandwiches or eaten simply with unsalted butter. The cinnamon rolls and cookies will make a hit with your sweet tooth. *13013 Bayne Rd., Leavenworth, tel. 509/548–7362. No reservations. Dress: casual. No credit cards. Inexpensive.*

Lodging

The number of hotels, motels, B&Bs, and long-term-rental cabins in Leavenworth has increased as the area has become more popular. **Bavarian Bedfinders** (309 8th St., Suite 1, Leavenworth 98826, tel. 509/548–4410 or 800/323–2920 in WA.) matches travelers with more than 100 facilities such as condominiums, private cabins, small lodges, and B&Bs, in Leavenworth and around the state, and it also books excursions and tours. Their services are free to guests.

For prices, *see* the Lodging chart in Seattle, *above.*

Der Ritterhof. This is a modern large hotel on the highway to Leavenworth from Seattle. Its 51 units, decorated in fairly standard-issue motel style, include suites that sleep six comfortably; some units have small kitchenettes. Amenities include a recreation area, barbecue pit, and volleyball and badminton courts on the lawn. The service is friendly and efficient. *190 Hwy. 2, 98826, tel. 509/548–5845 or 800/255–5845. 51 rooms. Facilities: outdoor heated pool, hot tubs. AE, MC, V. Moderate–Expensive.*

Pension Anna. This small, family-run Austrian-style pension in the middle of the village has a farmhouse atmosphere. Although it's newly built, it has a distinctly old-fashioned feel; rooms and suites are decorated with sturdy, antique pine furniture, with such added touches as fresh flowers and comforters on the beds. Two of the suites have whirlpool baths, and all except the ground-level rooms have small balconies. The two largest suites have fireplaces and handsome four-poster beds. A hearty European-style breakfast (cold cuts, meats, cheeses, soft-boiled eggs), included in the room price, is served in a breakfast room decorated in traditional European style with crisp linens, pine decor, dark green curtains, and (of course) a cuckoo clock. The staircases to the upper floors are quite steep. Two suites are in a 1913 onion dome steepled church building that has been relocated on the property. *926 Commercial St., 98826, tel. 509/548-6273. 14 units. Facilities: TV. AE, D, MC, V. Moderate–Expensive.*

Evergreen Motel. Popular with hikers and skiers, the Evergreen was built in the 1930s and still has a lot of the charm of the old-fashioned roadside inn it once was. Some of its two-bedroom suites have fireplaces and/or kitchens (though no utensils), while some have multiple beds and can sleep up to six comfortably. Thus, although there are only 26 units, the motel's capacity is about 80 guests. Complimentary Continental breakfast is offered by a very friendly staff, and the motel is one block from downtown. *1117 Front St., 98826, tel. 509/548-5515 or 800/327-7212. 26 rooms. AE, D, DC, MC, V. Moderate.*

Haus Rohrbach. This alpine-style B&B sits on the side of a hill overlooking its own pool and hot tub, the village of Leavenworth, and the valley beyond. The center of activity here is a large lodgelike room with a wood stove, a kitchen area, and tables for dining, playing games, socializing, or just taking in the view. Guest rooms have double or queen-size beds (some have a sofabed or daybed, as well), down comforters, and pine furniture. The suites offer king-size beds, whirlpool tubs, a gas fireplace, easy chairs, and small but fully equipped kitchens. The full breakfast served here typically features Dutch babies or sourdough pancakes and sausage. *12882 Ranger Rd., Leavenworth, 98826, tel. 509/548-7024. 9 rooms with bath, 4 rooms share 2 baths, 3 suites. Facilities: outdoor pool, outdoor hot tub. AE, D, MC, V. Moderate.*

Linderhoff Motor Inn. This small place at the west end of Leavenworth recently updated its facilities, making it one of the nicest in town for the money. It offers a variety of options: standard rooms, honeymoon suites with whirlpool tubs and fireplaces, and townhouse units that sleep up to eight and have fully equipped kitchens and two bathrooms. In contrast to the Bavarian-style exterior, with its overflowing flower boxes, guest rooms are decorated in a contemporary style of soft colors and feature locally crafted pine furnishings. The complimentary Continental breakfast choices of fresh fruit juice and locally baked muffins and Danishes can be taken back to the rooms or eaten outside on the inn's balcony. *690 Hwy. 2, Leavenworth 98826, tel. 509/548-5283. 26 units. Facilities: outdoor pool, outdoor hot tub. AE, MC, V. Moderate.*

Edelweiss Hotel. This is an unpretentious hotel above the restaurant of the same name. Small rooms, plainly furnished and with either shared or private baths, are available. This is not the place to go for a romantic weekend, but if you're on a budget and simply need a place to lay your head, the Edelweiss's price ($15 for a single room, no windows or TV) is hard to beat in this hotel-hungry town. The service is genial if sometimes harried, and the staircase is steep. *843 Front St., 98826, tel. 509/548-7015. 14 units. MC, V. Inexpensive.*

4 Vancouver

Updated by Loralee Wenger

Vancouver is a young city, even by North American standards. While three to four hundred years of settlement may make cities like Québec and Halifax historically interesting to travelers, Vancouver's youthful vigor attracts visitors to its powerful elements that have not yet been ground down by time. Vancouver is just over a hundred years old; it was not yet a town in 1870, when British Columbia became part of the Canadian confederation. The city's history, such as it is, remains visible to the naked eye: Eras are stacked east to west along the waterfront like some century-old archaeological dig—from cobbled, late-Victorian Gastown to shiny postmodern glass cathedrals of commerce grazing the sunset.

The Chinese were among the first to recognize the possibilities of Vancouver's setting. They came to British Columbia during the 1850s seeking the gold that inspired them to name the province *Gum-shan*, or Gold Mountain. They built the Canadian Pacific Railway that gave Vancouver's original townsite a purpose—one beyond the natural splendor that Royal Navy Capt. George Vancouver admired during his lunchtime cruise around its harbor on June 13, 1792. The transcontinental railway, along with its Great White Fleet of clipper ships, gave Vancouver a full week's edge over the California ports in shipping tea and silk to New York at the dawn of the 20th century.

Vancouver's natural charms are less scattered than in other cities. On clear days, the mountains appear close enough to touch. Two 1,000-acre wilderness parks lie within the city limits. The salt water of the Pacific and fresh water direct from the Rocky Mountain Trench form the city's northern and southern boundaries.

Bring a healthy sense of reverence when you visit: Vancouver is a spiritual place. For its original inhabitants, the Coast Salish peoples, it was the sacred spot where the mythical Thunderbird and Killer Whale flung wind and rain all about the heavens during their epic battles—how else to explain the coast's occasional climatic fits of temper? Devotees of a later religious tradition might worship in the sepulchre of Stanley Park or in the polished, incense-filled quiet of St. James Anglican Church, designed by English architect Sir Adrian Gilbert Scott and perhaps Vancouver's finest building.

Vancouver has a level of nightlife possible only in a place where the finer things in life have never been driven out to the suburbs and where sidewalks have never rolled up at 5 PM. There is no shortage of excellent hotels and restaurants here either. But you can find good theater, accommodations, and dining almost anywhere these days. Vancouver's *real* culture consists of its tall fir trees practically downtown and its towering rock spires close by, the ocean at your doorstep, and people from every corner of the earth all around you.

Essential Information

Arriving and Departing by Plane

Airport and Airlines
International Airports

Vancouver International Airport is on an island about 14 kilometers (9 miles) south of downtown. The main terminal building has three levels: departures, international arrivals, and domestic arrivals; a small south terminal building services flights to secondary destinations within the province. **American Airlines** (tel. 800/433–7300), **Continental** (tel. 800/525–0280), **Delta** (tel. 604/221–1212), **Horizon Air** (800/547–9308), and **United** (tel. 800/241–6522) fly into the airport. The two major domestic airlines are **Air Canada** (tel. 604/688–5515) and **Canadian Airlines** (tel. 604/279–6611).

Other Facilities Air BC (tel. 604/688-5515) offers 30-minute harbor-to-harbor service (downtown Vancouver to downtown Victoria) several times a day. Planes leave from near the Bayshore Hotel. Helijet Airways (tel. 604/273–1414) has helicopter service from downtown Vancouver to downtown Victoria and Whistler. The heliport is near Vancouver's Pan Pacific Hotel.

Between the Airport and Downtown The drive from the airport to downtown is 20–45 minutes, depending on the time of day. Airport hotels offer free shuttle service to and from the airport.

By Bus The **Airport Express** (tel. 604/261–2299) bus leaves the domestic arrivals level of the terminal building every 15 minutes in summer and every 30 minutes in winter, stopping at major downtown hotels and the bus depot. It operates from 5:30 AM until 12:30 AM. The fare is $8.25 one-way and $14 round-trip.

By Taxi Taxi stands are in front of the terminal building on domestic and international arrivals levels. Taxi fare to downtown is about $24. Area cab companies are Yellow (tel. 604/681–3311) and Black Top (tel. 604/681–2181).

By Limousine Limousine service from **Airlimo** (tel. 604/273–1331) costs about the same as a taxi to downtown: The current rate is about $28.

Arriving and Departing

By Car From the south, I–5 from Seattle becomes **Highway 99** at the U.S.–Canada border. Vancouver is a three-hour drive from Seattle. Avoid border crossings during peak times: holidays and weekends.

Highway 1, the **Trans-Canada Highway,** enters Vancouver from the east. If you enter the city after rush hour (8:30 AM), you should not have a problem with traffic.

By Ferry **BC Ferries** operates two major ferry terminals outside Vancouver. From Tsawwassen to the south (an hour's drive from downtown), ferries sail to Victoria and Nanaimo on Vancouver Island and through the Gulf Islands (the small islands between the mainland and Vancouver Island). From Horseshoe Bay (30 minutes north from downtown), ferries sail a short distance up the coast and to Nanaimo on Vancouver Island. Call (tel.604/685–1021) for departure and arrival times.

Sealink Express (tel. 604/687–6925) takes passengers by high-speed catamaran from downtown Vancouver to downtown Victoria in 2½ hours. The two boats each seat 302 people and have such airplane-type amenities as movies, work tables, and headphones for music; there are also fax machines, telephones, two snack bars, a children's playroom, and a newsstand on board. Tickets cost $32.95 one-way, $59.95 round-trip.

By Train The Pacific Central Station (1150 Station St.) is the hub for rail, bus, and SkyTrain service. The **VIA Rail** (tel. 800/561–8630) station is at Main Street and Terminal Avenue. VIA provides service through the Rockies to Banff. Passenger trains leave

Vancouver Exploring *(Boxes Refer to Detail Maps)*

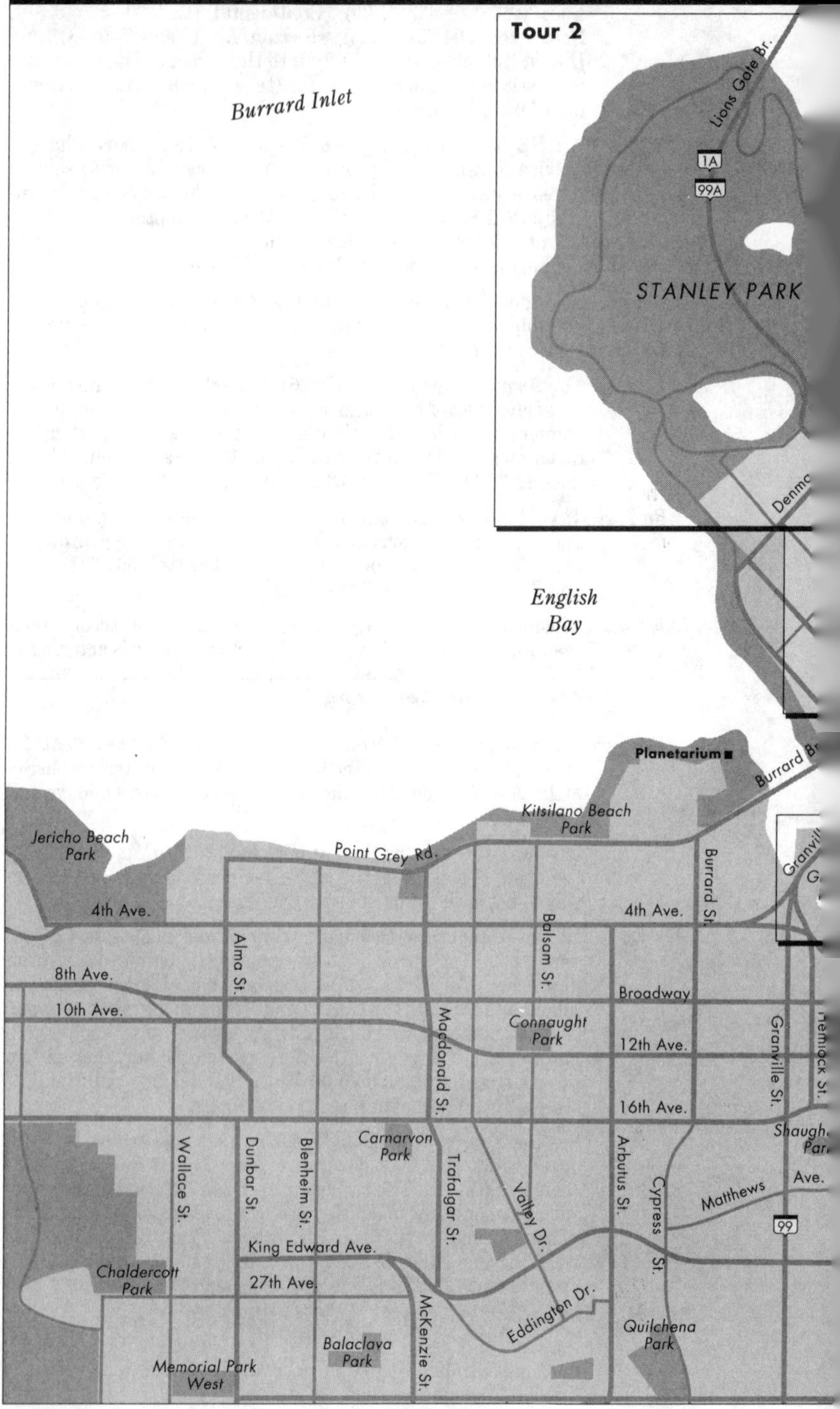
Tour 2
Burrard Inlet
Lions Gate Br.
1A
99A
STANLEY PARK
Denma
English Bay
Planetarium
Burrard Br
Kitsilano Beach Park
Jericho Beach Park
Point Grey Rd.
4th Ave.
Alma St.
Balsam St.
4th Ave.
Burrard St.
8th Ave.
Broadway
10th Ave.
Macdonald St.
Connaught Park
12th Ave.
Granville St.
16th Ave.
Wallace St.
Dunbar St.
Blenheim St.
Carnarvon Park
Trafalgar St.
Valley Dr.
Arbutus St.
Cypress St.
Matthews
Ave.
99
King Edward Ave.
Chaldercott Park
27th Ave.
McKenzie St.
Eddington Dr.
Quilchena Park
Balaclava Park
Memorial Park West

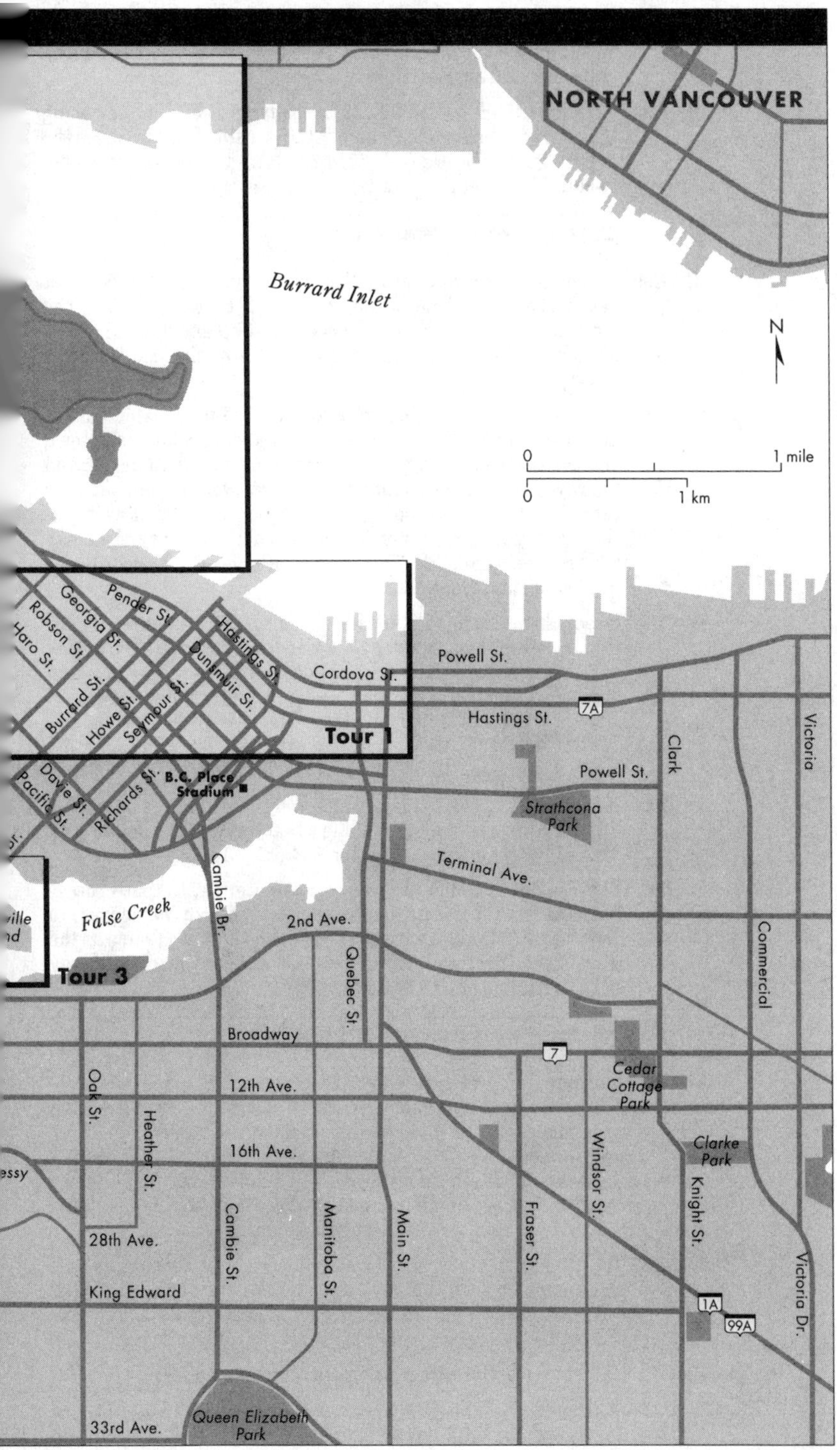
NORTH VANCOUVER
Burrard Inlet
N
0
1 mile
0
1 km
Pender St.
Georgia St.
Robson St.
Haro St.
Hastings St.
Dunsmuir St.
Burrard St.
Howe St.
Seymour St.
Cordova St.
Powell St.
7A
Hastings St.
Tour 1
Clark
Victoria
Powell St.
Davie St.
Pacific St.
Richards St.
B.C. Place Stadium
Strathcona Park
Terminal Ave.
Cambie Br.
False Creek
2nd Ave.
Quebec St.
Commercial
Tour 3
Broadway
7
Oak St.
12th Ave.
Cedar Cottage Park
Heather St.
16th Ave.
Windsor St.
Clarke Park
Knight St.
28th Ave.
Cambie St.
Manitoba St.
Main St.
Fraser St.
Victoria Dr.
King Edward
1A
99A
33rd Ave.
Queen Elizabeth Park

the **BC Rail** (tel. 604/631–3500) station in North Vancouver for Whistler and the interior of British Columbia. There is no Amtrak service from Seattle.

By Bus **Greyhound** (tel. 604/662–3222) is the biggest bus line servicing Vancouver. The Pacific Central Station (1150 Station St.) is the depot. **Quick Shuttle** (tel. 604/526–2836) bus service runs between Vancouver and Seattle six times a day.

Getting Around Vancouver

By Car Although no freeways cross Vancouver, rush-hour traffic is not yet horrendous. The worst rush-hour bottlenecks are the North Shore bridges, the George Massey Tunnel on Highway 99 south of Vancouver, and Highway 1 through Coquitlam and Surrey.

By Subway Vancouver has a one-line, 25-kilometer (15-mile) rapid transit system called **SkyTrain,** which travels underground downtown and is elevated for the rest of its route to New Westminster and Surrey. Trains leave about every five minutes. Tickets must be carried with you as proof of payment, and are sold at each station from machines; correct change is not necessary. You may use transfers from SkyTrain to SeaBus and BC Transit buses (*see below*) and vice versa.

By Bus Exact change is needed to ride the buses: $1.50 adults, 75¢ for senior citizens and children 5–13. Books of 25 tickets are sold at convenience stores and newsstands; look for a red, white, and blue "Fare Dealer" sign. Day passes, good for unlimited travel after 9:30 AM, cost $4.50 for adults. They are available from fare dealers and any SeaBus or SkyTrain station. Transfers are valid for 90 minutes and allow travel in both directions.

By Taxi It is difficult to hail a cab in Vancouver; unless you're near a hotel, you'd have better luck calling a taxi service. Try **Yellow** (tel. 604/681–3311) or **Black Top** (tel. 604/681–2181).

By SeaBus The **SeaBus** is a 400-passenger commuter ferry that crosses Burrard Inlet from the foot of Lonsdale (North Vancouver) to downtown. The ride takes 13 minutes and costs the same as the transit bus. With a transfer, connection can be made with any BC Transit bus or SkyTrain.

Important Addresses and Numbers

Tourist Information **Vancouver Travel Infocentre** (200 Burrard St., tel. 604/683–2000) provides maps and information about the city and is open in summer, daily 8–6; in winter, Monday–Saturday 9–5. A kiosk in Pacific Centre Mall is open daily in summer, Monday–Saturday 9:30–5, Sunday noon–5; in winter, Monday–Saturday 9–5. Eaton's department store downtown also has a tourist information counter that is open all year.

Embassies There are no embassies in Vancouver, only consulates and trade commissions: **United States** (1075 W. Pender St., tel. 604/685–4311) and **United Kingdom** (800–1111 Melville St., tel. 604/683–4421). For a complete listing, see the Yellow Pages.

Emergencies Call 911 for **police, fire department,** and **ambulance.**

Hospitals and Clinics **St. Paul's Hospital** (1081 Burrard St., tel. 604/682–2344), a downtown hospital, has an emergency ward. **Medicentre** (1055

Dunsmuir St., lower level, tel. 604/683–8138), a drop-in clinic on the lower level of the Bentall Centre, is open weekdays.

Dentist The counterpart to Medicentre is **Dentacentre** (1055 Dunsmuir St., lower level, tel. 604/669–6700), which is next door and is also open weekdays.

Late-Night Pharmacy **Shopper's Drug Mart** (1125 Davie St., tel. 604/685–6445) is open until midnight every night except Sunday, when it closes at 9.

Road Emergencies **BCAA** (tel. 604/293–2222) has 24-hour emergency road service for members of AAA or CAA.

Travel Agencies **American Express Travel Service** (1040 W. Georgia St., tel. 604/669–2813), **Hagen's Travel** (210–850 W. Hastings St., tel. 604/684–2448), and **P. Lawson Travel** (409 Granville St., tel. 604/682–4272).

Opening and Closing Times

Banks traditionally are open Monday–Thursday 10–3 and Friday 10–6, but many banks have extended hours and are open on Saturday, particularly outside of downtown.

Museums are generally open 10–5, including Saturday and Sunday. Most are open one evening a week as well.

Department store hours are Monday–Wednesday and Saturday 9:30–6, Thursday and Friday 9:30–9, and Sunday noon–5. Many smaller stores are also open Sunday. Robson Street and Chinatown are particularly good for Sunday shopping.

Guided Tours

Orientation **Gray Line** (tel. 604/879-3363), the largest tour operator, offers the 3½-hour Grand City bus tour year-round. Departing from the Hotel Vancouver, the tour includes Stanley Park, Chinatown, Gastown, English Bay, and Queen Elizabeth Park and costs about $31. **Westcoast City and Nature Sightseeing** (tel. 604/451-5581) accommodates up to 24 people in vans that run a 3½-hour City Highlights Tour for $27 (pickup available from any downtown location). A short city tour (2½ hours) is offered by **Vance Tours** (tel. 604/941-5660) in minibuses and costs $29.

The **Vancouver Trolley Company** (tel. 604/451-5581) runs turn-of-the-century–style trolleys through Vancouver from April to October on a 1½-hour narrated tour of Stanley Park, Gastown, English Bay, the Vancouver Museum, Granville Island, Queen Elizabeth Park, Science World, and Chinatown, among other sights. A day pass allows you to complete one full circuit, getting off and on as often as you like. Start the trip at any of the sights and buy a ticket on board. It's a perfect way to deal with a rainy day in Vancouver. Adult fare is $15, children's $7.

North Shore tours usually include any or several of the following: a gondola ride up Grouse Mountain, a walk across the Capilano Suspension Bridge, a stop at a salmon hatchery, the Lonsdale Quay Market, and a ride back to town on the SeaBus. Half-day tours cost about $35 and are offered by **Landsea Tours** (tel. 604/255–7272), **Harbour Ferries** (tel. 604/687–9558), **Gray Line** (tel. 604/879-3363), and **Pacific Coach Lines** (tel. 604/662–7575).

Air Tours Tour the mountains and fjords of the North Shore by helicopter for $165 per person (minimum of three people) for 45 minutes: Vancouver Helicopters (tel. 604/270–1484) flies from the Harbour Heliport downtown. Or see Vancouver from the air for $60 for 20 minutes: Harbour Air's (tel. 604/688–1277) seaplanes leave from beside the Bayshore Hotel.

Boat Tours The Royal Hudson, Canada's only functioning steam train, heads along the mountainous coast up Howe Sound to the logging town of Squamish. After a break to explore, you sail back to Vancouver via the MV *Britannia*. This highly recommended excursion costs about $45, takes 6½ hours, and is organized by **Harbour Ferries** (tel. 604/687–9558). Reservations are necessary.

The **SS *Beaver*** (tel. 604/682–7284), a replica of a Hudson Bay fur-trading vessel that ran aground here in 1888, offers two trips. One is the Harbour Sunset Dinner Cruise, a four-hour trip with a barbecue dinner; the other is a four-hour daytime trip up Indian Arm with salmon for lunch. Each is about $50 and reservations are necessary for both.

Harbour Ferries (tel. 604/687–9558) takes a 1½-hour tour of Burrard Inlet in a paddlewheeler, and costs about $20.

Fraser River Connection (tel. 604/525–4465) will take you on a four-hour tour of a fascinating working river—past log booms, tugs, and houseboats. Ride from New Westminster to Fort Langley, aboard a convincing replica of an 1800s-era paddlewheeler, for about $25.

Personal Guides **Early Motion Tours** (tel. 604/687–5088) covers Vancouver in a Model-A Ford convertible that comfortably seats about four people. For about $60, up to four people can take an hour-long trip around downtown, Chinatown, and Stanley Park.

AAA Horse & Carriage (tel. 604/681–5115) has a 50-minute tour of Stanley Park, along the waterfront, and through a cedar forest and a rose garden for about $10.

Exploring Vancouver

The heart of Vancouver—which includes the downtown area, Stanley Park, and the West End high-rise residential neighborhood—sits on a peninsula bordered by English Bay and the Pacific Ocean to the west; by False Creek, an inlet on which you will find Granville Island, to the south; and to the north by Burrard Inlet, the working port of the city, past which loom the North Shore mountains. The oldest part of the city—Gastown and Chinatown—lies at the edge of Burrard Inlet, around Main Street, which runs north–south and is roughly the dividing line between the east side and the west side. All the avenues, which are numbered, have east and west designations.

Highlights for First-Time Visitors

Chinatown, Tour 1: Downtown Vancouver
English Bay, Tour 2: Stanley Park
Granville Island, Tour 3: Granville Island
Stanley Park, Tour 2: Stanley Park

Tour 1: Downtown Vancouver

Numbers in the margin correspond to points of interest on the Tour 1: Downtown Vancouver map.

You can logically begin your downtown tour in either of two
1 ways. If you're in for a day of shopping, amble down **Robson Street** (*see* Shopping, *below*), where you'll find any item from souvenirs to high fashions, from espresso to sushi.

2 If you opt otherwise, start at **Robson Square,** built in 1975 and designed by architect Arthur Erickson to be the gathering place of downtown Vancouver. The complex, which functions from the outside as a park, encompasses the Vancouver Art Gallery and government offices and law courts that have been built under landscaped walkways, a block-long glass canopy, and a waterfall that helps mask traffic noise. An ice-skating rink and restaurants occupy the below-street level.

3 The **Vancouver Art Gallery** that heads the square was a neoclassical-style 1912 courthouse until Erickson converted it in 1980. Notice some details: lions that guard the majestic front steps and the use of columns and domes—features borrowed from ancient Roman architecture. In back of the old courthouse, a more modest staircase now serves as a speakers' corner. *750 Hornby St., tel. 604/682–5621. Admission: $4.50 adults, $2.50 students and senior citizens; free Thurs. eve. Open Mon.–Wed., and Sat. 10–5; Thurs. 10–9; Sun. noon–5.*

4 Directly across Hornby Street is the **Hotel Vancouver** (1939), one of the last of the railway-built hotels. (The last one built was the Chateau Whistler, in 1989.) Reminiscent of a medieval French castle, this château style has been incorporated into hotels throughout almost every major Canadian city. With the onset of the depression, construction was halted here, and the hotel was finished only in time for the visit of King George VI in 1939. It has been renovated twice: During the 1960s it was unfortunately modernized, but the more recent refurbishment is more in keeping with the spirit of what is the most recognizable roof on Vancouver's skyline. The exterior of the building has carvings of malevolent gargoyles at the corners, an ornate chimney, Indian chiefs on the Hornby Street side, and an assortment of grotesque mythological figures.

5 **Christ Church Cathedral** (1895), across the street from the Hotel Vancouver, is the oldest church in Vancouver. The tiny church was built in a Gothic style with buttresses and pointed arched windows and looks like the parish church of an English village. By contrast, the cathedral's rough-hewn interior is that of a frontier town, with Douglas-fir beams and carpenter woodwork that offers excellent acoustics for the frequent vespers, carol services, and Gregorian chants presented here. *690 Burrard St., tel. 604/682–3848.*

6 **Cathedral Place,** on the corner of Hornby and Georgia streets, is a spectacular office tower adjacent to Christ Church Cathedral. Three large sculptures of nurses at the corners of the building are replicas of the statues that graced the art deco Georgia Medical-Dental Building, the site's previous structure.

A restored terra-cotta arch—formerly the front entrance to the medical building—and frieze panels showing scenes of indi-

Tour 1: Downtown Vancouver

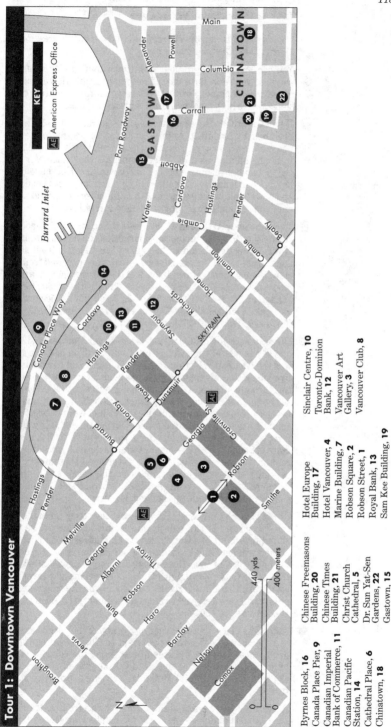

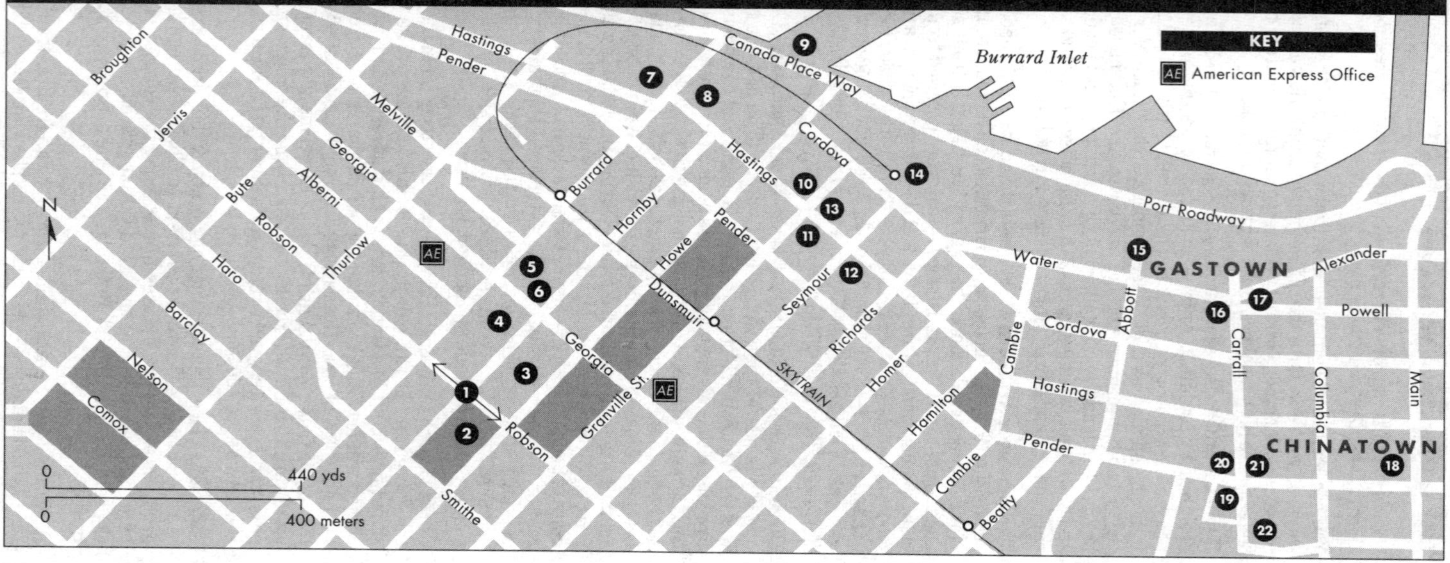

KEY

AE American Express Office

Burrard Inlet

GASTOWN

CHINATOWN

Main
Alexander
Powell
Columbia
Carrall
Abbott
Cordova
Water
Hastings
Pender
Cambie
Hamilton
Homer
Richards
Seymour
SKYTRAIN
Dunsmuir
Granville St.
Georgia
Smithe
Robson
Howe
Hornby
Burrard
Hastings
Pender
Melville
Georgia
Thurlow
Alberni
Robson
Haro
Barclay
Nelson
Comox
Bute
Jervis
Broughton
Port Roadway
Canada Place Way

N

440 yds
400 meters

Byrnes Block, **16**
Canada Place Pier, **9**
Canadian Imperial
Bank of Commerce, **11**
Canadian Pacific
Station, **14**
Cathedral Place, **6**
Chinatown, **18**

Chinese Freemasons
Building, **20**
Chinese Times
Building, **21**
Christ Church
Cathedral, **5**
Dr. Sun Yat-Sen
Gardens, **22**
Gastown, **15**

Hotel Europe
Building, **17**
Hotel Vancouver, **4**
Marine Building, **7**
Robson Square, **2**
Robson Street, **1**
Royal Bank, **13**
Sam Kee Building, **19**

Sinclair Centre, **10**
Toronto-Dominion
Bank, **12**
Vancouver Art
Gallery, **3**
Vancouver Club, **8**

viduals administering care now grace the **Canadian Craft Museum,** across the courtyard. Originally founded in 1980, but opened on this site in 1992, the Craft Museum is the first national cultural facility dedicated to craft—historical and contemporary, functional and decorative. Craft embodies the human need for artistic expression in everyday life, and examples here range from elegantly carved utensils with decorative handles to colorful hand-spun and hand-woven garments. The three-level museum offers exhibits, workshops, and the Gallery Shop, which specializes in, of course, Canadian crafts. The restful courtyard is a quiet place to take a break. *639 Hornby St., tel 604/687–8266. Admission: $2.50 adults, $1.50 senior citizens and students, children under 12 free. Open Mon.–Sat. 9:30–5:30, Sun. and holidays noon–5.*

Cathedral Place also is the site of the **Sri Lankan Gem Museum,** which opened in 1993. The museum features a floor of 900 polished agates set in aggregate, and some $5 million worth of gemstones, including moonstones, rubies, lapis, diamonds, garnets, jade, and emeralds. Many of the gems are from Sri Lanka. *150 925 W. Georgia St., tel. 604/662–7708. Admission: $5 (proceeds go to the Vancouver Symphony Orchestra). Open Mon.–Sat. 10:30–5:30.*

7 The **Marine Building** (1931), at the foot of Burrard Street, is Canada's best example of Art Deco style. Terra-cotta bas reliefs depict the history of transportation: Airships, biplanes, steamships, locomotives, and submarines are figured. These motifs were once considered radical and modernistic adornments, because most buildings were still using classical or Gothic ornamentation. From the east, the Marine Building is reflected in bronze by 999 West Hastings, and in silver from the southeast by the Canadian Imperial Bank of Commerce. Stand on the corner of Hastings and Hornby streets for the best view of the Marine Building.

A nice walk is along Hastings Street—the old financial district. Until the 1966–1972 period, when the first of the bank towers and underground malls on West Georgia Street were developed, this was Canada's westernmost business terminus. The temple-style banks, businessmen's clubs, and investment houses survive as evidence of the city's sophisticated architectural advances prior to World War I.
8 The **Vancouver Club,** built between 1912 and 1914, was a gathering place for the city's elite. Its architectural design is reminiscent of private clubs in England that were inspired by Italian Renaissance palaces. The Vancouver Club is still the private haunt of some of the city's businessmen. *915 W. Hastings St., tel. 604/685–9321.*

9 The foot of Howe Street, north of Hastings, is **Canada Place Pier.** Originally built on an old cargo pier to be the off-site Canadian pavilion in Expo '86, Canada Place was later converted into Vancouver's Trade and Convention Center. It is dominated at the shore end by the luxurious Pan Pacific Hotel (*see* Lodging, *below*), with its spectacular three-story lobby and waterfall. The convention space is covered by a fabric roof shaped like 10 sails, which has become a landmark of Vancouver's skyline. Below is a cruise ship facility, and at the north end are an Imax theater, a restaurant, and an outdoor performance space. A promenade runs along the pier's west side with views of the Burrard Inlet harbor and Stanley Park. *999 Canada Pl., tel. 604/688–8687.*

Time Out Across the street and accessible via an enclosed walkway is the luxurious **Waterfront Centre Hotel,** a 23-story glass structure that opened in 1992. The lobby, lounge, and restaurant offer stunning views of Burrard Inlet; at night, the casual Herons Lounge with a fireplace features relaxing piano music. Weather permitting, you can enjoy the view even more from the patio outside Herons Restaurant, where the menu offers local and regional Pacific Rim specialties. *900 Canada Place Way, tel. 604/691-1991.*

Just next door to the Waterfront Centre Hotel is the **Tourism Vancouver Infocentre** (200 Burrard St., tel. 604/682–2222), with brochures and personnel to answer questions, as well as an attractive Northwest Coast native art collection.

10 Walk back up to Hastings and Howe streets to the **Sinclair Centre.** Vancouver's outstanding architect, Richard Henriquez, has knitted four government office buildings (built 1905–1939) into an office-retail complex. The two Hastings Street buildings—the 1905 post office with the elegant clock tower and the 1913 Winch Building—are linked with the Post Office Extension and Customs Examining Warehouse to the north. Painstaking and very costly restoration involved finding master masons—the original terrazzo suppliers in Europe—and uncovering and refurbishing the pressed-metal ceilings.

Walking a bit farther up Hastings, at Granville Street, will reveal one of Vancouver's oldest and most impressive charter
11 banks, the former **Canadian Imperial Bank of Commerce** headquarters (1906–1908); the columns, arches, and details are of
12 typically Roman influence. The **Toronto-Dominion Bank,** one block east, is of the same style but was built in 1920.

Backtrack directly across from the CIBC on Hastings Street to
13 the more Gothic **Royal Bank.** It was intended to be half of a symmetrical building that was never completed, due to the depression. Striking, though, is the magnificent hall, ecclesiastical in style, reminiscent of a European cathedral.

14 At the foot of Seymour Street is the **Canadian Pacific Station,** the third and most pretentious of three Canadian Pacific Railway passenger terminals. Constructed in 1912–1914, this terminal replaced the other two as the western terminus for Canada's transcontinental railway. After Canada's railways merged, the station became obsolete until a 1978 renovation turned it into an office-retail complex and SeaBus terminal. Murals in the waiting rooms show passengers what kind of scenery to expect on their journeys across Canada.

From Seymour Street, pick up Water Street, on your way to
15 **Gastown.** Named after the original townsite saloon keeper, "Gassy" Jack Deighton, Gastown is where Vancouver originated. Deighton arrived at Burrard Inlet in 1867 with his Indian wife, a barrel of whiskey, and few amenities. A statue of Gassy Jack stands on the north side of Maple Tree Square, the intersection of five streets, where he built his first saloon.

When the transcontinental train arrived in 1887, Gastown became the transfer point for trade with the Orient and was soon crowded with hotels and warehouses. The Klondike gold rush encouraged further development until 1912, when the "Golden Years" ended. The 1930s–1950s saw hotels being converted into rooming houses and the warehouse district shifting elsewhere. The area gradually became unattended and run-down. However, both Gastown and Chinatown were declared historic areas and have been revitalized.

16 The **Byrnes Block** building was constructed on the corner of Water and Carrall streets (the site of Gassy Jack's second saloon) after the 1886 Great Fire. The date is just visible at the top of the building above the door where it says "Herman Block," which was its name for a short time. The extravagantly detailed Alhambra Hotel that was situated here was luxury class for the time, at a cost of a dollar a night.

Tucked behind 2 Water Street are **Blood Alley** and **Gaoler's Mews.** Once the site of the city's first civic buildings—the constable's cabin and courthouse, and a two-cell log jail—today the cobblestone street with antique streetlighting is the home of architectural offices.

17 The **Hotel Europe** (1908–1909), a flatiron building at Powell and Alexander streets, was billed as the best hotel in the city and was Vancouver's first reinforced concrete structure. Designed as a functional commercial building, the hotel lacks ornamentation and fine detail, a style unusually utilitarian for the time.

From Maple Tree Square, walk three blocks up Carrall Street
18 to Pender Street, where **Chinatown** begins. There was already a sizable Chinese community in British Columbia because of the 1858 Cariboo gold rush in central British Columbia, but the biggest influx from China occurred in the 1880s, during construction of the Canadian Pacific Railway, when 15,000 laborers were imported. The Chinese were among the first inhabitants of Vancouver, and some of the oldest buildings in the city are in Chinatown.

Even while doing the hazardous work of blasting the railbed through the Rocky Mountains, the Chinese were discriminated against. The Anti-Asiatic Riots of 1907 stopped growth in Chinatown for 50 years, and immigration from China was discouraged by more and more restrictive policies, climaxing in a $500 head tax during the 1920s.

In the 1960s the city council was planning bulldozer urban renewal for Strathcona, the residential part of Chinatown, and freeway connections through the most historic blocks of Chinatown were charted. Fortunately, the plans were halted, and today Chinatown is an expanding, vital district fueled by investment from Vancouver's most notable newcomers—immigrants from Hong Kong. It is best to view the buildings in Chinatown from the south side of Pender Street, where the Chinese Cultural Center stands. From here you'll get a view of important details that adorn the upper stories. The style of architecture in Vancouver's Chinatown is patterned on that of Canton and won't be seen in any other Canadian cities.

The corner of Carrall and East Pender streets, now the western boundary of Chinatown, is one of the neighborhood's most his-
19 toric spots. Standing at 8 West Pender Street is the **Sam Kee Building,** recognized by *Ripley's Believe It or Not!* as the narrowest building in the world, at just 6 feet wide. The 1913 structure still exists, with its bay windows overhanging the street and a basement that burrows under the sidewalk.

20 The **Chinese Freemasons Building** (1901) at 1 West Pender Street has two completely different styles of facades: The side

facing Chinatown displays a fine example of Cantonese-imported recessed balconies; on the Carrall Street side, the standard Victorian style common throughout the British Empire is displayed. It was in this building that Dr. Sun Yat-sen hid for months from the agents of the Manchu dynasty while he raised funds for its overthrow, which he accomplished in 1911.

21 Directly across Carrall Street is the **Chinese Times Building,** constructed in 1902. Inside, there is a hidden mezzanine floor from which police officers could hear the clicking sounds of clandestine mah-jongg games played after sunset. Attempts by vice squads to enforce restrictive policies against the Chinese gamblers proved fruitless, because police were unable to find the players, who were hidden on the secret floor.

22 Planning for the **Chinese Cultural Center** and **Dr. Sun Yat-sen Gardens** (1980–1987) began during the late 1960s; the first phase was designed by James Cheng, a former associate of Arthur Erickson. The cultural center has exhibition space, classrooms, and meeting rooms. The Dr. Sun Yat-sen Gardens, located behind the cultural center, were built by 52 artisans from Suzhou, the Garden City of the People's Republic. The gardens incorporate design elements and traditional materials from several of that city's centuries-old private gardens and are the first living classical Chinese gardens built outside China. As you walk through the gardens, remember that no power tools, screws, or nails were used in the construction. Free guided tours are offered throughout the day; telephone for times. *Dr. Sun Yat-sen Gardens. 578 Carrall St., tel. 604/689–7133. Admission: $3.50 adults, $2.50 senior citizens and students, $7 families. Open May–Sept., daily 10–8; Oct.–Apr., daily 10–4:30.*

Tour 2: Stanley Park

Numbers in the margin correspond to points of interest on the Tour 2: Stanley Park map.

A 1,000-acre wilderness park just blocks from the downtown section of a major city is a rarity but is one of Vancouver's major attractions. In the 1860s, due to a threat of American invasion, the area that is now Stanley Park was designated a military reserve (though it was never needed). When the city of Vancouver was incorporated in 1886, the council's first act was to request that the land be set aside for a park. In 1888 permission was granted and the grounds were named Stanley Park after Lord Stanley, then governor general of Canada (the same person after whom hockey's Stanley Cup is named).

An afternoon in Stanley Park gives you a capsule tour of Vancouver that includes beaches, the ocean, the harbor, Douglas fir and cedar forests, and a good look at the North Shore mountains. The park sits on a peninsula, and along the shore is a pathway 9 kilometers (5½ miles) long called the seawall. You can walk or bicycle all the way around or follow the shorter route suggested below.

Bicycles are for rent at the foot of Georgia Street near the park entrance. Cyclists must ride in a counterclockwise direction and stay on their side of the path. A good place for pedestrians
23 to start is at the foot of Alberni Street beside **Lost Lagoon.** Go through the underpass and veer right to the seawall.

Tour 2: Stanley Park

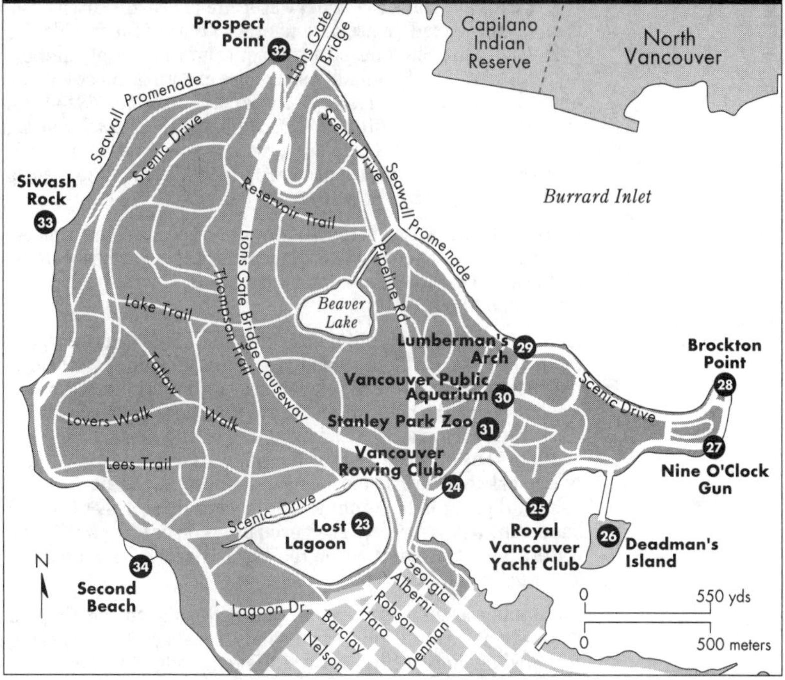

24 The old wood structure that you pass is the **Vancouver Rowing Club,** a private athletic club (established 1903); a bit farther
25 along is the **Royal Vancouver Yacht Club.**

26 About ½ kilometer (⅓ mile) away is the causeway to **Deadman's Island,** a former burial ground for the local Salish Indians and the early settlers. It is now a small naval training base called the HMCS *Discovery* that is not open to the public. Just ahead
27 is the **Nine O'Clock Gun,** a cannonlike apparatus that sits by the water's edge. Originally used to alert fishermen to a curfew ending weekend fishing, now it automatically signals every night at 9.

28 Farther along is **Brockton Point** and its small but functional lighthouse and foghorn. The **totem poles,** which are situated more inland, make a popular photo spot for tourists. Totem poles were not carved in the Vancouver area; they were brought to the park from the north coast of British Columbia and were carved by the Kwakiutl and Haida peoples late in the last century. These cedar poles with carved animals, fish, birds, or mythological creatures were like family coats-of-arms or crests.

29 At kilometer 3 (mile 2) is **Lumberman's Arch,** a huge log archway dedicated to the workers in Vancouver's first industry. Beside the arch is an asphalt path that leads back to Lost Lagoon, for those who want a shorter walk. (It's about a third of the dis-
30 tance.) This path also leads to the **Vancouver Public Aquarium.**

Also part of this attraction is the humid Amazon rain-forest gallery, through which you can walk, with its piranhas, giant cockroaches, alligators, tropical birds, and jungle vegetation. Other displays show the underwater life of coastal British Columbia, the Canadian arctic, and other areas of the world. The Clamshell Gift Shop next to the aquarium is one of the best spots in town for high-quality souvenirs and gifts, most with an emphasis on natural history. *Aquarium, tel. 604/682–1118. Admission: $8.50 adults, $7.25 senior citizens and youths, $5.25 children 5–12. Open daily in summer 9:30–8; daily in winter 10–5:30. Clamshell open July–Labor Day, daily 9:30–8; rest of year, daily 10–5:30.*

31 Next to the aquarium is the **Stanley Park Zoo,** a friendly place, easily seen in an hour or two. Except for the polar bears, most of the animals are small—monkeys, seals, exotic birds, penguins, and playful otters.

About 1 kilometer (¾ mile) farther is the **Lions Gate Bridge**—the halfway point of the seawall. On the other side of the bridge
32 is **Prospect Point,** where you can see cormorants in their seaweed nests on the ledges along the cliffs. The large black diving birds are recognized by their long necks and beaks; when not nesting, they often perch atop floating logs or boulders. Another remarkable bird found along the shore in the park is the beautiful great blue heron, which reaches up to 4 feet tall and has a wing span of 6 feet. The heron preys on passing fish in the waters here; the oldest heron rookery in British Columbia is in the trees around the zoo.

Continuing around the seawall you will come to the **English Bay** side and the beginning of sandy beaches. The imposing
33 rock just offshore is **Siwash Rock.** Legend tells of a young Indian who, about to become a father, bathed persistently to wash his sins away so that his son could be born pure; for his devotion he was blessed by the gods and immortalized in the shape of Siwash Rock. Two small rocks, said to be his wife and child, are just up on the cliff above the site.

Time Out Along the seawall is one of Vancouver's best restaurants, the **Teahouse at Ferguson Point.** Set on the great lawn among Douglas fir and cedar trees, the restaurant is the perfect stopover for a summer weekend lunch or brunch. If you want just a snack, a park concession stand is also at Ferguson Point.

The next attraction along the seawall is the large saltwater pool
34 at **Second Beach.** In the summer it is a children's pool with lifeguards, but during winter the pool is drained and skateboarders perform stunts. At the pool you can take a shortcut back to Lost Lagoon. To take the shortcut, walk along the perpendicular road behind the pool, which cuts into the park. The wood footbridge that's ahead will lead you to a path along the south side of the lagoon and to your starting point at the foot of Alberni or Georgia street.

If you continue along the seawall, it will emerge out of the park into a high-rise residential neighborhood, the **West End.** You can walk back to Alberni Street along Denman Street, where there are plenty of places to stop for coffee, ice cream, or a drink.

Tour 3: Granville Island

Numbers in the margin correspond to points of interest on the Tour 3: Granville Island map.

Granville Island was just a sandbar until World War I, when the federal government dredged False Creek for access to the sawmills that lined the shore. The sludge from the creek was heaped up onto a sandbar to create Granville Island so that it could house the much-needed industrial- and logging-equipment plants for British Columbia. By the late 1960s, however, many of the businesses that had once flourished on Granville Island had deteriorated. Buildings were rotted, rat-infested, and dangerous. In 1971, the federal government bought up leases from businesses that wanted to leave, and offered an imaginative plan to refurbish the island. A public market was introduced, and marine activities and artisans' studios were supported. The opposite shore of False Creek was the site of the 1986 World's Fair and is now part of the largest urban redevelopment plan in North America.

The small island has no residents except for a small houseboat community. Most of the previously used industrial buildings and tin sheds have been retained but are painted in upbeat reds, yellows, and blues. Through a committee of community representatives, the government regulates the types of businesses that settle on Granville Island; most of the businesses permitted here involve food, crafts, marine activities, and the arts.

Access on foot to Granville Island starts with a 15-minute walk from downtown Vancouver to the south end of Thurlow Street. From a dock behind the Vancouver Aquatic Center, the Granville Island ferry leaves every six minutes for the short trip across False Creek to the Granville Island Public Market. These pudgy boats are a great way to see the sights on False Creek, but for a longer ferry ride, go to the Maritime Museum (1905 Ogden St., tel. 604/737–2211), where visitors can board the wheelhouse of a tugboat and chart the coastal waters of British Columbia. For more information, call Granville Island Ferries (tel. 604/684–7781).

Another way to reach the island is to take a 20-minute ride on a BC Transit (tel. 604/261–5100) bus. Take a UBC, Granville, Arbutus, Cambie, or Oak bus from downtown to Granville and Broadway, and transfer to the Granville Island bus No. 51. Parking is limited, but if you must take a car, go early in the week and early in the day to avoid crowds. Parking is free for one to three hours; an alternative is to pay for parking in the garages on the island if you can find a space.

35 The ferry to Granville Island will drop you off at the **Granville Island Public Market,** where food stalls are enclosed in the 50,000-square-foot building. Since the government allows no chain stores, each outlet is unique, and most are of good quality. You probably won't be able to leave the market without a snack, espresso, or fixings for a lunch out on the wharf. Don't miss the charcoal-grilled oysters from **Sea-kist,** fish chowder or bouillabaisse from the **Stock Market,** fresh fudge at **Olde World Fudge,** or smoked salmon from the **Salmon Shop.** Year-round you'll see mounds of raspberries, strawberries, blueberries, and even more exotic fruits like persimmons and lychees. On

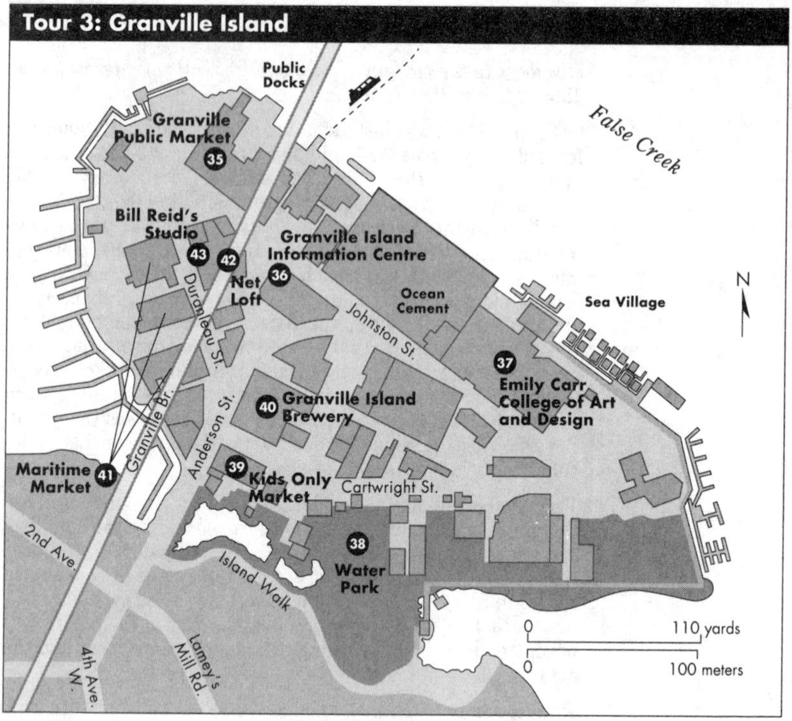

the water side of the market is lots of outdoor seating. *Public Market, tel. 604/666-6477. Open June–Aug., daily 9–6; closed Mon. Sept.–May except holidays.*

36 The **Granville Island Information Centre,** kitty-corner to the market, is a good place to get oriented to the island. Maps are available, and a slide show depicts the evolution of Granville Island. Ask here about special-events days; perhaps there's a boat show, outdoor concert, dance performance, or some other happening. *1592 Johnston St., tel. 604/666-5784. Open daily 9–6.*

Continue walking south on Johnston Street, along a clockwise loop of the island. Next is **Ocean Cement,** one of the last of the island's former industries; its lease does not expire until the year 2004.

37 Next door is the **Emily Carr College of Art and Design.** Just inside the front door, to your right, is the **Charles H. Scott Gallery,** which hosts contemporary multimedia exhibits. *1399 Johnston St., tel. 604/687-2345. Admission free. Open daily 11–5, Thurs. 11–8.*

Past the art school, on the left, is one of the only **houseboat communities** in Vancouver; others have been banned by the city because of problems with sewage and property taxes. The owners of this community appealed the ban and won special status. Take the boardwalk that starts at the houseboats and continues partway around the island.

As you circle around to Cartwright Street, stop in **Kakali** at number 1249, where you can watch the process of making fine handmade paper from all sorts of materials like blue jeans, herbs, and sequins. Another unusual artisan on the island is the **glassblower** at 1440 Old Bridge Street, around the corner.

The next two attractions will make any child's visit to Granville Island a thrill. First, on Cartwright Street, is the children's
38 **water park,** with a wading pool, sprinklers, and a fire hydrant made for children to shower one another. A bit farther down,
39 beside Isadora's restaurant, is the **Kids Only Market,** with two floors of small shops selling toys, arts-and-crafts materials, dolls, records and tapes, chemistry sets, and other sorts of kid stuff. *Water park. 1318 Cartwright St., tel. 604/665–3425. Admission free. Open June–Aug., daily 10–6. Kids Only Market. 1496 Cartwright St., tel. 604/689–8447. Open daily 10–6.*

40 At the **Granville Island Brewery,** next door, you can take a half-hour tour every afternoon; at the end of the tour, sample the Granville Island lager that is produced here and sold locally in most restaurants. *Tel. 604/688–9927. Admission free. Tours daily at 1 and 3.*

Cross Anderson Street and walk down Duranleau Street. On your left, the scuba-diving pool in **Adrenalin Sports** marks the
41 start of the **Maritime Market,** a string of businesses all geared to the sea. The first walkway to the left, Maritime Mews, leads to marinas and dry docks. There are dozens of outfits in the Maritime Market that charter boats (with or without skippers) or run cruise-and-learn trips.

Another way to take to the water is by kayak. Take a lesson or rent a kayak from **Ecomarine Ocean Kayak Center** (1668 Duranleau St., tel. 604/689–7575). Owner John Dowd is considered *the* expert on Pacific Northwest ocean kayaking.

Time Out **Bridges** (1696 Duranleau St., tel. 604/687–4400), in the bright yellow building across from the market, is a good spot to have lunch, especially on a warm summer's day. Eat on the spacious deck that looks out on the sailboats, fishing boats, and other water activities.

The last place to explore on Granville Island is the blue building
42 next to Ecomarine on Duranleau Street, the **Net Loft.** The loft is a collection of small, high-quality stores—good places to find a gift to take home: a bookstore, crafts store/gallery, kitchenware shop, postcard shop, custom-made hat shop, handmade paper store, British Columbian native Indian gallery, do-it-yourself jewelry store, and more reside here.

43 Behind Blackberry Books, in the Net Loft complex, is the **Bill Reid's studio,** belonging to British Columbia's most respected Haida Indian carver. His *The Raven and the First Men,* which took five carvers more than three years to complete, is in the Museum of Anthropology (*see* Other Museums, *below*); Reid's Pacific Northwest Coast Indian artworks are world renowned. Although you can't visit the studio, there are large windows through which you can look.

Since you have come full circle, you can either take the ferry back to downtown Vancouver or stay for dinner and catch a play at the **Arts Club** (tel. 604/687–1644) or the **Waterfront Theater** (tel. 604/685–6217).

Other Museums

The **Maritime Museum** traces the history of marine activities on the west coast. Permanent exhibits depict the port of Vancouver, the fishing industry, and early explorers; the model ships on display are a delight. Traveling exhibits vary but always have a maritime theme. Guided tours are led through the double-masted schooner *St. Roch,* the first ship to sail in both directions through the treacherous Northwest Passage. A changing variety of restored heritage boats from different cultures are moored behind the museum, and a huge Kwakiutl totem pole stands out front. *North foot of Cypress St., tel. 604/737–2211. Admission: $5 adults, $2.50 children, students, and senior citizens, $8 families. Open daily 10–5, closed Mon. in winter. Access available by the Granville Island Ferries.*

The **Museum of Anthropology,** focusing on the arts of the Pacific Northwest Indians, is Vancouver's most spectacular museum. It's situated on the campus of the University of British Columbia and housed in an award-winning glass-and-concrete structure designed by Arthur Erickson. In the Great Hall are large and dramatic totem poles, ceremonial archways, and dugout canoes—all adorned with carvings of frogs, eagles, ravens, bears, and salmon. Also showcased are exquisite carvings of gold, silver, and argillite (a black stone found in the Queen Charlotte Islands), as well as masks, tools, and costumes from many other cultures. Also in the museum is a ceramics wing, which houses about 600 pieces from 15th- to 19th-century Europe. *6393 N.W. Marine Dr., tel. 604/822–3825. Admission: $5 adults, $2.50 students 6–18 and senior citizens; free Tues. evenings. Open Tues. 11–9, Wed.–Sun. 11–5.*

Science World is in a gigantic shiny dome that was built for Expo 86 for an Omnimax Theater—the world's largest dome screen. The hands-on museum encourages visitors to touch and participate in the theme exhibits. A special gallery, the Search Gallery, is aimed at younger children, as are the fun-filled demonstrations given in Center Stage. *1455 Quebec St., tel. 604/687–7832. Admission to Science World: $7 adults, $4.50 senior citizens and children. Admission to Omnimax is the same; for admission to both you get a discount. Open weekdays 10–5, Sat.10–9.*

Vancouver Museum displays permanent exhibits that focus on the city's early history and native art and culture. Life-size replicas of an 1897 Canadian Pacific Railway passenger car, a trading post, and a Victorian parlor, as well as a real dugout canoe are highlights. Also on the site are the planetarium and observatory (*see* Off the Beaten Track, *below*). *1100 Chestnut St., tel. 604/736–7736. Admission: $5 adults, $2.50 senior citizens and children. Open Tues.–Sun. 10–5 in winter, daily 10–5 in summer.*

Other Parks and Gardens

Nitobe Garden is a small (2.4-acre) garden that is considered the most authentic Japanese garden outside Japan. The circular path around the park symbolizes the cycle of life and provides a tranquil view from every direction. In April and May cherry blossoms are the highlight, and in June the irises are magnificent. *1903 West Mall, Univ. of B.C., tel. 604/822–4208.*

Admission: $2 adults, $1.25 senior citizens and students, free Wed. and every day Oct. 11–Mar. 17. Open daily 10–dusk in summer; Mon.–Fri. in winter; phone for specific closing times.

Pacific Spirit Park (W. 16th Ave., tel. 604/224–5739) is a 1,000-acre park that is bigger and more rugged than Stanley Park. Pacific Spirit's only amenities are 61 kilometers (30 miles) of trails, a few washrooms, and a couple of signboard maps. Go for a wonderful walk in the west coast woods—it's hard to believe that you are only 15 minutes from downtown Vancouver.

Queen Elizabeth Park has lavish gardens and lots of grassy picnicking spots. Illuminated fountains; the botanical Bloedel Conservatory, with tropical and desert zones and 20 species of free-flying tropical birds; and other facilities including 20 tennis courts, lawn bowling, pitch and putt, and a restaurant are on the grounds. *Cambie St. and 25th Ave., tel. 604/872–5513. Admission to conservatory: $2.85 adults, $1.40 senior citizens and students, $5.70 families. Open May–Sept., weekdays 9–8, weekends 10–9; Oct.–Apr., daily 10–5.*

Van Dusen Botanical Garden was a 55-acre golf course but is now the grounds of one of the largest collections of ornamental plants in Canada. Native and exotic plant displays include the shrubbery maze and the rhododendrons in May and June. For a bite to eat, stop into Sprinklers Restaurant (tel. 604/261–0011), on the grounds. *5251 Oak St. at 37th Ave., tel. 604/266–7194. Admission: $4.50 adults, $2.25 senior citizens and children 13–18, $9 families; half-price off-season. Garden open 10–dusk.*

Vancouver for Free

Among the public galleries and museums that offer free admission on certain days are: The **Vancouver Art Gallery** (750 Hornby St., tel. 604/682–5621) is free on Thursday evenings; the **Museum of Anthropology** (6393 N.W. Marine Dr., tel. 604/822–3825) is free Tuesday evenings; the **Vancouver Museum** (1100 Chestnut St., tel. 604/736–7736) is free on the first Thursday evening of every month (it is also free every Tuesday for senior citizens).

The **University of British Columbia Botanical Garden** and **Nitobe Garden** (tel. 604/822–4208), a well-established Japanese garden also at UBC, are free on Wednesday and all winter.

What to See and Do with Children

Take your pint-size chef out to Sunday brunch at **Griffin's** (900 W. Georgia St., tel. 604/684–3131), the bistro-style restaurant in the Hotel Vancouver, where the little ones don small-person-size aprons and make their own pancakes and churn ice cream.

Stanley Park Zoo (*see* Tour 2: Stanley Park, *above*).

The **miniature steam train** in Stanley Park, just five minutes northwest of the aquarium, is a big hit with children as it chugs through the forest.

Splashdown Park (Hwy. 17, just before the Tsawwassen Ferry causeway, tel. 604/943–2251), 38 kilometers (24 miles) outside

Vancouver, is a giant waterslide park with 11 slides (for toddlers to adults), heated water, picnic tables, and minigolf.

Richmond Nature Park (No. 5 Rd. exit from Hwy. 99, tel. 604/273–7015), with its displays and games in the Nature House, is geared toward children. Guides answer questions and give tours. Since the park sits on a natural bog, rubber boots are recommended if it's been wet, but a boardwalk around the duck pond makes some of the park accessible to strollers and wheelchairs.

Maplewood Farms (405 Seymour River Pl., tel. 604/929–5610), a 20-minute drive from downtown Vancouver, is set up like a small farm, with all the barnyard animals for children to see and pet. Cows are milked every day at 1:15.

Kids Only Market (*see* Tour 3: Granville Island, *above*).

The Planetarium (1100 Chestnut St., tel. 604/736–3656), on the same site as the Vancouver Museum in Vanier Park, has astronomy shows each afternoon and evening, and laser rock music shows later in the night.

Science World (*see* Other Museums, *above*).

Vancouver Public Aquarium (*see* Tour 2: Stanley Park, *above*).

Off the Beaten Track

On the North Shore you can get a taste of the mountains and test your mettle at the **Lynn Canyon Suspension Bridge** (Lynn Headwaters Regional Park, North Vancouver, tel. 604/987–5922), which hangs 240 feet above Lynn Creek. Also on the North Shore is the **Capilano Fish Hatchery** in the Regional Park (4500 Capilano Park Rd., tel. 604/666–1790), with exhibits about salmon.

If the sky is clear, the telescope at the **Gordon Southam Observatory** (1100 Chestnut St., in Vanier Park, tel. 604/738–2855) will be focused on whatever stars or planets are worth watching that night. While you're there, visit the planetarium on the site. Open Friday, Saturday, Sunday, and holiday evenings.

The **Beatles Museum** (456 Seymour St., tel. 604/685–8841) exhibits memorabilia from the early years of the Fab Four. Admission is $3, and the museum is open daily 10–6, Sunday noon–6.

Shopping

Unlike many cities where suburban malls have taken over, Vancouver has a downtown area that is still lined with individual boutiques and specialty shops. Stores are usually open daily and on Thursday and Friday nights, and Sundays noon to 5.

Shopping Districts

The immense **Pacific Center Mall,** in the heart of downtown, connects Eaton's and The Bay department stores, which stand at opposite corners of Georgia and Granville streets. Pacific Center is on two levels and is mostly underground.

A new commercial center has developed around **Sinclair Center** (*see* Tour 1, *above*), which caters to sophisticated and upscale tastes.

On the opposite side of Pacific Center is **Robson Street,** stretching from Burrard to Bute streets, and chockablock with small stores and cafés. Vancouver's liveliest street is not only for the fashion conscious, it also provides many excellent corners for people watching.

Two other shopping districts, one on **West 41st Avenue** between West Boulevard and Larch Street in Kerrisdale and the other on **West 10th** from Discovery Street west, are both in upscale neighborhoods and have high-quality shops and restaurants.

Fourth Avenue, from Burrard to Balsam streets, offers an eclectic mix of stores (from sophisticated women's clothing to surfboards and Jams).

In addition to the Pacific Center Mall, **Oakridge Shopping Center** at Cambie Street and 41st Avenue has chic, expensive stores that are fun to browse.

Ethnic Districts **Chinatown** (*see* Tour 1, *above*)—centered on Pender and Main streets—is an exciting and animated place for restaurants, exotic foodstuffs, and distinctive architecture.

Commercial Drive (around East 1st Avenue) is the heart of the Italian community, here called **Little Italy.** You can sip cappuccino in coffee bars where you may be the only one speaking English, or buy sun-dried tomatoes, real Parmesan, or an espresso machine.

The **East Indian shopping district** is on Main Street around 50th Avenue. Curry houses, sweet shops, grocery stores, and sari shops abound.

A small **Japantown** on Powell Street at Dunlevy Street is made up of grocery stores, fish stores, and a few restaurants.

Department Stores

The biggest department stores in Vancouver, **Eaton's, Holt Renfew,** and **The Bay,** are Canadian owned and located downtown and at most malls.

Flea Markets

A huge flea market (703 Terminal Ave., tel. 604/685–0666), with more than 300 stalls, is held Saturday, Sunday, and holidays from 8 to 4. It is easily accessible from downtown via SkyTrain, if you exit at the Main Street station.

Auctions

On Wednesday at noon and 7 PM, auctions are held at Love's (1635 W. Broadway, tel. 604/733–1157). Maynard's (415 W. 2nd Ave., tel. 604/876–6787) has home furnishings auctions on Wednesday at 7 PM. Phone for times of art and antiques auctions.

Specialty Stores

Antiques A stretch of antiques stores runs along Main Street from 19th to 35th avenues. On 10th Avenue near Alma are a few antiques stores that specialize in Canadiana, including **Folkart Interiors** (3715 W. 10th Ave.) and **Old Country Antique Co.** (3720 W. 10th Ave.). Also try **Canada West** (3607 W. Broadway). For very refined antiques, see **Artemis** (321 Water St.) in Gastown. For Oriental rugs, go to Granville Street between 7th and 14th avenues.

Art Galleries There are many private galleries throughout Vancouver. The best of them are **Buschlen-Mowatt** (1445 W. Georgia St., tel. 604/682–1234), **Diane Farris** (1565 W. 7th Ave., tel. 604/737–2629), **Equinox** (2321 Granville St., tel. 604/736–2405), and the **Heffel Gallery** (2247 Granville St., tel. 604/732–6505). Call all galleries before visiting to make sure they are open.

Books The best general bookstores are **Duthie's,** located downtown (919 Robson St.) and near the university (4444 W. 10th Ave.), and **Blackberry Books** (1663 Duranleau St.) on Granville Island.

Specialty bookstores include **The Travel Bug** (2667 W. Broadway) and **World Wide Books and Maps** (736 Granville St., downstairs) for travel books, **Vancouver Kidsbooks** (3083 W. Broadway), **Sportsbooks Plus** (230 W. Broadway), and **Pink Peppercorn** (2686 W. Broadway) for cookbooks, and **William McCarley** (213 Carrall St.) for design and architecture.

Most of the secondhand and antiquarian dealers, such as **William Hoffer** (60 Powell St.) and **Colophon Books** (407 W. Cordova St., upstairs), are in the Gastown area. A block or two away are **McLeod's** (455 W. Pender St. and around the corner at 432 Richards St.), **Ainsworth's** (321 W. Pender St.), and **Bond's** (319 W. Hastings St.). **Lawrence Books** (3591 W. 41st Ave.) is out of the way but is probably the best used-books bookstore in town.

Children's Stores An unusual children's store worth checking out is **The Imagination Market** (528 Powell St.), an oddball warehouse-type store selling recycled industrial goods for arts-and-crafts materials: barrels of metallic plastic, feathers, fluorescent-colored paper, buttons, bits of Plexiglas, and other materials by the bagful.

Clothing
Men Several high-quality men's clothing stores are in the business district: **Edward Chapman** (833 W. Pender St.) has conservative looks; **E.A. Lee** (466 Howe St.) is stylish; **Leone** (757 W. Hastings St.) is ultrachic.

A few blocks away, at Pacific Center, are **Harry Rosen, Eddie Bauer,** and **Holt Renfrew.** If your tastes are traditional, don't miss **George Straith** (900 W. Georgia St.) in the Hotel Vancouver.

On Robson Street, a more trendy shopping area, are **Boy's Co.** (No. 1080) and **Club Monaco** (No. 1153), for casual wear.

Outside downtown Vancouver there are two men's boutiques selling Italian imports: **Mondo Uomo** (2709 Granville St.) and **Boboli** (2776 Granville St.).

In Kerrisdale, three excellent men's clothing stores are **Finn's** (2159 W. 41st Ave.), **Hill's** (2125 W. 41st Ave.), and, across the street, **S. Lampman** (2126 W. 41st Ave.).

Women For women's fashions, visit **E.A. Lee** (466 Howe St.), **Wear Else?** (789 W. Pender St.), **Leone** (757 W. Hastings St.), and the more conservative **Chapy's** (833 W. Pender St.), all in the business district.

On Robson Street, look for **Margareta** (No. 948), **Alfred Sung** (No. 1143), **Club Monaco** (No. 1153), and a lingerie shop, **La Vie en Rose** (No. 1001). The two blocks between Burrard and Bute have six shoe stores.

Two expensive and very stylish import stores in South Granville are **Boboli** (2776 Granville St.) and **Bacci** (2788 Granville St.). Nearby, one of the largest and best shoe stores in town is **Freedman Shoes** (2867 Granville St.).

On the west side **Enda B.** (4346 W. 10th Ave.) and **Wear Else?** (2360 W. 4th Ave.) are the largest and best stores for high-quality fashions, but there's also **Bali Bali** for the more exotic (4462 W. 10th Ave.) and **Zig Zag** (4424 W. 10th Ave.) for fashion accessories.

Gifts Want something special to take home from British Columbia? The best places for good-quality souvenirs are the Vancouver Art Gallery (750 Hornby St.) and the Clamshell Gift Shop at the aquarium in Stanley Park. The Salmon Shop in the Granville Island Public Market will wrap smoked salmon for travel. In Gastown, Haida and Salish Indian art is available at Images for a Canadian Heritage (164 Water St.). Near Granville Island is Leona Lattimer (1590 W. 2nd Ave.), where the inside of her shop is built like an Indian longhouse and is full of Indian arts and crafts ranging from cheap to priceless.

Sports and the Outdoors

Participant Sports

Biking **Stanley Park** (*see* Tour 2 in Exploring Vancouver, *above*) is the most popular spot for family cycling. Rentals are available here from **Bayshore Bicycles** (745 Denman St., tel. 604/688–2453) or around the corner at **Stanley Park Rentals** (676 Chilco St., tel. 604/681–5581).

Another biking route is along the north or south shores of **False Creek.** Rent bikes at **Robson Cycles** (1840 Fir St., tel. 604/731–5552), near Granville Island.

Fishing You can fish for salmon all year in coastal British Columbia. **Sewell's Marina Horseshoe Bay** (6695 Nelson St., Horseshoe Bay, tel. 604/921–3474) organizes a daily four-hour trip on Howe Sound or has hourly rates on U-drives. **Bayshore Yacht Charters** (1601 W. Georgia St., tel. 604/691–6936) has a daily five-hour fishing trip; boats are moored five minutes from downtown Vancouver. **Island Charters** (Duranleau St., Granville Island, tel. 604/688–6625) arranges charters or boat shares and supplies all gear.

Golf Lower Mainland golf courses are open all year. **Fraserview Golf Course** (tel. 604/327–3717), a spacious course with fairways well defined by hills and mature conifers and deciduous trees, is the busiest course in the country. Fraserview is also the most central, about 20 minutes from downtown. **Seymour Golf and Country Club** (tel. 604/929–5491), on the south side of Mt. Seymour, on the North Shore, is a semiprivate club that is open to the public on Monday and Friday. One of the finest public courses in the country is **Peace Portal** (tel. 604/538–4818), near White Rock, a 45-minute drive from downtown.

Health and Fitness Clubs

Both the **YMCA** (955 Burrard St., tel. 604/681–0221) and the **YWCA** (580 Burrard St., tel. 604/683–2531) downtown have drop-in rates that let you participate in all activities for the day. Both have pools, weight rooms, and fitness classes; the YMCA has racquetball, squash, and handball courts. Two other recommended clubs are **Chancery Squash Club** (202–865 Hornby St., tel. 604/682–3752) and **Tower Courts Racquet and Fitness Club** (1055 Dunsmuir St., lower level, tel. 604/689–4424), both with racquetball courts, weight rooms, and aerobics.

Hiking

Pacific Spirit Park is a 1,000-acre wilderness park with 48 kilometers (30 miles) of hiking trails (*see* Other Parks and Gardens in Exploring Vancouver, *above*).

The **Capilano Regional Park** (*see* Off the Beaten Track, in Exploring Vancouver, *above*), on the North Shore, provides a scenic hike.

Jogging

The seawall around **Stanley Park** (*see* Tour 2 in Exploring Vancouver, *above*) is 9 kilometers (5½ miles) and gives an excellent minitour of the city. A shorter run of 4 kilometers (2½ miles) in the park is around **Lost Lagoon.**

Skiing

Cross-Country

The best cross-country skiing is at **Cypress Bowl Ski Area** (tel. 604/926–6007).

Downhill

Vancouver is two hours away from **Whistler/Blackcomb** (Whistler Resort Association, tel. 604/685–3650; snow report, tel. 604/687–7507), one of the top ski spots in North America.

There are three ski areas on the North Shore mountains, close to Vancouver, with night skiing. The snow is not as good as at Whistler, and the runs are generally used by novice, junior, and family skiers or those who want a quick ski after work. **Cypress Bowl** (tel. 604/926–5612; snow report, tel. 604/926–6007) has the most and the longest runs; **Grouse Mountain** (tel. 604/984–0661; snow report, tel. 604/986–6262) has extensive night skiing, restaurants, and bars; and **Mt. Seymour** (tel. 604/986–2261; snow report, tel. 604/986–3444) is the highest in the area, so the snow is a little better.

Water Sports

Kayaking

Rent a kayak from **Ecomarine Ocean Kayak Center** (tel. 604/689–7575) on Granville Island (*see* Tour 3 in Exploring Vancouver, *above*).

Rafting

The Thompson, the Chilliwack, and the Fraser are the principal rafting rivers in southwestern British Columbia. The Fraser River has whirlpools and big waves, but for frothing white water, try the Thompson and Chilliwack rivers. Trips range from three hours to several days. Some well-qualified outfitters that lead trips are **Kumsheen** (Lytton, tel. 604/455–2296; in British Columbia, 800/482–2269), **Hyak Wilderness Adventures** (Vancouver, tel. 604/734–8622), and **Canadian River Expeditions** (Vancouver, tel. 604/738–4449).

Sailing

Several charter companies offer a cruise-and-learn vacation, usually to the Gulf Islands. The five-day trip is a crash course teaching the ins and outs of sailing. **Sea Wing Sailing Group, Ltd.** (Granville Island, tel. 604/669–0840) and **Pacific Quest** (Granville Island, tel. 604/682–2205) offer this package.

Windsurfing

Boards can be rented at **Windsure Windsurfing School** (Jericho Beach, tel. 604/224–0615) and **Windmaster** (English Bay Beach, tel. 604/685–7245).

Spectator Sports

The **Vancouver Canucks** (tel. 604/254-5141) of the National Hockey League play in the Coliseum October–April. The **Canadians** (tel. 604/872-5232) play baseball in an old-time outdoor stadium in the Pacific Coast League. Their season runs April–September. The **B.C. Lions** (tel. 604/585-3323) football team scrimmages at the B.C. Place Stadium downtown June–November. Tickets are available from Ticketmaster (tel. 604/280-4444).

Beaches

An almost continuous string of beaches runs from Stanley Park to the University of British Columbia. Children and hardy swimmers can take the cool water, but most others prefer to sunbathe; these beaches are sandy, with grassy areas running alongside. Note that liquor is prohibited in parks and on beaches. For information on beaches, call the **Parks Department of the City of Vancouver** (tel. 604/681-1141).

Kitsilano Beach. Kits Beach, with a lifeguard, is the busiest of them all—transistor radios, volleyball games, and sleek young people are ever present. The part of the beach nearest the Maritime Museum is the quietest. Facilities include a playground, tennis courts, heated saltwater pool (good for serious swimmers to toddlers), concession stands, and many nearby restaurants and cafés.

Point Grey Beaches. Jericho, Locarno, and Spanish Banks begin at the end of Point Grey Road. This string of beaches has a huge expanse of sand, especially in the summer and at low tide. The shallow water here is warmed slightly by the sun and the sand and so is best for swimming. Farther out, toward Spanish Banks, you'll find the beach becomes less crowded, but the last concession stand and washrooms are at Locarno. If you keep walking along the beach just past Point Grey, you'll hit Wreck Beach, Vancouver's nude beach. It is also accessible from Marine Drive at the university, but there is a fairly steep climb from the beach to the road.

West End Beaches. Second Beach and Third Beach, along Beach Drive in Stanley Park, are large family beaches. Second Beach has a guarded saltwater pool. Both have concession stands and washrooms. Farther along Beach Drive, at the foot of Jervis Street, is Sunset Beach, a surprisingly quiet beach, considering the location. A lifeguard is on duty, but there are no facilities.

Dining

Among other allures, experiencing Vancouver's diverse gastronomical pleasures makes a visit to the city worthwhile. Restaurants appear throughout Vancouver—from the bustling downtown area to trendy beachside neighborhoods—making the diversity of the establishments' surroundings as enticing as the succulent cuisine they serve. A new wave of Chinese immigration and Japanese tourism has brought a proliferation of upscale Chinese and Japanese restaurants, offering dishes that would be at home in their own leading cities. Restaurants featuring Pacific Northwest fare—including homegrown regional favorites such as salmon and oysters, accompanied by British Columbia and Washington State wines—have become some of the city's leading attractions.

Highly recommended restaurants in each price category are indicated by a star ★.

Category	*Cost
Very Expensive	over $40
Expensive	$30—$40
Moderate	$20—$30

**per person, including appetizer, entrée and dessert; excluding drinks, service, and sales tax*

American

Isadora's. Not only does Isadora's offer good coffee, a menu that ranges from samosas to lox and bagels, and children's specials, but there is also an inside play area packed with toys. Rest rooms with changing tables accommodate families. In the summer, the restaurant opens onto Granville Island's waterpark, so kids can entertain themselves. Service can be slow, but Isadora's staff is friendly. *1540 Old Bridge St., Granville Island, tel. 604/681–8816. Reservations required for 6 or more. Dress: casual. MC, V. Closed dinner Mon. Sept.–May. Inexpensive.*

Nazarre BBQ Chicken. The best barbecued chicken in several hundred miles comes from this funky storefront on Commercial Drive. Owner Gerry Moutal massages his chickens for tenderness before he puts them on the rotisserie and bastes them in a mixture of rum and spices. Chicken comes with roasted potatoes and a choice of mild, hot, extra hot, or hot garlic sauce. You can eat in, at one of four rickety tables, or take out. *1408 Commercial Dr., tel. 604/251–1844. No reservations. Dress: casual. No credit cards. Inexpensive.*

Cambodian/ Vietnamese★

Phnom Penh Restaurant. A block away from the bustle of Keefer Street, the Phnom Penh is part of a small cluster of Southeast Asian shops on the fringes of Chinatown. Simple, pleasant decor abounds: arborite tables, potted plants, and framed views of Ankor Wat on the walls. The hospitable staff serves unusually robust Vietnamese fare, including crisp, peppery garlic prawns fried in the shell and slices of beef crusted with ground salt and pepper mixed in the warm beef salad. The decor in the new Broadway location is fancier and the food is every bit as good as at East Georgia Street. *244 E. Georgia St., tel. 604/682–5777; 955 W. Broadway, tel. 604/734–8898. No reservations for lunch; reservations for 5 or more only for dinner. Dress: casual. DC, MC. Closed Tues. Inexpensive.*

Chinese

★ **Kirin Mandarin Restaurant.** Kirin, located two blocks from most of the major downtown hotels, presents attentively served Chinese food in posh, elegant surroundings. Live fish in tanks set into the slate green walls remind one of an aquarium displayed in a lavishly decorated home. Drawn from a smattering of northern Chinese cuisines, dishes include Shanghai-style smoked eel, Peking duck, and Szechuan hot-and-spicy scallops. *1166 Alberni St., tel. 604/682–8833. Reservations advised. Dress: neat but casual. AE, DC, MC, V. Moderate.*

★ **The Pink Pearl.** In the world of Cantonese restaurants, biggest may very well be best: This 650-seat restaurant certainly wins

Downtown Vancouver Dining

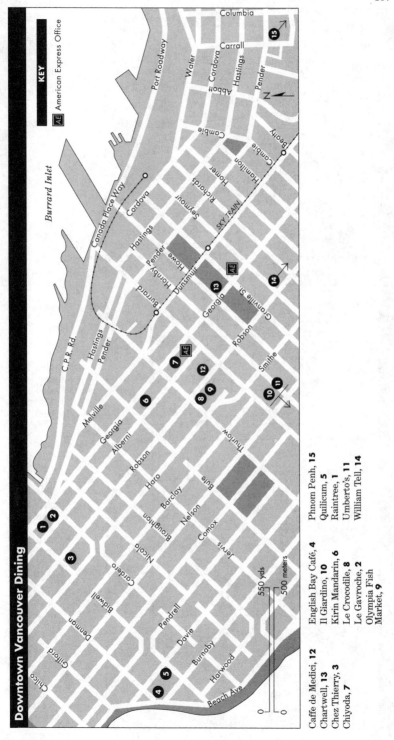

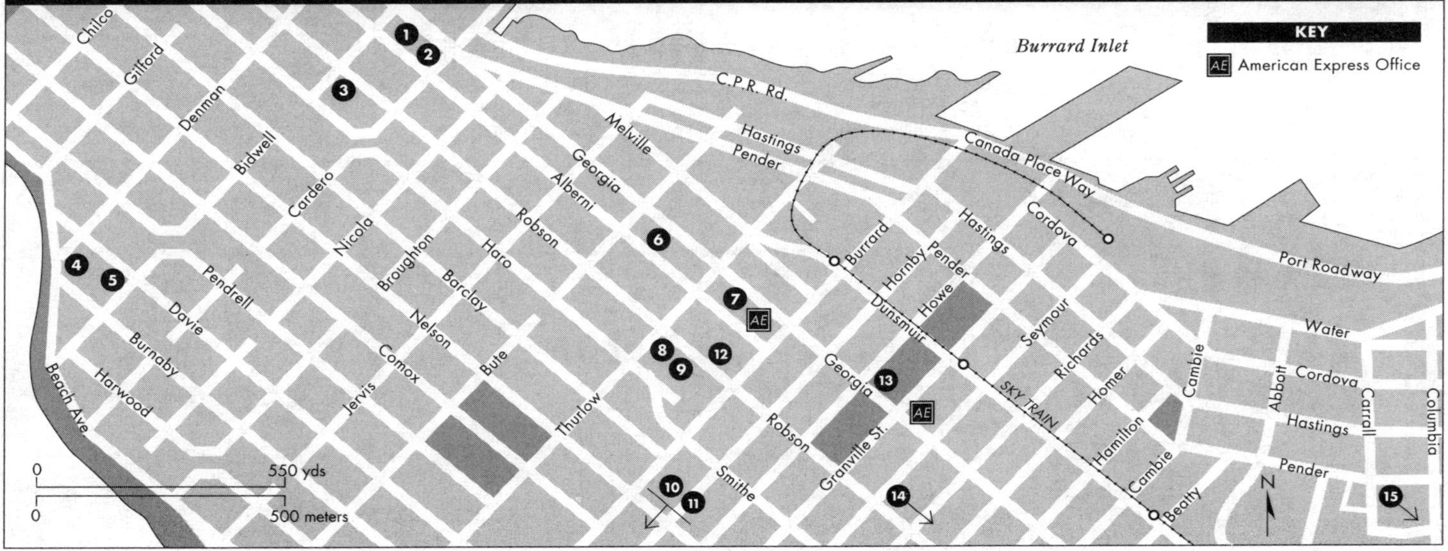

Caffe de Medici, **12**
Chartwell, **13**
Chez Thierry, **3**
Chiyoda, **7**
English Bay Café, **4**
Il Giardino, **10**
Kirin Mandarin, **6**
Le Crocodile, **8**
Le Gavroche, **2**
Olympia Fish Market, **9**
Phnom Penh, **15**
Quilicum, **5**
Raintree, **1**
Umberto's, **11**
William Tell, **14**

Greater Vancouver Dining

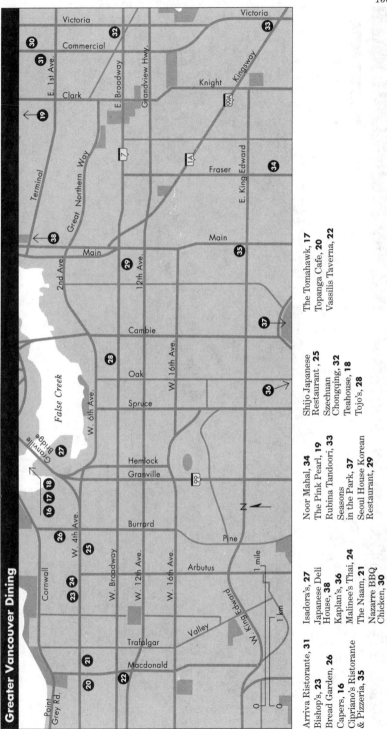

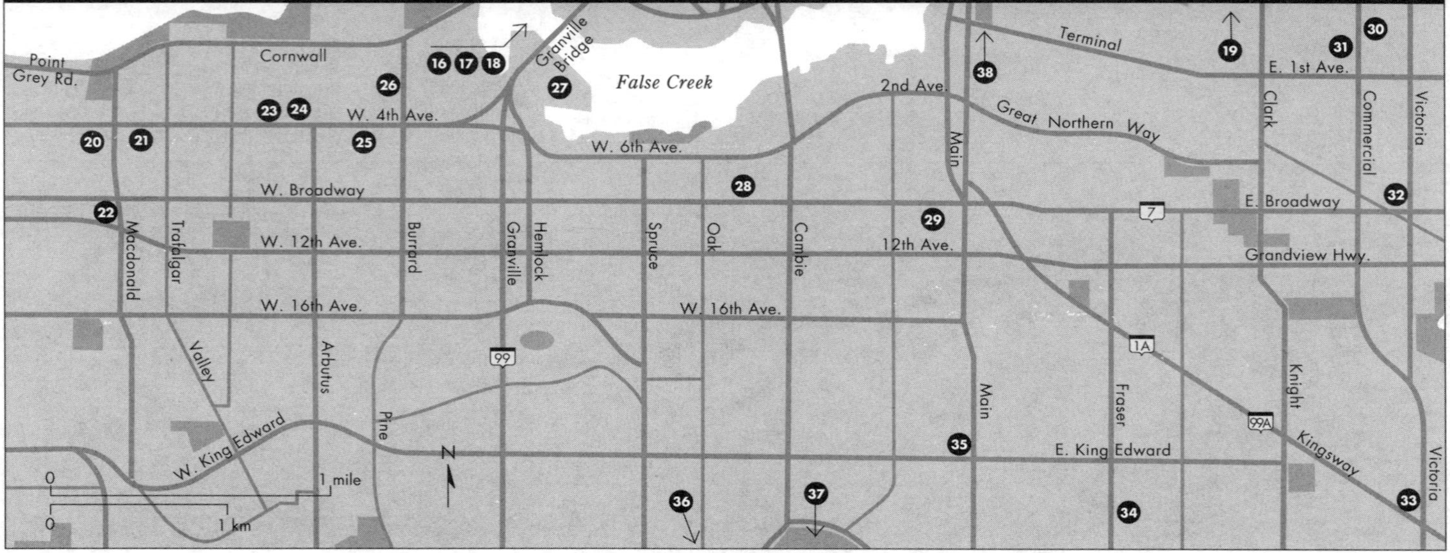

Arriva Ristorante, **31**
Bishop's, **23**
Bread Garden, **26**
Capers, **16**
Cipriano's Ristorante & Pizzeria, **35**
Isadora's, **27**
Japanese Deli House, **38**
Kaplan's, **36**
Malinee's Thai, **24**
The Naam, **21**
Nazarre BBQ Chicken, **30**
Noor Mahal, **34**
The Pink Pearl, **19**
Rubina Tandoori, **33**
Seasons in the Park, **37**
Seoul House Korean Restaurant, **29**
Shijo Japanese Restaurant , **25**
Szechuan Chongqing, **32**
Teahouse, **18**
Tojo's, **28**
The Tomahawk, **17**
Topanga Cafe, **20**
Vassilis Taverna, **22**

the prize in this city. The huge, noisy room features tanks of live seafood—crab, shrimp, geoduck, oysters, abalone, rock cod, lobsters, and scallops. Menu highlights include clams in black bean sauce, crab sautéed with five spices (a spicy dish sometimes translated as crab with peppery salt), and Pink Pearl's version of crispy-skinned chicken. Arrive early for dim sum on the weekend if you don't want to be caught in the lineup. *1132 E. Hastings St., tel.604/253-4316. Reservations advised. Dress: casual. AE, DC, MC, V. Moderate.*

Szechuan Chongqing. Although fancier Szechuan restaurants can be found, the continued popularity of this unpretentious, white-tablecloth restaurant in a revamped fried-chicken franchise speaks for itself. Try the Szechuan-style fried green beans, steamed and tossed with spiced ground pork, or the Chongqing chicken—a boneless chicken served on a bed of spinach cooked in dry heat until crisp, giving it the texture of dried seaweed and a salty, rich, and nutty taste. *2495 Victoria Dr., tel. 604/254-7434. Reservations advised. Dress: casual. AE, MC, V. Inexpensive.*

Continental

★ **Chartwell.** Named after Sir Winston Churchill's country home (a painting of which hangs over the green marble fireplace), the flagship dining room at the Four Seasons Hotel (*see* Lodging, *below*) looks like an upper-class British men's club. Floor-to-ceiling dark wood paneling, deep leather chairs to sink back in and sip claret, plus a quiet setting make this the city's top spot for a power lunch. The chefs cook robust, inventive Continental food with lighter offerings and a variety of low-calorie, low-fat entrées. A salad of smoked loin of wild boar comes sprinkled with hazelnuts; Wiener schnitzel with roast potatoes is a favorite. Conclude the meal with port and Stilton. *791 W. Georgia St., tel. 604/844-6715. Reservations advised. Jacket suggested. AE, DC, MC, V. Closed weekends for lunch. Expensive.*

Seasons in the Park. Seasons has a commanding view over the park gardens to the city lights and the mountains beyond. A comfortable room with lots of light wood, white tablecloths, and deep-pile carpeting, this restaurant in Queen Elizabeth Park serves a conservative Continental menu with standards such as grilled salmon with fresh mint and roast duck with Bing cherry sauce. *Queen Elizabeth Park, tel. 604/874-8008. Reservations advised. Dress: neat but casual. AE, MC, V. Closed Christmas Day. Expensive.*

★ **The Teahouse Restaurant at Ferguson Point.** The best of the Stanley Park restaurants is perfectly poised for watching sunsets over the water, especially from its newer wing, a glassed-in room that conveys a conservatorylike ambience. Although the teahouse has a less innovative menu than its sister restaurant—Seasons in the Park—certain specialties such as the cream of carrot soup, duck in cassis, and the perfectly grilled fish don't need any meddling. For dessert, there's baked Alaska—a natural for this restaurant. *Ferguson Point in Stanley Park, tel. 604/669-3281. Reservations required. Dress: neat but casual. AE, MC, V. Closed Christmas Day. Expensive.*

The William Tell. Silver underliners, embossed linen napkins, and a silver flower vase on each table set the tone of Swiss luxury. The William Tell's well-established reputation for excellent Continental food continues at its quarters on the main floor of the Georgian Court Hotel, located 10 minutes from the central business district. Chef Pierre Dubrelle, a member of the gold medal–winning Canadian team at the 1988 Culinary Olympics, offers locally raised pheasant with glazed grapes and red wine sauce, sautéed veal sweetbreads with red onion marmalade and marsala sauce, and the Swiss specialty *Buendnerfleisch* (paper-thin slices of air-dried beef). Professional and discreet service contributes to the restaurant's excellence. *765 Beatty St., tel. 604/688–3504. Reservations advised. Jacket required at dinner. AE, DC, MC, V. Expensive.*

★ **English Bay Café.** Downstairs, the English Bay Café is a noisy bistro serving eggs Benedict, pasta, and fish specialties such as snapper or clam-and-sausage pasta. Upstairs, in the more serious dining room, you'll find the chef's fondness for venison and racks of lamb. Regardless of the level, however, when you look out the windows, it's all the same: With English Bay just two lanes of traffic away, you're guaranteed a glorious view of the sunset. Both bars are substantial; the bistro offers a large choice of imported beers. Valet parking is available and well worth the money. *1795 Beach Ave., tel. 604/669–2225. Reservations required. Dress: casual downstairs; neat but casual upstairs. AE, DC, MC, V. Moderate.*

Deli/Bakery

The Bread Garden Bakery, Café & Espresso Bar. What began as a croissant bakery has taken over two neighboring stores and is now the ultimate Kitsilano 24-hour hangout. Salads, smoked salmon pizzas, quiches, elaborate cakes and pies, giant muffins, and cappuccino bring a steady stream of the young and fashionable. The Bread Garden To Go, next door, serves over-the-counter, but you may still be subjected to an irritatingly long wait in line; things just don't happen fast here. *1880 W. 1st Ave., tel. 604/ 738–6684; 812 Bute St., tel. 604/688–3213. No reservations. Dress: casual. MC, V. Inexpensive.*

★ **Kaplan's Deli, Restaurant and Bakery.** Tucked into a minimall on Oak Street (the road that leads to the Tsawwassen ferries and Seattle), Kaplan's is the traveler's last chance for authentic Jewish deli food before leaving town. Eat in at booths, or take your chopped liver, chopped herring, lox, and homemade corned beef with you. The bakery makes justly famous cinnamon buns. *5775 Oak St., tel. 604/263–2625. No reservations. Dress: casual. MC, V. Closed Jewish holidays. Inexpensive.*

East Indian

★ **Rubina Tandoori.** If one must single out the best East Indian food in the city, then Rubina Tandoori, 20 minutes from downtown, ranks as a top contender. The large menu spans most of the subcontinent's cuisines, and the especially popular *chevda* (East Indian salty snack) gets shipped to fans all over North America. Maître d' Shaffeen Jamal has a phenomenal memory for faces. Nonsmokers get the smaller, funkier back room with the paintings of coupling gods and goddesses; smokers get the big, upholstered banquettes in the new room. *1962 Kingsway, tel. 604/874–3621. Reservations advised on weekends. Dress: casual. MC, V. Closed lunch and Sun. Moderate.*

Noor Mahal. The only Lower Mainland restaurant that specializes in South Indian food, the Noor Mahal provides good-size portions at a reasonable price in authentic surroundings. The pink walls help to create the light and airy decor. Try a *dosa*—a lacy pancake made from bean, rice, and semolina flour, stuffed with curried potatoes, shrimp, or chicken—for lunch. Owners Susan and Paul Singh double as staff, so service can be slow and harried during busy periods. *4354 Fraser St., tel. 604/873–9263. Reservations advised on weekends. Dress: casual. AE, MC, V. Closed lunch. Inexpensive.*

French

★ **Le Gavroche.** Time has stood still in this charming turn-of-the-century house, where a woman dining with a man will be offered a menu without prices. Featuring classic French cooking, lightened—but by no means reduced—to nouvelle cuisine, Le Gavroche's menu also includes simple listings such as smoked salmon with blinis and sour cream. Other options may be as complex as smoked pheasant breast on a puree of celeriac, shallots, and wine with a light truffle sauce. The excellent wine list stresses Bordeaux. No reservations are necessary after 9:30, when the late-dessert menu is offered. Tables by the front window promise mountains-and-water views. *1616 Alberni St., tel. 604/685–3924. Reservations advised on weekends. Jacket and tie advised. AE, MC, V. Closed lunch, Sun., and holidays. Expensive.*

Chez Thierry. This cozy bistro on the Stanley Park end of Robson Street adds pizzazz to a celebration: Owner Thierry Damilano stylishly slashes open champagne bottles with a sword on request. The country-style French cooking emphasizes seafood. Try watercress and smoked salmon salad; fresh tuna grilled with artichokes, garlic, and tomatoes; and apple tarte Tatin for dessert. During the week the intimate dining room promises a relaxing meal; on the weekend, however, with every one of the 16 tables jammed, the restaurant gets noisy. *1674 Robson St., tel. 604/688–0919. Reservations required on weekends. Dress: casual. AE, DC, MC, V. Closed lunch and Dec. 24–26. Moderate.*

★ **Le Crocodile.** Why do people want to sit packed tighter than sardines in this tiny bistro? Because chef Michael Jacob serves extremely well cooked, simple food at very moderate prices. His Alsatian background shines with the caramelly, sweet onion tart. Anything that involves innards is superb, and even old standards such as duck à l'orange are worth ordering here. The one flaw? A small, overpriced wine list. *909 Burrard St., tel. 604/669–4298. Reservations required. Dress casual. AE, DC, MC, V. Closed Sat. lunch and Sun. Moderate.*

Greek

Vassilis Taverna. The menu in this family-run restaurant, located in the heart of the city's small Greek community, is almost as conventional as the decor: checked tablecloths and mandatory paintings of white fishing villages and the blue Aegean Sea. At Vassilis, though, even standards become memorable due to the flawless preparation. The house specialty is a deceptively simple *kotopoulo* (a half-chicken, pounded flat, herbed, and charbroiled); the lamb fricassee with artichoke hearts and broad beans in an egg-lemon sauce is more complicated, though not necessarily better. Save room for a *navarino*, a creamy custard square topped with whipped cream and ground nuts. *2884 W. Broadway, tel. 604/733–3231. Reservations advised on weekends. Dress: casual. AE, DC, MC, V. Closed Mon. and lunch Sat. and Sun. Moderate.*

Health Food

★ **Capers.** Hidden in the back of the most lavishly handsome health food store in the Lower Mainland, Capers (open for breakfast, lunch, and dinner) drips with earth-mother chic: wood tables, potted plants, and heady smells from the store's bakery. Breakfast starts weekdays at 7:30, weekends at 8. Eggs and bacon? Sure, but Capers serves free-range eggs, as well as bacon without additives. Feather-light blueberry pancakes crammed with berries star here. The view of the water compensates for service that can be slow and forgetful. *2496*

Marine Dr., W. Vancouver, tel. 604/925–3316. No reservations. Dress: casual. MC, V. Closed dinner Sun. Inexpensive.

The Naam Restaurant. Vancouver's oldest alternative restaurant is now open 24 hours, so those needing to satisfy a late-night tofu-burger craving, rest easy. The Naam has left its caffeine- and alcohol-free days behind and now serves wine, beer, cappuccino, and wicked chocolate desserts, along with the vegetarian stir-fries. Wood tables and kitchen chairs make for a homey atmosphere. On warm summer evenings, the outdoor courtyard at the back of the restaurant welcomes diners. *2724 W. 4th Ave., tel. 604/738–7151. Reservations required for 6 or more. Dress: casual. MC, V. Inexpensive.*

Italian

★ **Caffe de Medici.** It takes shifting gears as you leave the stark concrete walls of the Robson Galleria behind and step into this elegant restaurant with its ornate molded ceilings, rich green velvet curtains and chair coverings, and portraits of the de Medici family. But after a little wine, an evening's exposure to courtly waiters, and a superb meal, you may begin to wish the outside world conformed more closely to this peaceful environment. Although an enticing antipasto table sits in the center of the room, consider the *Bresaola* (air-dried beef marinated in olive oil, lemon, and pepper) as a worthwhile appetizer. Try the rack of lamb in a mint, mustard, and Martini & Rossi sauce. Any of the pastas is a safe bet. *1025 Robson St., tel. 604/669–9322. Reservations advised. Jacket advised. AE, DC, MC, V. Closed lunch Sat. and Sun. Expensive.*

Il Giardino di Umberto, Umberto's. First came Umberto's, a Florentine restaurant serving classic northern Italian food, installed in a century-old Vancouver home at the foot of Hornby Street. Then, next door, Umberto Menghi built Il Giardino, a sunny, light-splashed restaurant styled after a Tuscan house. This restaurant features braided breast of pheasant with polenta and reindeer fillet with crushed peppercorn sauce. Il Giardino attracts a regular young, moneyed crowd, while Umberto's is more quiet and sedate. Fish is treated either Italian style—rainbow trout grilled and served with sun-dried tomatoes, black olives, and pine-nuts—or with a taste of the Far East, as in yellow-fin tuna grilled with wasabi butter. *Il Giardino, 1382 Hornby St., tel. 604/669–2422. Umberto's, 1380 Hornby St., tel. 604/687–6316. Reservations advised. Dress: neat but casual. AE, DC, MC, V. Umberto's closed lunch and Sun., Mon. Il Giardino closed lunch Sat. and Sun. Expensive.*

Arriva Ristorante. Commercial Drive Italian restaurants, like Chinese restaurants in Chinatown, are best looked at with a skeptical eye. The best of the breed are elsewhere, and what's left is often found cranking out North Americanized travesties of the home country's food. Arriva is one Little Italy restaurant that's worth the drive, and it's a welcome find if you've spent the day shopping in Italian groceries. There's a version of spaghetti and meatballs on the menu, ziti with spicy squid sauce, and a fusili with wild game—"Bambi and Bugs Bunny," as the waiters have affectionately coined it. The antipasto plate includes a heaping order of octopus, shrimp, roasted red peppers, cheese, sausage, and fat lima beans in an herby marinade. Don't miss the orange sherbet served in a hollowed-out orange for dessert. *1537 Commercial Dr., tel. 604/251–1177. Reservations advised. Dress: casual. AE, DC, MC, V. Closed lunch Sat. and Sun. Moderate.*

Griffin's. Sunday brunch here was rated as top entertainment in 1992 by the daily newspaper, *The Province*. The ambience is fun, energetic, and kid-oriented: Kids in aprons (provided by the restaurant) whip up their own pancakes and take turns churning ice cream for dessert. The rest of the week the emphasis is on the adult crowd. This brasserie uniquely blends the charm of old Italy with the flair of sophisticated design and fresh, regional ingredients. Squash-yellow walls, bold black-and-white tiles, and splashy food art by Mary Frances Tuck enhance Griffin's liveliness. The hotel's gargoyles are repeated in stenciling on the walls and in the red, yellow, and green carpet. The brasserie features an open kichen that prepares inspirational cuisine, including buffet selections such as convict bread, a round loaf stuffed with soft, fresh goat cheese, olives, tomatoes, and peppers in olive oil; smoked salmon; chicken pasta al pesto; and baked Pacific black cod with herbed crumbs. There's a pizza buffet on Saturday. *900 W. Georgia St., tel. 604/684–3131. Reservations advised. Dress: casual but neat. AE, DC, MC, V. Moderate*

Cipriano's Ristorante & Pizzeria. Formerly a Greek pizza parlor, Cipriano's has been transformed into an Italian restaurant, with green-white-and-red walls representing the Italian flag, Mama-mia!—inexpensive and hearty Italian food is the mainstay here, including good pizza, even better pasta, and the "Pappa" lasagna. *3995 Main St., tel. 604/879–0020. Reservations accepted. Dress: casual. V. Closed lunch and Mon. Inexpensive.*

Japanese
★
Tojo's. Hidekazu Tojo is a sushi-making legend here. His handsome blond-wood tatami rooms, on the second floor of a new green-glass tower in the hospital district on West Broadway, provide proper ambience for intimate dining, but Tojo's 10-seat sushi bar stands as the centerpiece. With Tojo presiding, it is a convivial place for dinner and offers a ringside seat for watching the creation of edible art. Although tempura and teriyaki dinners will satisfy, the seasonal menu is more exciting. In October, ask for *dobbin mushi*, a soup made from pine mushrooms that's served in a teapot. In spring, try sushi made from scallops and pink cherry blossoms. *777 W. Broadway, No. 202, tel. 604/872–8050. Reservations advised on weekends. Dress: neat but casual. AE, DC, MC, V. Closed lunch and Sun.; Dec. 24–26. Expensive.*

Chiyoda. The robata bar curves like an oversize sushi bar through Chiyoda's main room: On one side are the customers and an array of flat baskets full of the day's offerings; on the other side are the robata chefs and grills. There are 35 choices of things to grill, from squid, snapper, and oysters to eggplant, mushrooms, onions, and potatoes. The finished dishes, dressed with sake, soy, or *ponzu* sauce, are dramatically passed over on the end of a long wooden paddle. If Japanese food means only sushi and tempura to you, check this out. *1050 Alberni St., tel. 604/688–5050. Reservations accepted. Dress: casual. AE, MC, V. Closed lunch Sat. and Sun.; closed Sun. off-season. Moderate.*

Shijo Japanese Restaurant. Shijo has an excellent and very large sushi bar, a smaller robata bar, tatami rooms, and a row of tables overlooking bustling Fourth Avenue. The epitome of modern urban Japanese chic is conveyed through the jazz music, handsome lamps with a patinated bronze finish, and lots of black wood. Count on creatively prepared sushi, eggplant *dengaku* topped with light and dark miso paste and broiled, and shiitake *foil yaki* (fresh shiitake mushrooms cooked in foil with *ponzu* sauce). *1926 W. 4th Ave., tel. 604/732–4676. Reservations advised. Dress: casual. AE, MC, V. Closed lunch, Sat. and Sun. Moderate.*

Japanese Deli House. The least expensive sushi in town is served in this high-ceilinged room on the main floor of a turn-of-the-century building on Powell Street, once the heart of Vancouver's Japantown. Along with the standard sushi-bar menu, Japanese Deli House makes a pungent but tender, hot ginger squid appetizer from baby squid caught off the Thai coast, and a geoduck appetizer in mayonnaise worth wandering off the beaten path for. The food is especially fresh and good if you can make it an early lunch: Nigiri sushi and sushi rolls are made at 11 AM for the 11:30 opening. *381 Powell St., tel. 604/681–6484. No reservations. Dress: casual. No credit cards. Closed lunch Mon. Inexpensive.*

Korean

Seoul House Korean Restaurant. The shining star in a desperately ugly section of East Broadway, Seoul House is a bright restaurant, decorated in Japanese style, that serves a full menu of Japanese and Korean food. The best bet is the Korean barbecue, which you cook at your table. A barbecue dinner of marinated beef, pork, chicken, or fish comes complete with a half dozen side dishes—*kim chee* (Korea's national pickle), salads, stir-fried rice, and pickled vegetables—as well as soup and rice. Service can be chaotic in this very popular restaurant. *36 E. Broadway, tel. 604/874–4131. Reservations advised. Dress: casual. MC, V. Closed lunch Sun. Inexpensive.*

Mexican

Topanga Cafe. Arrive before 6:30 or after 8 PM to avoid waiting in line for this 40-seat Kitsilano classic. The California-Mexican food hasn't changed much in the 15 years the Topanga has been dishing up fresh salsa and homemade tortilla chips. Quantities are still huge and prices are low. Kids can color blank menu covers while waiting for food; a hundred or more of the clientele's best efforts are framed and on the walls. *2904 4th Ave., tel. 604/ 733–3713. No reservations. Dress: casual. MC, V. Closed Sun. Inexpensive.*

Nouvelle

★ **Bishop's.** John Bishop established Vancouver's most influential restaurant in 1987 by serving West Coast Continental cuisine with an emphasis on British Columbia seafood. Penne with grilled eggplant, roasted peppers, and basil pasta cohabit the menu with medallions of venison, rack of lamb, and beef tenderloin. The small white rooms—their only ornament some splashy, expressionist paintings—are favored by Pierre Trudeau and by Robert De Niro when he's on location in Vancouver. *2183 W. 4th Ave., tel. 604/738–2025. Reservations required. Dress: casual. AE, DC, MC, V. Closed 1st week in Jan., lunch Sat. and Sun. Expensive.*

Pacific Northwest

Quilicum. Only a few blocks from English Bay, this downstairs "longhouse" serves the original Northwest Coast cuisine: bannock bread, baked sweet potato with hazelnuts, alder-grilled salmon, and soapberries for dessert. Try the authentic but odd dish—oolichan grease—that's prepared from candlefish. Native music is piped in, and Northwest Coast masks (for sale) peer out from the walls. *1724 Davie St., tel. 604/681–7044. Reservations advised. Dress: casual. AE, MC, V. Closed lunch Sat.–Tues. Moderate.*

★ **The Raintree.** This cool, spacious restaurant offers a local menu and wine list, which features vintages from British Columbia,

Washington, and Oregon. Raintree bakes its own bread, makes luxurious soups, and offers old favorites such as a slab of apple pie for dessert. With main courses, which change daily depending on market availability, the kitchen, focusing on healthy choices, teeters between willfully eccentric and exceedingly simple. Specials could include Queen Charlotte abalone and side-stripe shrimps, stir-fried with scallions and spinach in chamomile essence; and grilled lamb chops with a mint and pear puree. Leon's Bar and Grill, on the ground floor, stocks local beers and a respectable number of single-malt scotches. The pub-food menu includes organic-beef burgers and vegetarian chili. The $14 fixed-price Sunday brunch features ricotta and apple-stuffed French toast, sockeye salmon hash, and apricot-hazelnut pancakes, plus several other courses. *1630 Alberni St., tel. 604/688–5570. Reservations advised on weekends. Dress: casual. AE, DC, MC, V. Closed lunch Sat. and Dec. 24–26. Moderate.*

The Tomahawk. North Vancouver was mostly trees 66 years ago, when the Tomahawk first opened. Over the years, the original hamburger stand grew and mutated into part Northwest Coast Indian kitsch museum, part gift shop, and part restaurant. Renowned for its Yukon breakfast—five slices of back bacon, two eggs, hash browns, and toast—the Tomahawk also serves gigantic muffins, excellent French toast, and pancakes. The menu switches to oysters, trout, and burgers named after Indian chiefs for lunch and dinner. *1550 Philip Ave., tel. 604/988–2612. No reservations. Dress: casual. AE, MC, V. Inexpensive.*

Seafood

Olympia Fish Market and Oyster Co. Ltd. Some of the city's best fish-and-chips are fried in this tiny shop located behind a fish store in the middle of the Robson Street shopping district. The choice is halibut, cod, prawns, calamari, and whatever's on special in the store, served with genuine—never frozen—french fries. *1094 Robson St., tel. 604/685–0716. No reservations. Dress: casual. DC, V. Inexpensive.*

Thai

★ **Malinee's Thai.** The city's most consistently interesting Thai food can be found in this typically Southeast Asian–style room, tapestries adorning the walls. The owners, two Canadians who lived several years in Thailand, can give you detailed descriptions of every dish on the menu. Steamed fish with ginger, pickled plums, and red chili sauce is on the regular menu; a steamed whole red snapper marinated in oyster sauce, ginger, cilantro, red pepper, and lime juice is a special worth ordering when available. *2153 W. 4th Ave., tel. 604/737–0097. Reservations advised. Dress: casual. AE, DC, MC, V. Closed lunch. Moderate.*

Lodging

Lodging has become a major business for Vancouver, a fairly young city that hosts a lot of Asian businesspeople who are used to an above-average level of service. Although by some standards pricey, properties here are highly competitive, and you can expect the service to reflect this trend.

Highly recommended lodgings in each price category are indicated by a star ★.

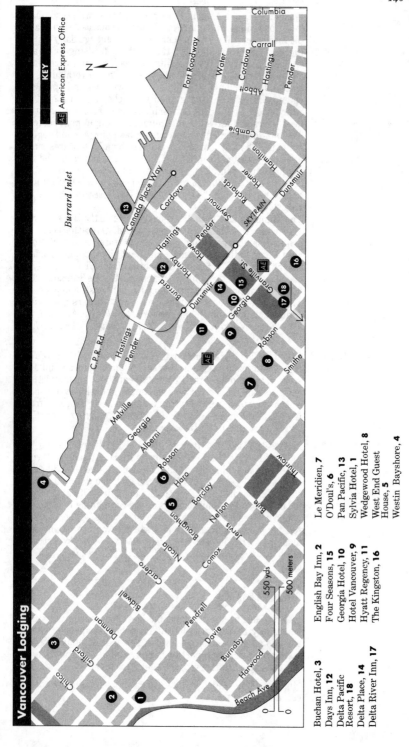

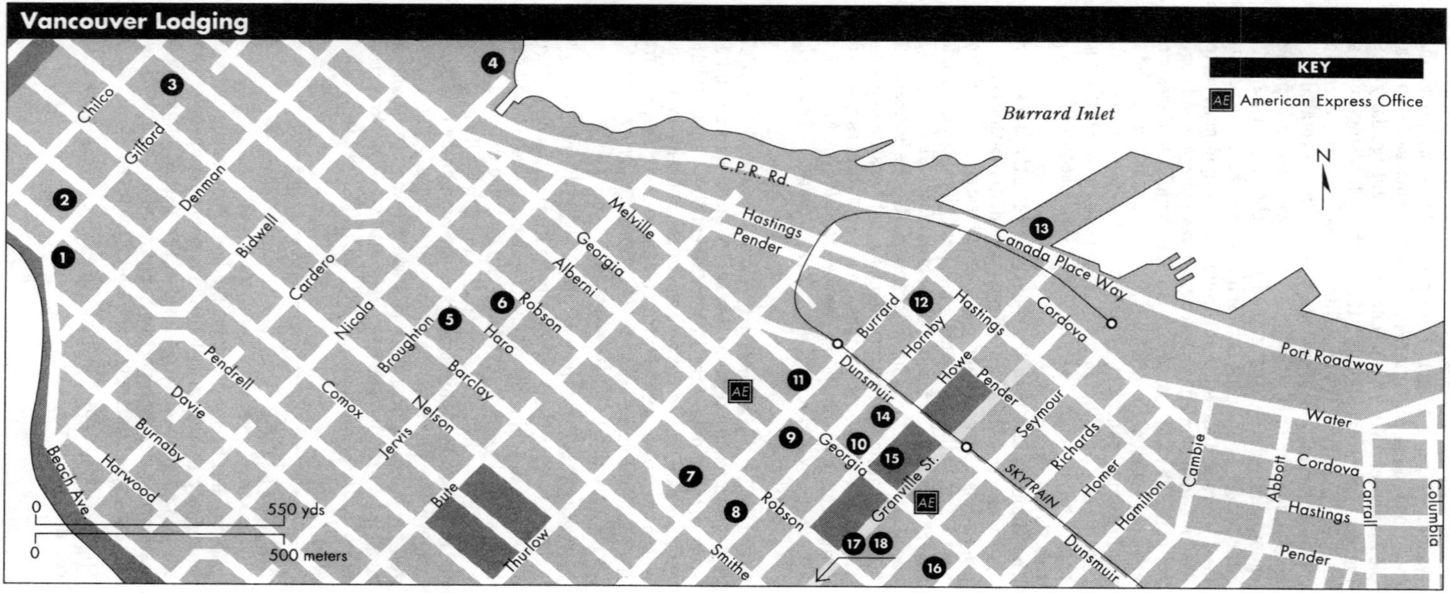

Buchan Hotel, **3**
Days Inn, **12**
Delta Pacific Resort, **18**
Delta Place, **14**
Delta River Inn, **17**
English Bay Inn, **2**
Four Seasons, **15**
Georgia Hotel, **10**
Hotel Vancouver, **9**
Hyatt Regency, **11**
The Kingston, **16**
Le Meridien, **7**
O'Doul's, **6**
Pan Pacific, **13**
Sylvia Hotel, **1**
Wedgewood Hotel, **8**
West End Guest House, **5**
Westin Bayshore, **4**

Category	Cost*
Very Expensive	over $180
Expensive	$140–$180
Moderate	$90–$139
Inexpensive	under $90

**All prices are for a standard double room for two, excluding 10% provincial accommodation tax, 15% service charge, and 7% GST.*

Very Expensive

Four Seasons. This 28-story hotel is adjacent to the Vancouver Stock Exchange and is attached to the Pacific Centre shopping mall. Standard rooms are not large; corner deluxe or deluxe Four Seasons rooms are recommended. Expect tasteful and stylish decor in the rooms and hallways, providing a calm mood despite the bustling hotel. A huge sun deck and indoor-outdoor pool are part of the complete health club facilities. Service is outstanding, and the Four Seasons has all the amenities. The formal dining room, Chartwell (see Dining, above), is one of the best in the city. *791 W. Georgia St., V6C 2T4, tel. 604/689–9333; in Canada, 800/268–6282; in the U.S., 800/332–3442; fax 604/844–6744. 317 rooms, 68 suites. Facilities: restaurant, café, bars, indoor-outdoor pool, sun deck, weight room, aerobics classes, sauna, Jacuzzi, ping-pong. AE, DC, MC, V.*

★ **Le Meridien.** This property feels more like an exclusive guest house than a large hotel: Its lobby has sumptuously thick carpets, enormous displays of flowers, and a newsstand situated discreetly down the hall. The rooms are even better, furnished with rich, dark woods reminiscent of 19th-century France. Bathrobes, slippers, and umbrellas in the room attest to the attention to detail here. Despite the size of this hotel, the Le Meridien in Vancouver has achieved and maintained a level of intimacy and exclusivity. The **Café Fleuri** serves one of the best Sunday brunches in town (plus a chocolate buffet on Thursday, Friday, and Saturday evenings), and **Le Club,** a fine French restaurant, is a special-occasion place. Lots of leather, dark wood, wingback chairs, and a fireplace give the **Gerard** bar the feel of a refined gentlemen's club. *845 Burrard St., V6Z 2K6, tel. 604/682–5511, fax 604/682–5513. 350 doubles, 47 suites. Facilities: restaurant, café, bar, business center, health club with pool, Jacuzzi, sauna, steam room, tanning bed, masseuse, salon, weights, exercise equipment, adjoining apartment hotel. AE, DC, MC, V.*

★ **Pan Pacific.** Canada Place sits on a pier right by the financial district and houses the luxurious Pan Pacific Hotel (built in 1986 for the Expo), the Vancouver Trade and Convention Centre, and a cruise-ship terminal. The lobby has a dramatic three-story atrium with a waterfall, and the lounge, restaurant, and café all have huge expanses of glass, so that you are rarely without a harbor view or mountain backdrop. Earthtones and Japanese detail give the rooms an understated elegance. Make sure you get a room that looks out on the water. The health club has a $15 fee that's well worth the price. The Pan Pacific is a grand, luxurious, busy hotel, but it is not a pick for an intimate weekend getaway. *300–999 Canada Pl., V6C 3B5, tel. 604/662–8211; in Canada, 800/663–1515; in the U.S., 800/937–1515; fax 604/685–8690. 468 doubles, 40 suites. Facilities: 3 restaurants, bar, health club with indoor track, sauna, steam room, state-*

of-the-art aerobics equipment, weights, massage and Shiatsu, sports lounge with wide-screen TV, squash, racquetball, and paddle-tennis courts, heated outdoor pool. AE, DC, MC, V.

Expensive–Very Expensive

Westin Bayshore. This hotel is the closest thing to a resort that you'll find in the downtown area. Because the Bayshore is perched right on the best part of the harbor, because it is a five-minute walk from Stanley Park, because of the truly fabulous view, and because of its huge outdoor pool, sun deck, and grassy areas, it is the perfect place to stay during the summer, especially for a family. The tower is the newer section, so rooms there are better furnished and larger and offer the best views of the water. The café is okay, and Trader Vic's, the hotel's dining room, is a pleasant, Polynesian-style experience. There are also several neighborhood restaurants. *1601 W. Georgia St., V6G 2V4, tel. 604/682–3377 or 800/228–3000; fax 604/691–6959. 481 doubles, 38 suites, 2 floors for the disabled. Facilities: restaurant, café, bars, free shuttle service downtown, bicycle rentals, marina with fishing and sailing charters, health club with indoor and outdoor pools, Jacuzzi, sun deck, masseur, sauna, pool table. AE, DC, MC, V.*

Expensive

Delta Pacific Resort & Conference Center. It's not a view or a shoreline that makes this place (five minutes from the airport) a resort, it's the facilities on the 12-acre site: three swimming pools (one indoor), four all-year tennis courts with a pro (matching list for partners), an outdoor fitness circuit, squash courts, aqua-exercise classes, outdoor volleyball nets, golf practice nets, a play center for children, summer camps for 5- to 12-year-olds, and a playground. In spite of the hotel's enormity, the atmosphere is casual and friendly. There are two guest-room towers and a few low-rise buildings for convention facilities. The resort was renovated in 1991–92, so guest rooms are modern with contemporary decor and pleasant color schemes. The Japanese restaurant is expensive and not the best value. *10251 St. Edwards Dr., V6X 2M9, tel. 604/278–9611; in Canada, 800/268–1133; in the U.S., 800/877–1133; fax 604/276–1122. 460 doubles, 4 suites. Facilities: restaurant, café, bar, shuttle to airport and shopping center, meeting rooms. AE, DC, MC, V.*

Delta Place. This 18-story hotel was built in 1985 by the luxurious Hong Kong Mandarin chain but was sold to Delta Hotels in 1987. Although the rates went down, the surroundings did not change: The lobby is still restrained and tasteful—one has to look for the registration desk. A slight Oriental theme is given to the deluxe furnishings, and dark, rich mahogany is everywhere. Most rooms have small balconies, and the studio suites are recommended since they are much roomier and only slightly more expensive than a standard room. Continental breakfast is included with your stay. The business center has secretarial services, work stations, cellular phones for rent, and small meeting rooms. The restaurant and bar are adequate and the location is perfect; the business and shopping district is a five-minute walk away. *645 Howe St., V6C 2Y9, tel. 604/687–1122; in Canada, 800/268–1133; in the U.S., 800/877–1133; fax 604/643–7267. 181 doubles, 16 suites. Facilities: restaurant, bar, squash and racquetball courts, lap pool, weight room. AE, DC, MC, V.*

Delta River Inn. This hotel, on the edge of the Fraser River, is two minutes from the airport. Rooms on the south side get the best view. Although renovations began in 1990, the River Inn still has a way to go to compete with others in the price range: The rooms here just don't have the style and pizzazz of the others. The hotel's draw lies in its proximity to the airport and its attachment to the marina, which organizes fishing charters so there are things for guests to do here. Food does not seem to be a priority with Delta. *3500 Cessena Dr., V7B 1C7, tel. 604/278–1241; in Canada, 800/268–1133; in the U.S., 800/877–1133; fax 604/276–1975. 410 doubles, 6 suites. Facilities: jogging route, outdoor pool, free shuttle to airport, shopping center, and extensive health club at the nearby Delta Pacific Resort. AE, DC, MC, V.*

★ **Hotel Vancouver.** The Hotel Vancouver, which opened in 1939 by the Canadian National Railway, is one of the grand old ladies of the chateau-style hotels that appear across Canada. Its copper roof dominates the city's skyline, and the hotel itself commands a regal position in the center of town across from the art gallery and Cathedral Place. Even the standard guest rooms lend an air of prestige with mahogany furniture, TVs in armoires, attractive linens, and the original, deep bathtubs. The whole design is by far more classic than what you'll find at the Hyatt Regency or the Four Seasons. The hotel's two floors of Entrée Gold feature extra services and amenities, including complimentary breakfast in a private, luxurious lounge. Entrée Gold suites are spacious with French doors, graceful wingback chairs, and fine mahogany furniture. The style and elegance of the Hotel Vancouver especially leave their mark on these floors. The hotel features the Roof Restaurant, which offers spectacular views with fine dining and dancing to live entertainment nightly. Reservations for Griffin's, the hotel's bistro-style restaurant—one of the most popular eateries in the city—are a must; there's a pizza buffet Saturday and a Tex-Mex Sunday brunch where children get into the act, making pancakes and churning ice cream. *900 W. Georgia St., V6C 2W6, tel. 604/684–3131 or 800/441–1414; fax 604/662–1937. 466 doubles, 42 suites, rooms for guests with disabilities. Facilities: 2 restaurants, 2 bars, two-line telephones, health club with lap pool, exercise machines, tanning bed, sun deck. AE, CB, DC, MC, V.*

Hyatt Regency. The 34-story hotel, which opened in 1973, completed an $11 million renovation in 1992. The Hyatt's standard rooms are the largest in the city and have been decorated in deep, dramatic colors and dark wood. Ask for a corner room with a balcony on the north or west side. The lobby, with its four-story atrium, however, can't escape the feel of a large convention hotel. For a small fee, the Regency Club gives you the exclusivity of three floors accessed by keyed elevators, your own concierge, a private lounge with a stereo and large TV, complimentary breakfast, 5 PM hors d'oeuvres, and evening pastries. Robes and special toiletries are also in the Regency Club rooms. For a hotel restaurant, Fish & Co. is unusual in that the room is casual, the atmosphere fun, and the food good. The Gallery Lounge is one of the most pleasant in town. Health club facilities include outdoor heated pool, saunas, exercise machine, and access to a nearby fitness center with racquetball and squash courts. *655 Burrard St., V6C 2R7, tel. 604/687–6543 or 800/233–1234, fax 604/689–3707. 612 doubles, 34 suites. Facilities: restaurant, café, 2 bars, health club. AE, DC, MC, V.*

O'Doul's. This conveniently situated hotel on a lively street, with loads of shops and restaurants, is only a five-minute walk from either the heart of downtown or Stanley Park. It's a great location if you're traveling with teenagers who want time on their own. Among mid-range hotels, this is one of the more thoughtful: Public areas are very well maintained, and to insure extra security guests must use their room keys to operate the elevators. The rooms aren't what you'd expect, either: The decor is modern, with pastel color schemes. Deluxe rooms (with king-size beds) face Robson Street and are worth the price, especially off-season, when rates plummet. *1300 Robson St., V6E 1C5, tel. 604/684–8461 or 800/663–5491, fax 604/684–8326. 119 doubles, 11 suites. Facilities: 3 telephones in every room, pool, Jacuzzi, steam rooms, exercise machines. AE, DC, MC, V.*

Waterfront Centre Hotel. This dramatically elegant, 23-story glass hotel opened in 1991 across from Canada Place, the Convention Centre, and the cruise-ship terminal—all of which can be reached from the hotel by an enclosed walkway. Views from the caramel-colored lobby and many of the guest rooms are of Burrard Inlet; other guest rooms look out onto the mountains. The Entrée Gold floor has a lounge, terrace, and includes a concierge, board room, shoe-shine service, deluxe breakfast, cocktail-hour canapes, and honor bar. All guest rooms are attractively furnished with contemporary artwork, minibars, and armoires concealing the TV. A pleasant place for guests to enjoy a drink is Herons Lounge, off of the lobby area. But as the evening progresses, the activity usually moves into Herons Restaurant, where a Mediterranean ambience prevails and guests can watch their meals being prepared in the open kitchen and rotisserie. Sundays here are high spirited, as live Gospel singers entertain and inspire during a lavish brunch that includes imaginative dishes and decadent desserts. The property's health club includes a whirlpool, enclosed walkway to an outdoor heated pool, a variety of exercise equipment, a steam room, and massage services. *900 Canada Place Way, V6C 3L5, tel. 604/691–1991 or 800/441–1414; fax 604/691–1999. 460 doubles, 29 suites. Facilities: restaurants, health club, whirlpool, heated outdoor pool, steam room. AE, CB, DC, MC, V.*

★ **Wedgewood Hotel.** This hotel upholds its reputation for being a small, elegant property run by an owner who fervently cares about her guests. The intimate lobby is decorated in fine detail with polished brass, beveled glass, a fireplace, and tasteful artwork. All the extra touches are here, too: nightly turndown service, afternoon ice delivery, dark-out drapes, flowers growing on the balcony, terry-cloth robes, and morning newspaper. No tour groups or conventions stop here; the Wedgewood's clients are almost exclusively corporate, except on weekends, when the place turns into a couple's retreat. Health facilities are next door at the excellent Chancery Squash Club. The lounge and restaurant couldn't be better. It's a treasure. *845 Hornby St., V6Z 1V1, tel. 604/689–7777 or 800/663–0666, fax 604/688–3074. 60 doubles, 33 suites. Facilities: 2 restaurants, bar, use of the adjacent Chancery Squash Club with 7 squash courts, weight room, aerobics, sauna, and whirlpool. AE, DC, MC, V.*

Moderate **Days Inn.** For the businessperson looking for a bargain, this location is tops. The six-story hotel, which opened as the Abbotsford in 1920, is the only moderately priced hotel in the business core. Recent renovations of the guest rooms and the lobby have made this accommodation even more agreeable. Although it's a basic hotel, rooms are bright, clean, and functional; standard units are very large, but there is no room service and few amenities. Suites 310, 410, 510, and 610 have a harbor view. The bar, the **Bombay Bicycle Club,** is a favorite with businesspeople. *921 W. Pender St., V6C 1M2, tel. 604/681–4335, fax 604/681–7808. 74 doubles, 11 suites. Facilities: restaurant, 2 bars, free overnight parking. AE, DC, MC, V.*

★ **English Bay Inn.** The newly renovated 1930s Tudor house in which this inn sits is one block from the ocean and Stanley Park in a quiet residential part of the West End. The five small guest rooms—each with private bath—have wonderful sleigh beds with matching armoires, Ralph Lauren linen, and alabaster lighting fixtures. The common areas are generous and elegantly furnished: The sophisticated but cozy parlor has wingback chairs, a fireplace, and French doors opening onto the front garden. A small, sunny English country garden graces the back of the inn. Breakfast is served in a rather formal dining room furnished with a Gothic dining room suite, a fireplace, and an 18th-century grandfather clock. *1968 Comox St., V6G 1R4, tel. 604/683–8002. 5 rooms. Facilities: off-street parking. AE, MC, V.*

★ **Hotel Georgia.** This handsome 12-story hotel, built in 1927, has such Old World features as a dark-wood-paneled lobby, ornate brass elevators, and a subdued, genteel atmosphere. Although it's lacking in extra amenities, the Georgia is a reliable and satisfactory deal. Rooms are small but well furnished, with nothing worn around the edges. Executive rooms have an almost separate seating area; rooms facing the art gallery have the best views. From this hotel (situated across from the Four Seasons) it's a five-minute walk to the business district. *801 W. Georgia St., V6C 1P7, tel. 604/682–5566 or 800/663–1111, fax 604/682–8192. 310 doubles, 4 suites. Facilities: restaurant, 3 bars. AE, DC, MC, V.*

★ **West End Guest House.** Judge this lovely Victorian house, built in 1906, by its gracious front parlor, cozy fireplace, and early 1900s furniture rather than by its bright pink exterior. Most of the small but extraordinarily handsome rooms have high brass beds, antiques, gorgeous linens, and dozens of old framed pictures of Vancouver. However, avoid the basement rooms. All units have phones, TVs, modern bathrooms, and newly papered walls. There's a veranda for people watching, and a back deck for sunbathing. A full breakfast is included and can be served in bed. The inn's genial host, Evan Penner, has learned that it is the little things that make the difference, including a predinner glass of sherry, duvets and feather mattress-pads, terry bathrobes, hand-knit slippers, turn-down service, and a goodnight tart. The inn is in a residential neighborhood that is a 15-minute walk from downtown and Stanley Park and two minutes from Robson Street. This is a nonsmoking establishment. *1362 Haro St., V6E 1G2, tel. 604/681–2889, fax 604/688–8812. 7 rooms. Facilities: off-street parking. AE, MC, V.*

Inexpensive

★ **Buchan Hotel.** This three-story 1930s building is conveniently set in a tree-lined residential street a block from Stanley Park, a block from shops and restaurants on Denman Street, and a 15-minute walk from the liveliest part of Robson Street. The hallways appear a bit institutional, but the rooms are bright and clean. Furnishings, in good condition, consist of a color TV and a wood-grained arborite desk and chest of drawers. The rooms are small and the bathrooms tiny. None of the rooms have phones and you have to park on the street, but with this location you probably won't use your car much. Rooms on the east side are brightest and overlook a park; front corner rooms are the biggest. A popular restaurant with an eclectic menu is in the basement and is open for dinner. *1906 Haro St., V6G 1H7, tel. 604/685–5354 or 800/668–6654, fax 604/685–5367. 60 rooms, 30 with private bath. Facilities: TV lounge, laundry room. AE, DC, MC, V.*

The Kingston. The Kingston is a small budget hotel in a location convenient for shopping. It is an old-style, four-story hotel, with no elevator—the type of establishment you'd find in Europe. The Spartan rooms are small and immaculate and share a bathroom down the hall. All rooms have phones but no TVs. Rooms on the south side are brighter. Continental breakfast is included. *757 Richards St., V6B 3A6, tel. 604/684–9024, fax 604/684–9917. 60 rooms, 7 with bath. Facilities: sauna, coin-op laundry, TV lounge, free nighttime parking. AE, MC, V.*

★ **Sylvia Hotel.** Perhaps the Sylvia Hotel is the best bargain in Vancouver, but don't count on staying here June–August unless you've booked six months ahead. What makes this hotel so popular are its low rates and near-perfect location: about 25 feet from the beach, 200 feet from Stanley Park, and a 20-minute walk from downtown. Vancouverites are particularly fond of the eight-story ivy-covered brick building—it was once the tallest building in the West End and the first to open a cocktail bar in the city, in 1954. It's part of the local history and was declared a protected heritage building in the 1970s. Rooms are unadorned and have basic plain furnishings that have probably been around for more than 20 years—not much to look at, but the view and price make it worthwhile. Suites are huge, and all have kitchens, making this a perfect family accommodation. There is little difference between the old and new wings. *1154 Gilford St., V6G 2P6, tel. 604/681–9321. 97 doubles, 18 suites. Facilities: restaurant, lounge, parking. AE, DC, MC, V.*

The Arts and Nightlife

For information on events, look in the entertainment section of the *Vancouver Sun;* also, Thursday's paper has complete listings in the **"What's On"** column, and there's the **Arts Hotline** (tel. 604/684–ARTS). For tickets to major events, book through **Ticketmaster** (tel. 604/280–3311).

The Arts

Theater The **Vancouver Playhouse** (Hamilton St., tel. 604/872–6622) is the most established venue in Vancouver. The **Arts Club Theatre** (tel. 604/687–1644), with two stages on Granville Island (1585 Johnston St.) and performances all year, is the most active. Both feature mainstream theatrical shows. **Carousel Theater** (tel. 604/669–3410), which performs off-off Broadway shows at the Waterfront Theatre (1405 Anderson St.) on Granville Island, and **Touchstone** (tel. 604/687–8737), at the Firehall Theater (280 E. Cordova St.), are smaller but lively companies. The **Back Alley Theatre** (751 Thurlow St., tel. 604/688–7013) hosts **Theatresports,** a hilarious improv event. The **Vancouver East Cultural Centre** (1895 Venables St., tel. 604/254–9578) is a multipurpose performance space that always hosts high-caliber shows.

Music The **Vancouver Symphony Orchestra** (tel. 604/684–9100) and the **CBC Orchestra** (tel. 604/662–6000) play at the restored **Orpheum Theatre** (601 Smithe St.). Choral groups like the **Bach Choir** (tel. 604/921–8012), the **Cantata Singers** (no tel.), and the **Vancouver Chamber Choir** (tel. 604/738–6822) play a major role in Vancouver's classical music scene. The **Early Music Society** (tel. 604/732–1610) performs medieval, renaissance, and baroque music throughout the year and hosts the Vancouver Early Music Summer Festival, one of the most important early music festivals in North America. Concerts by the **Friends of Chamber Music** (no tel.) and the **Vancouver Recital Society** (tel. 604/736–6034) are always of excellent quality.

Vancouver Opera (tel. 604/682–2871) stages four productions a year, usually in October, January, March, and May, at the **Queen Elizabeth Theatre** (600 Hamilton St.). Productions are high caliber with both local and imported talent.

Dance Watch for **Ballet BC's Dance Alive!** series, presenting visiting or local ballet companies (from the Kirov to Ballet BC). Most performances by these companies can be seen at the Orpheum or the Queen Elizabeth Theatre (*see above*). Local modern dance companies worth seeing are **Karen Jamison, Judith Marcuse,** and **JumpStart.**

Film Two theaters have distinguished themselves by avoiding the regular movie fare: **Ridge Theatre** (3131 Arbutus St., tel. 604/738–6311), which generally plays foreign films and rerun double-bills, and **Pacific Cinémateque Pacifique** (1131 Howe St., tel. 604/688–3456), which goes for even more esoteric foreign and art films. The **Vancouver International Film Festival** (tel. 604/685–0260) is held in September and October in several theaters around town.

Nightlife

Bars and Lounges **The Gérard Lounge** (845 Burrard St., tel. 604/682–5511) at Le Meridien Hotel is probably the nicest in the city because of its fireplaces, wingback chairs, dark wood, and leather. For spectacular views, head up to the **Roof Lounge** (900 W. Georgia St., tel. 604/684–3131), in the Hotel Vancouver, where a pianist plays nightly. The **Bacchus Lounge** (845 Hornby St., tel. 604/689–7777) in the Wedgewood Hotel is stylish and sophisticated. The **Gallery Lounge** (655 Burrard St., tel. 604/687–6543) in the Hyatt is a genteel bar, with lots of windows letting in the sun and giving views of the action on the bustling street. The **Garden Lounge** (791 W. Georgia St., tel. 604/689–9333) in the Four Seasons is bright and airy with greenery and a waterfall, plus big soft chairs you won't want to get out of. For a more lively atmosphere, try **Joe Fortes** (777 Thurlow St., 604/669–1940), or **Night Court** (801 W. Georgia St., tel. 604/682–5566) in the Georgia Hotel.

The **English Bay Café** (1795 Beach Ave., tel. 604/669–2225) is the place to go to catch the sunset over English Bay. **La Bodega** (1277 Howe St., tel. 604/684–8815), beneath the Château Madrid, is a popular Spanish tapas bar.

Two bars on Granville Island catering to the after-work crowd are **Bridges** (tel. 604/687–4400), near the Public Market, and the upscale **Pelican Bay** (tel. 604/683–7373), in the Granville Island Hotel, at the other end of the island. The **Backstage**

Lounge (1585 Johnston St., tel. 604/687–1354), behind the main stage at the Arts Club Theatre, features one of the largest selections of scotches in town, and is the hangout for local and touring musicians and actors.

Music

Discos While discos come and go, lines still form every weekend at **Richard's on Richards** (1036 Richards St., tel. 604/687–6794) for live and taped Top-40 music.

Jazz A jazz and blues hotline (tel. 604/682–0706) gives you current information on concerts and clubs. **Carnegie's** (1619 W. Broadway, tel. 604/733–4141), and the **Alma Street Café** (2505 Alma St., tel. 604/222–2244), both restaurants, are traditional venues with good mainstream jazz. The **Glass Slipper** (185 E. 11th Ave., tel. 604/877–0066) has mainstream to contemporary jazz with a more underground atmosphere.

Rock The **Town Pump** (66 Water St., tel. 604/683–6695) is the main venue for local and touring rock bands. The **Soft Rock Café** (1925 W. 4th Ave., tel. 604/736–8480) is decidedly more upscale. There's live music with dinner. The **86th Street Music Hall** (750 Pacific Blvd., tel. 604/683–8687) serves up big-name bands. The **Commodore Ballroom** (870 Granville St., tel. 604/681–7838), a Vancouver institution, has been restored to its original, art deco style and offers live music ranging from B.B. King to zydeco bands.

Casinos A few casinos have been licensed recently in Vancouver, and proceeds go to local charities and arts groups. No alcohol is served. Downtown there are the **Royal Diamond Casino** (535 Davie St., tel. 604/685–2340) and the **Great Canadian Casino** (2477 Heather St., tel. 604/872–5543) in the Holiday Inn.

Comedy Yuk Yuks (750 Pacific Blvd., tel. 604/687–5233) is good for a few laughs. Punchlines Comedy Theatre (15 Water St., tel. 604/684–3015), another fun place, is in Gastown.

Excursion to Victoria

Important Addresses and Numbers

Tourist Information **Tourism Victoria** (812 Wharf St., Victoria V8W 1T3, tel. 604/382–2127 or 800/663–3883).

Emergencies Dial **911** in Victoria.

Hospitals **Victoria General Hospital** (35 Helmcken St., tel. 604/727–4181).

Late-Night Pharmacies All-night pharmacies are unknown in British Columbia, even in the largest cities, although some pharmacies do offer after-hours emergency numbers. Generally, emergency prescriptions can be filled through major hospitals. McGill and Orme Pharmacies (649 Fort St., tel. 604/384–1195) could provide assistance.

Arriving and Departing by Plane

Airports and Airlines **Victoria International Airport** serves Victoria. **Air Canada** (tel. 604/360–9074; in the U.S., 800/458–5811) and **Canadian Airlines International** (tel. 604/382–6111; in the U.S., 800/426–7000) are the two dominant carriers. **Air B.C.** (tel. 604/360–9074; in the U.S., 800/663–0522) provides both airport-to-airport and harbor-to-harbor service from Vancouver to Victoria at least hourly. Both flights take about 35 minutes. **Air B.C.** is the major regional line and runs daily flights between Seattle and Victoria. **Helijet Airways** (tel. 604/382–6222) helicopter service is available from downtown Vancouver to downtown Victoria.

Arriving and Departing by Car, Bus, and Boat

By Car The TransCanada Highway, Route 1, runs south from Nanaimo to Victoria. Route 14 connects Sooke to Port Renfrew, on the West Coast of Vancouver Island, with Victoria.

By Bus **Greyhound** (tel. 604/388–5348; in Seattle, 206/624–3456) connects destinations throughout British Columbia with cities and towns throughout the Pacific North Coast.

By Boat **BC Ferries** (tel. 604/656–0757) travel year-round from Tsawwassen, just south of Vancouver, to Swartz Bay, a 30-minute trip by car or bus from Victoria.

Sealink Express (tel. 604/687–6925) offers high-speed (2 ½-hour) catamaran service between downtown Vancouver and downtown Victoria. One-way fares for adults are $32.95, and round-trip is $59.95.

There is year-round passenger service (closed Christmas) between Victoria and Seattle via the ***Victoria Clipper*** (tel. 800/888–2535).

Washington State Ferries (tel. in Victoria, 604/656–1551; in Seattle, 206/464–6400) cross daily, year-round, between Sidney, just north of Victoria, and Anacortes, WA. **Black Ball Transport** (tel. in Victoria, 604/386–2202; in Seattle, 206/622–2222) operates between Victoria and Port Angeles, WA.

Getting Around

For the most part, Victoria is a walker's city; most of its main attractions are downtown or are a few blocks from the core. Attractions on the outskirts of downtown can easily be reached by bus or a short cab ride (though taxis can be alarmingly expensive). In the summer you have the added option of horse-drawn carriage, bicycle, boat, or double-decker bus tours.

By Bus The **BC Transit System** (tel. 604/382–6161) runs a fairly extensive service throughout Victoria and the surrounding areas, with an all-day pass that costs $4 for adults, $3 for students and senior citizens. Passes are sold at many outlets in downtown Victoria, including Eaton Centre and Harbour Square Ticket Centre.

Guided Tours

Tally-ho Horsedrawn Tours (tel. 604/479–1113) offers visitors a get- acquainted session with downtown Victoria that includes Beacon Hill Park.

Exploring Victoria

Numbers in the margin correspond to points of interest on the Downtown Victoria map.

Victoria, originally Fort Victoria, was the first European settlement on Vancouver Island and is the oldest city on Canada's west coast. It was chosen in 1842 by James Douglas to be the Hudson's Bay Company's most western outpost, and it became the capital of British Columbia in 1868. Today it's a compact seaside town laced with tea shops and gardens. Though it's quite touristy during the high summer season, it's also at its prettiest, with flowers hanging from turn-of-the-century building posts and strollers feasting on the beauty of Victoria's natural harbor.

1 A logical place to begin this tour is at the **Visitors Information Centre,** located on the waterfront. *812 Wharf St., tel. 604/382–2127. Open July, Aug., daily 9–9; May, June, Sept., Oct., daily 9–7; Nov.–Apr., daily 9–5.*

2 Just across the way is the **Empress Hotel,** which originally opened in 1908, and is a symbol both of the city and of the Canadian Pacific Railway. Designed by Francis Rattenbury, whose works dot Victoria, the property is another of the great châteaux built by Canadian Pacific, the still-current owners who also built the Château Frontenac in Québec City, Château Laurier in Ottawa, and Château Lake Louise in Alberta. The $45 million face-lift was a hot topic of discussion in traditional Victoria, though not all of the comments have been positive: For contrast, take a pleasant stroll through the modern, elegantly designed Victoria Conference Centre at the south end of the Empress. Criticism aside, the ingredients that made the 488-room hotel a tourist attraction in the past are still alive. Stop in for high tea—served at hour-and-a-half intervals during the afternoon. *721 Government St., tel. 604/384–8111. Proper dress required; no jeans, shorts, or T-shirts.*

Around the corner from the Empress is **Miniature World,** on Humboldt Street, where small replicas of people, trains, and historic events are displayed. The exhibit seems at times like a mix of fact and fiction, with the models laid out so delicately. *649 Humboldt St., tel. 604/385–9731. Admission: $6.50 adults, $5.50 children 12–17, $4.50 children 4–11, disabled persons with escort free. Open mid-June–mid-Sept., daily 8:30–10 PM; mid-Sept.–mid-June, daily 9–5.*

A short walk around the harbor leads you to the old CPR Steamship Terminal, also designed by Rattenbury and com-
3 pleted in 1924. Today it is the **Royal London Wax Museum,** housing more than 200 wax figures, including replicas of Queen Victoria, Elvis, and Marilyn Monroe. *470 Belleville St., tel. 604/388–4461. Admission: $6.50 adults, $5.50 students and senior citizens, $3.50 children 5–12. Open May–Aug., daily 9–9; Sept.–Apr., daily 9–5.*

4 Next to the wax museum is the **Pacific Undersea Gardens,** where more than 5,000 marine specimens are on display in their natural habitat. You also get performing scuba divers and a giant Pacific octopus. Unfortunately, there are no washrooms, and the site is not wheelchair accessible. *490 Belleville St., tel. 604/382–5717. Admission: $6 adults, $5.50 senior citizens, $4.50 children 12–17, $2.75 children 5–11. Open Oct.–end of May, daily 10–5; summer, daily 9–9; closed Christmas. Shows run about every 45 minutes.*

5 Across Belleville Street is the **Legislative Parliament Buildings** complex. The stone-exterior building, completed in 1897, domi-

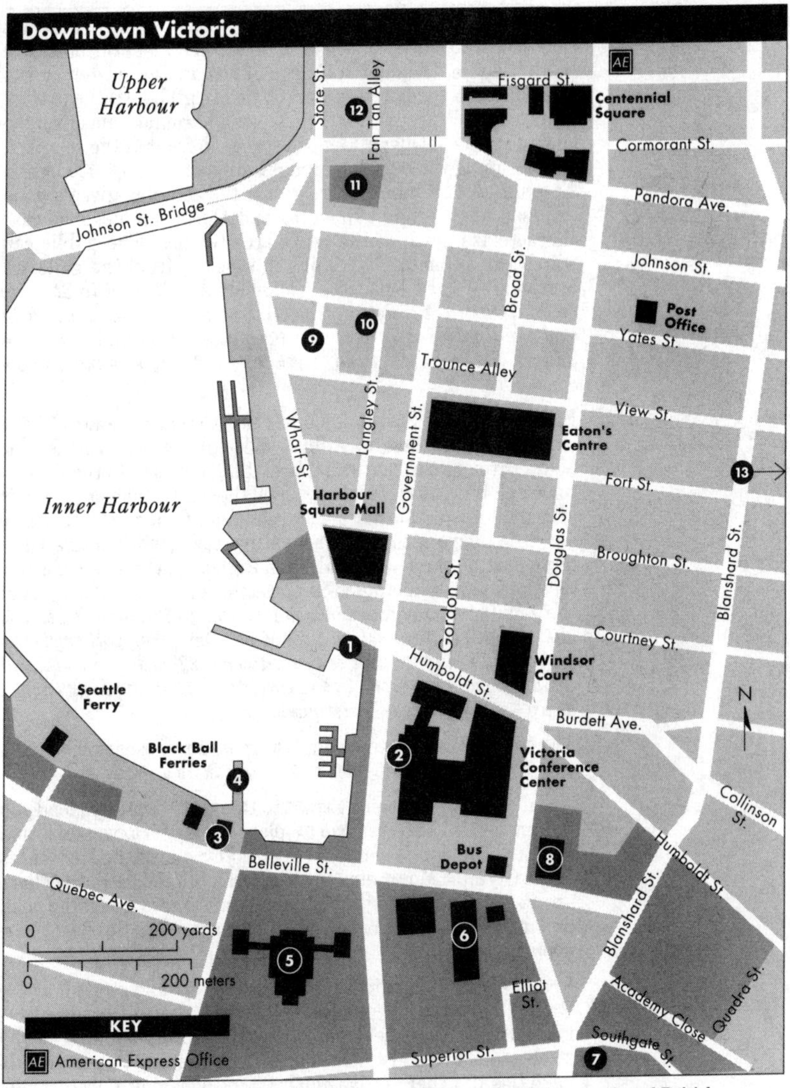

Bastion Square, **9**
Beacon Hill Park, **7**
Chinatown, **12**
Craigdarroch Castle, **13**
Crystal Gardens, **8**
Empress Hotel, **2**
Legislative/ Parliament Buildings, **5**
Maritime Museum, **10**
Market Square, **11**
Pacific Undersea Garden, **4**
Royal British Columbia Museum, **6**
Royal London Wax Museum, **3**
Visitors Information Centre, **1**

nates the inner harbor and is flanked by two statues: Sir James Douglas, who chose the location of Victoria, and Sir Matthew Baille Begbie, the man in charge of law and order during the gold-rush era. Atop the central dome is a gilded statue of Captain George Vancouver, who first sailed around Vancouver Island; a statue of Queen Victoria stands in front of the complex; and outlining the building at night are more than 3,000 lights. Another of Rattenbury's creations, the complex gives a good example of the rigid symmetry and European elegance that characterize much of the city's architecture. The public can watch the assembly, when it's in session, from the galleries overlooking the Legislative Chamber. *501 Belleville St., tel. 604/387–3046. Admission free. Tours run several times daily and are conducted in at least 4 languages in summer and 3 in winter. Open Sept.–June, weekdays 8:30–5; summer, daily 8:30–5:30.*

6 Follow Belleville Street one block east to reach the **Royal British Columbia Museum.** Adults and children can wander for hours through the centuries, back 12,000 years. In the prehistoric exhibit, you can actually smell the pines and hear the calls of mammoths and other ancient wildlife. Other exhibits allow you to explore a turn-of-the-century town, with trains rumbling past; in the Kwakiutl Indian Bighouse, the smell of cedar envelops you, while piped-in potlatch songs tell the origins of the genuine ceremonial house before you. *675 Belleville St., tel. 604/387–3014. Admission: Free Mon., Oct.–Apr.; otherwise $5 adults, $3 students and senior citizens, $2 children 6–18 and disabled persons. Open Oct.–Apr., daily 10–5:30; May–Sept., daily 9:30–7; closed Christmas.*

The **Newcombe Theatre** behind the museum presents slide talks and films. *Tel. 604/387–5822. Admission by donation.*

A walk east on Belleville Street to Douglas Street will lead you
7 to **Beacon Hill Park,** a favorite place for joggers, walkers, and cyclists. The park's southern lawns offer one of the best views of the Olympic Mountains and the Strait of Juan de Fuca. There are also lakes, walking paths, abundant flowers, a wading pool, petting zoo, and an outdoor amphitheater for Sunday-afternoon concerts.

From the park, go north on Douglas Street and stop off at the
8 **Crystal Gardens.** Opened in 1925 as the largest swimming pool in the British Empire, this glass-roof building—now owned by the provincial government—is home to flamingos, macaws, 75 varieties of other birds, hundreds of blooming flowers, penguins, and monkeys. At street level there are several boutiques and Rattenbury's Restaurant, one of Victoria's well-frequented establishments. *713 Douglas St., tel. 604/381–1213. Admission: $3 adults, $2 children 6–16 and senior citizens. Open Oct.–Apr., daily 10–5:30; summer, daily 9–9.*

From Crystal Gardens continue on Douglas Street going north
9 to View Street, west to **Bastion Square,** with its gas lamps, restaurants, cobblestone streets, and small shops. This is the spot James Douglas chose as the original Fort Victoria in 1843 and the original Hudson's Bay Company trading post. Today fashion boutiques and restaurants occupy the old buildings. At the Wharf Street end of the square are some benches where you can rest your feet and catch a great view of the harbor. While you're here, you may want to stop in at what was Victoria's

10 original courthouse but is now the **Maritime Museum of British Columbia.** Dugout canoes, model ships, Royal Navy charts, photographs, uniforms, and ship's bells chronicle Victoria's seafaring history. A seldom-used 100-year-old cage lift, believed to be the oldest in North America, ascends to the third floor. In 1995, however, a new museum is scheduled to open and replace this facility. *28 Bastion Sq., tel. 604/385–4222. Admission: $5 adults, $3 children 12–17, $2 children 6–11. Open Oct. 1–May 31, daily 9:30–4:30; June 1–Sept. 30, daily 9–6. Closed Christmas and New Year's Day.*

West of Government Street, between Pandora Avenue and
11 Johnson Street, is **Market Square,** offering a variety of specialty shops and boutiques and considered one of the most picturesque shopping districts in the city. At the turn of the century this area—once part of Chinatown—provided everything a visitor desired: food, lodging, entertainment. Today the square has been restored to its original, pre-1900s character.

Just around the corner from Market Square is Fisgard Street,
12 the heart of one of the oldest **Chinatowns** in Canada. It was the Chinese who were responsible for building much of the Canadian Pacific Railway in the 19th century, and their influences still mark the region. If you enter Chinatown from Government Street, you'll walk under the elaborate **Gate of Harmonious Interest,** made from Taiwanese ceramic tiles and decorative panels. Along the street, merchants display fragile paper lanterns, embroidered silks, imported fruits, and vegetables. **Fan Tan Alley,** situated just off Fisgard Street, holds claim not only to being the narrowest street in Canada but also to having been the gambling and opium center of Chinatown, where mahjongg, fantan, and dominoes games were played.

A 15-minute walk or a short drive east on Fort Street will take
13 you to Joan Crescent, where **Craigdarroch Castle** stands. This lavish mansion was built as the home of British Columbia's first millionaire, Robert Dunsmuir, who oversaw coal mining for the Hudson's Bay Company. (He died before the castle's completion in about 1890.) Recently converted into a museum depicting turn-of-the-century life-style, the castle is strikingly authentic, with elaborately framed landscape paintings, stained-glass windows, carved woodwork—precut in Chicago for Dunsmuir and sent by rail—and rooms for billiards and smoking. The location offers a wonderful view of downtown Victoria from the fifth-floor tower; guided tours are given. *1050 Joan Crescent, Victoria, tel. 604/592–5323. Admission: $5.50 adults, $4.50 students, children under 12 by donation. Open mid-June–Aug., daily 9–7:30; Sept.–mid-June, daily 10–5.*

What to See and Do with Children

Anne Hathaway's Cottage, tucked away in a unique English village complex, is a full-size replica of the original thatched home in Stratford-Upon-Avon, England. The building and the 16th-century antiques inside are typical of Shakespeare's era. The Olde England Inn, on the grounds, is a pleasant spot for tea or a traditional English-style meal. You can also stay ($68–$184; AE, DC, MC, V) in one of the 50 antiques-furnished rooms, some complete with four-poster beds. *429 Lampson St., Victoria, V9A 5Y9, tel. 604/388–4353. Admission: $5.75 adults, $3.50 senior citizens and children 8–17, children under 8 free.*

Open June–Sept., daily 9–9; rest of year, daily 10–4. Guided tours leave from the inn during the winter and directly from the cottage in summer. From downtown Victoria, take the Munro bus to the door.

Pacific Undersea Gardens (*see* Exploring Victoria, *above*).

Swan Lake Christmas Hill Nature Sanctuary. This 23-acre lake, set within 110 acres of open fields and wetlands out Blanshard Street, is 10 minutes from downtown. From the 1½-mile chip trail and floating boardwalk, birders can spot a variety of waterfowl in winter and nesting birds in the tall grasses. Children will enjoy the displays and games in the nature house. *3873 Swan Lake Rd. (take the No. 70/No. 75 bus), tel. 604/479–0211. Admission free. Open year-round; nature House open Mon.–Fri. 8:30–4; weekends and holidays 12–4.*

Off The Beaten Track

Butchart Gardens, situated on the 130-acre Butchart estate about 21 kilometers (13 miles) north of downtown Victoria, offers more than 700 varieties of flowers and includes Italian, Japanese, and English rose gardens. During the summer, many of the exhibits are illuminated at night. Once a limestone quarry, the grounds were transformed in 1904 when Canadian cement pioneer Robert Butchart began building bridges and walkways and planting shrubs and flowers on the 50-acre (20-hectare) site. The grounds are lighted with beautiful displays during the Christmas season. Also on the premises are a gift shop, teahouse, and restaurants. *800 Benvenuto Ave., Victoria, tel. 604/652–5256. Admission: $9.50 adults, $5 children 12–17, $1 children under 12 excluding GST.*

Shopping

Shopping in Victoria is easy: Virtually everything can be found in the downtown area, beginning at the Empress and walking north along Government Street. In succession you'll hit **Roger's Chocolates** (tel. 604/384–7021), for fine chocolates; **George Straith Ltd.** (tel. 604/384–6912), for woolens; **Edinburgh Tartan Shop** (tel. 604/388–9312), for traditional Scottish clothing and accessories; **Gallery of the Arctic** (tel. 604/382–9012), for good-quality Inuit art; **Munro's Books** (tel. 604/382–2464), for the best selection of Victoriana in the city; and **Old Morris Tobacconist, Ltd.** (tel. 604/382–4811), for unusual pipe tobacco blends.

On the block of Douglas Street behind the Empress are shops like the exclusive **G. Gagliano of Florence,** with beautiful Italian leather goods; **LeJame Fashions,** with clothing designed and manufactured in Victoria, and the **Stephen Lowe Art Gallery.** Handy, also, is the **Currency Exchange,** which is open daily. The **Eaton Centre** at Government and Fort streets is both a department store and a series of small boutiques, with a total of 140 shops and restaurants. Market Square, between Johnson and Pandora, has three stories of specialty shops.

At last count, Victoria had 60-plus **antiques shops** specializing in coins, stamps, estate jewelry, rare books, crystal, china, furniture, or paintings and other works of art. A short walk on Fort Street going away from the harbor will take you to **Antique Row** between Blanshard and Cook streets. **Waller Antiques** (tel. 604/388–6116) and **Newberry Antiques** (tel. 604/388–

7732) offer a wide selection of furniture and collectibles. You will also find antiques on the west side of Government Street near the **Old Town.**

A 10-minute drive (or the No. 1/No. 2 bus) from downtown out Fort Street to Oak Bay Avenue will take you to one of the few residential shopping areas that is not a mall. The **Oak Bay Village** is great for browsing, buying, or an afternoon *cuppa'*. Start at the corner of Oak Bay and Foul Bay and work your way east toward the water.

Sports and Outdoor Activities

Golf Though **Victoria Golf Club** (1110 Beach Dr., Victoria, tel. 604/598–4321) is private, it's open to other private-club members. This windy course is the oldest (built in 1893) in British Columbia and offers a spectacular view of the Strait of Juan de Fuca. **Uplands Golf Club** (3300 Cadboro Bay Rd., Victoria, tel. 604/592–1818) is a flat, semiprivate course (it becomes public after 2). **Cedar Hill Municipal** (1400 Derby Rd., Victoria, tel. 604/595–3103) is a public course with up-and-down terrain. **Royal Oak Golf Club** (4680 Elk Lake Dr., Victoria, tel. 604/658–1433) is the newest nine-hole course in the area. **Gorge Vale Golf Club** (1005 Craigflower Rd., Victoria, tel. 604/386–3401) is a semiprivate course but is open to the public. It has punitive traps and a deep gorge that eats up golf balls. **Glen Meadows Golf and Country Club** (1050 McTavish Rd., Sidney, tel. 604/656–3921), situated near the ferry terminal, is a semiprivate course that's open to the public at select times.

Dining and Lodging

Dining For prices see Dining chart for Vancouver, *above*.

Chez Daniel. One of Victoria's old standbys, Chez Daniel offers dishes that are rich, though the nouvelle influence has found its way into a few of the offerings. The interior, following a burgundy color scheme, seems to match the traditional rich, caloric cuisine. The wine list is varied, and the menu has a wide selection of basic dishes: rabbit, salmon, duck, steak. This is a restaurant where you linger for the evening in the romantic atmosphere. *2524 Estevan Ave., tel. 604/592–7424. Reservations advised. Jacket advised. AE, MC, V. Closed lunch and Sun.–Mon. Expensive.*

Chez Pierre. Established in 1973, this is the oldest French restaurant in Victoria, and the downtown location, combined with an intimate, rustic decor, creates a pleasant ambience. House specialties include *canard à l'orange* (duckling in orange sauce), rack of lamb, and British Columbia salmon. Although a tourist destination, this restaurant has managed to maintain its high quality over the years. *512 Yates, tel. 604/388–7711. Reservations advised. Dress: casual but neat. AE, MC, V. Closed lunch and Sun.–Mon. Moderate–Expensive.*

Swan's Café. Here's a good choice for a casual meal with Mediterranean and pan-Pacific flair. Inside the historic building in which the café is housed are lavish bouquets of fresh flowers and original artwork collected by owner Michael Williams. Creatively prepared salads and succulent stir-fries are recommended. The brew pub on the premises sometimes features live music and is the busiest pub in the city. *506 Pandora Ave., tel.*

604/361–3310. Reservations accepted. Dress: casual. MC, V. Moderate–Expensive.

Camilles. This restaurant is romantic, intimate, and one of the few West Coast–cuisine restaurants in Victoria. House specialties such as chicken Napoli, papaya brochettes (prawns wrapped around chunks of papaya in a lime and jalapeño marinade), phyllo-wrapped salmon (fresh fillet of salmon in phyllo pastry) are all served in generous portions. Camilles also has an extensive wine cellar, uncommon in Victoria. *45 Bastion Sq., tel. 604/381–3433. Reservations advised. Dress: casual but neat. MC, V. Closed lunch and Sun.–Mon. Moderate.*

French Connection. Located in one of Victoria's Heritage homes, built in 1884, the restaurant has maintained the character of the time. From the outside, ornate details indicate the French tradition that you will find in the service and on the menu. The food is prepared with care, with an emphasis on the sauces. *512 Simcoe St., tel. 604/385–7014. Reservations required. Dress: casual. AE, MC, V. Closed Sat.–Mon. lunch and Sun. Moderate.*

★ **La Ville d'Is.** This historic brick building houses one of the best seafood restaurants in Victoria. Both the quality and price are right. Run by Michel Duteau, a Brittany native, the restaurant is cozy and friendly, with an outside café open May–October. An extensive, imaginative wine list features bottles from the Loire Valley that go well with the seafood, rabbit, lamb, and beef tenderloin specials. Try the *perche de la Nouvelle Zélande* (orange roughie in muscadet with herbs) or lobster soufflé for a unique taste. *26 Bastion Sq., tel. 604/388–9414. Reservations advised. Dress: casual but neat. AE, MC, V. Closed Sun. and Jan. Moderate.*

★ **Pagliacci's.** If you want Italian food, Pagliacci's is a must. Featured are dozens of pasta dishes, quiches, veal, and chicken in marsala sauce with fettuccine. The pastas are freshly made in-house. The orange-color walls are covered with photos of Hollywood stars, so there's always something to look at here. *1011 Broad St., tel. 604/386–1662. No reservations. Dress: casual. MC, V. Moderate.*

Blethering Place. Next to a teddy bear shop in Oak Bay is this clubby, neighborhood restaurant populated by dignified ladies sipping afternoon tea and blethering over crumpets, tarts, and scones. The menu points out that "blethering" is Scottish for "voluble, senseless talking." Later, neighborhood families stroll in for a dinner of steak-and-kidney pie, East Indian curries, and wonderfully rich desserts. Wines from British Columbia are featured. *2250 Oak Ave., tel. 604/598–1413. Reservations advised. Dress: casual but neat. AE, MC, V. Inexpensive–Moderate.*

Don Mee's. A large neon sign signals guests to Don Mee, a traditional Chinese restaurant. The long, red staircase leads to an expansive, comfortable restaurant for entrées such as sweet-and-sour chicken, almond duck, and bean curd with broccoli. *538 Fisgard St., tel. 604/383–1032. Reservations accepted. Dress: casual. MC, V. Inexpensive–Moderate.*

Le Petite Saigon. This is a small, intimate café-style restaurant, offering a quiet dining experience with beautifully presented meals and a fare that is primarily Vietnamese, with a touch of French. The crab, asparagus, and egg swirl soup is a specialty of the house, and combination meals are cheap and tasty. *1010 Langley St., tel. 604/386–1412. Dress: casual. AE, MC, V. Closed Sat. lunch and Sun. Inexpensive–Moderate.*

Cafe Mexico. Hearty portions of Mexican food, such as *pollo chipolte* (grilled chicken with melted cheddar and spicy sauce, on a bed of rice) are served inside this spacious, redbrick dining establishment, situated just off the waterfront. Bullfight ads and cactus plants decorate the restaurant and reinforce its character and Mexican theme. *1425 Store St., tel. 604/386–5454. Reservations accepted. Dress: casual. AE, MC, V. Inexpensive.*

Periklis. Standard Greek cuisine is offered in this warm, taverna-style restaurant, but there are also steaks and ribs on the menu. On the weekends you can enjoy Greek and belly dancing, but be prepared for the hordes of people who come for the entertainment. *531 Yates St., tel. 604/386–3313. Reservations accepted. Dress: casual. Closed weekend lunch; during summer, open Sat. lunch. AE, MC, V. Inexpensive.*

★ **Six-Mile-House.** This 1855 carriage house is a Victoria landmark. The brass, carved oak moldings and stained glass set a festive mood for the evening. The menu is constantly changing but always features seafood selections and burgers. Try the cider or one of the many international beers offered. *494 Island Hwy., tel. 604/478–3121. Reservations accepted. Dress: casual. MC, V. Inexpensive.*

Lodging

Category	Cost*
Very Expensive	over $180
Expensive	$110–$179
Moderate	$70–$109
Inexpensive	under $70

**All prices are for a standard double room for two, excluding 10% provincial accommodation tax, service charge, and 7% GST.*

★ **The Empress Hotel.** This is Victoria's dowager queen with a face-lift. First opened in 1908, the hotel underwent a $45 million dollar renovation in 1989 that enhanced its Edwardian charm, updated existing guest rooms, and added some 45 new ones. Stained glass, carved archways, and hardwood floors are used effectively. The Empress dominates the inner-harbor area and is the city's primary meeting place for politicians, locals, and tourists. From the Lobby Lounge, guests can have a splendid view of the harbor. Afternoon tea has been a tradition here since 1908, but it's so popular today, reservations are a must. The Bengal Lounge is full of colonial charm from British India, including a stuffed Bengal tiger, overhead fans, and mosquito netting. *721 Government St., V8W 1W5, in Canada, tel. 604/384–8111 or 800/268–9411; in the U.S., 800/828–7447; fax 604/381–4334. 481 rooms. Facilities: 2 restaurants, café, 2 lounges, conference center, indoor pool, sauna, health club, in-room movies, cable TV, Christmas discount, family discount. AE, DC, MC, V. Very Expensive.*

★ **Abigail's.** A Tudor country inn with gardens and crystal chandeliers, Abigail's is not only lovely but also conveniently located four blocks east of downtown. All guest rooms are prettily detailed with a contemporary color schemes. Down comforters, together with Jacuzzis and fireplaces in some, add to the pampering atmosphere. There's a sense of elegant informality about the hotel, noticed especially in the guest library and sitting room, where you'll want to spend an hour or so relaxing in the evening. Breakfast, included in the room rate, is served from 8 to 9:30 in the downstairs dining room. *906 McClure St., V8V 3E7, tel. 604/388–5363; fax 604/361–1905. 16 rooms. MC. Expensive.*

★ **The Beaconsfield Inn.** Built in 1875 and restored in 1984, the Beaconsfield has retained its Old World charm. Dark mahogany wood appears throughout the house; down comforters and some canopy beds and claw-foot tubs adorn the rooms, reinforcing the Edwardian style of this residentially situated inn. Some of the rooms have fireplaces and Jacuzzis. An added plus is the guest library and conservatory/sun room. Full breakfast, with homemade muffins, and a cocktail hour (6–7 PM), with sherry, cheese, and fruit, are included in the room rates. *998 Humboldt St., V8V 2Z8, tel. 604/384–4044; fax 604/361–1908. 12 rooms. Facilities: library, Jacuzzi. MC. Expensive.*

The Bedford Hotel. This European-style hotel, located in the heart of downtown, is reminiscent of San Francisco's small hotels, with personalized service and strict attention to details. In keeping with the theme, rooms follow an earthen color scheme, and many have goose-down comforters, fireplaces, and Jacuzzis. Meeting rooms and small conference facilities are available also, making this a good businessperson's lodging. An extensive breakfast is included in the room rate. *1140 Government St., V8W 1Y2, tel. 604/384–6835 or 800/665–6500; fax 604/386–8930. 40 rooms. Facilities: restaurant, pub. AE, MC, V. Expensive.*

Chateau Victoria. This 19-story hotel, situated across from Victoria's new Conference Centre, near the inner harbor and the Royal British Columbia Museum, promises wonderful views from its upper rooms and its rooftop restaurant. Following a Victorian motif, the rooms are warm and spacious, some with balconies or sitting areas and kitchenettes. *740 Burdett Ave., V8W 1B2, tel. 604/382–4221 or 800/663–5891; fax 604/380–1950. 178 rooms. Facilities: restaurants, lounge, indoor pool, whirlpool, meeting rooms, courtesy vans to ferry, access to health club. AE, MC. Expensive.*

Dashwood Manor. If you want a quiet place with a great view, this is it. Located on the waterfront next to Beacon Hill Park, this Heritage Tudor mansion, built in 1912 on property once owned by Governor Sir James Douglas, offers panoramic views of the Strait of Juan de Fuca and the Olympic Mountains. This B&B lacks some of the charm that many offer because the parlor and dining rooms have been made into guest quarters. The only place for guests to congregate is in the tiny office, where sherry or wine is offered in the afternoon. Three guest rooms have fireplaces, and all rooms come with a fully stocked frig; and breakfast is "make your own." *1 Cook St., V8V 3W6, tel. 604/385–5517. 14 rooms. AE, MC. Expensive.*

★ **Holland House Inn.** Two blocks from the inner harbor, legislative buildings, and ferry terminals, this nonsmoking hotel has a sense of casual elegance. Some of the individually designed rooms have original fine art created by the owner, and some have four-poster beds and fireplaces. All rooms have private baths, and all but two have their own balconies. A gourmet breakfast is served and included in room rates. You'll recognize the house by the picket fence around it. *595 Michigan St., V8V 1S7, tel. and fax 604/384–6644. 10 rooms. Facilities: lounge. AE, DC, MC, V. Expensive.*

★ **Hotel Grand Pacific.** This is one of Victoria's newest and finest hotels, with a lot of mahogany woodwork and an elegant ambience. Overlooking the harbor, and adjacent to the legislative buildings, the hotel accommodates business and vacationing people looking for comfort, convenience, and great scenery; all rooms have terraces, with views of either the harbor or the Olympic Mountains. The health club is elaborate, equipped with Nautilus, racquetball court, and sauna. *450 Québec St., V8V 1W5, tel. 604/386-0450 or 800/663-7550; fax 604/383-7603. 149 rooms. Facilities: restaurant, lounge, sauna, whirlpool, fitness center, convention facilities, underground parking, indoor pool. AE, D, DC, MC, V. Expensive.*

Mulberry Manor. This Tudor mansion is a special place for a number of reasons: It is the last building to have been designed by Victoria architect Simon McClure; the grounds were designed and, until recently, maintained by a gardener at the world-famous Butchart Gardens; the manor has been restored and decorated to magazine-cover perfection with antiques, sumptuous linens, and tiled baths. Hosts Susan and Tony Temple are charming and provide gourmet breakfasts with homemade jams and great coffee. *611 Foul Bay Rd., V8S 1H2, tel. 604/370-1918. 2 rooms, 2 suites. MC, V. Expensive.*

Ocean Pointe Resort. Set across the "blue bridge" from downtown Victoria, the resort, with a northern European ambience, opened in the summer of 1992 on the site of an old shingle mill and an area once claimed by the Songhees natives. Public rooms and half of the guest rooms offer romantic evening views of downtown Victoria and the parliament buildings, bedecked with some 3,000 twinkling lights. Guest rooms are spacious and some feature floor-to-ceiling windows and small balconies. The property offers a rich cache of amenities, including hydrotherapy, micronized marine algae body wrap, massages, aerobics, and beauty treatments in the spa. There are salads and sandwiches in the Boardwalk Café; steaks and seafood in the Boardwalk Brasserie; and Pacific Northwest and Continental entrées, along with low-calorie, low-fat spa cuisine in the Victorian Restaurant. *45 Songhees Rd., Victoria V9A 6T3, tel. 604/360-2999 or 800/667-4677; fax 604/360-1041. 213 rooms, 37 housekeeping suites w/kitchens. Facilities: 3 restaurants, lounge, 3 tennis courts, whirlpool, sauna, exercise room, indoor pool, squash and racquetball court, beauty parlor, supervised playroom. Reservations advised in restaurant. MC, V. Expensive.*

Victoria Regent Hotel. Originally built as an apartment, this is now a posh, condo-living hotel that offers views of the harbor or city. The outside is plain, with a glass facade, but the interior is sumptuously decorated with warm earth tones and modern furnishings; each apartment has a living room, dining room, deck, kitchen, and one or two bedrooms with bath. *1234 Wharf St., V8W 3H9, tel. 604/386-2211 or 800/663-7472; fax 604/386-2622. 47 rooms, including 32 suites. Facilities: restaurant, free parking, laundromat. AE, D, DC, MC, V. Expensive.*

Oak Bay Beach Hotel. This Tudor-style hotel in Oak Bay, on the southwest side of the Saanich Peninsula, is well removed from the bustle of downtown. There's a wonderful atmosphere here, though; the hotel, situated oceanside, overlooks the Haro Strait and catches the setting sun. The interior decor is as dreamy as the grounds, with antiques and flower prints decorating the rooms. The restaurant, Tudor Room by the Sea, is average, but the bar with its cozy fireplace is truly romantic.

1175 Beach Dr., V8S 2N2, tel. and fax 604/598–4556. 51 rooms. Facilities: restaurant, pub, yacht for cruises, access to health club. AE, DC, MC, V. Moderate–Very Expensive.

Admiral Motel. Located on the Victoria harbor and along the tourist strip, this motel is right where the action is, although it is relatively quiet in the evening. If you're looking for a basic, clean lodging, the Admiral is just that. The amicable owners take good care of the newly refurbished rooms, and small pets are permitted. *257 Belleville St., V8V 1X1, tel. 604/388–6267. 29 rooms, 23 with kitchens. Facilities: cable TV, free parking, laundry. AE, D, MC, V. Inexpensive–Moderate.*

★ **Craigmyle Guest House.** At this typical English-style bed-and-breakfast you'll find a casual, homey feeling without expensive designer touches. In the shade of Craigdarroch Castle, about 2 kilometers (1 mile) from the downtown core, this lodge, built in 1913, has a special view of the castle. The rooms are small and simple, but most units have a private bath. The main lounge features high ceilings and a huge fireplace. A hearty English-style breakfast, with homemade preserves, porridge, and eggs is served. Hosts are very friendly and chatty. *1037 Craigdarroch Rd., V8S 2A5, tel. 604/595–5411, fax 604/370–5276. 19 rooms, 15 with private bath. MC, V. Inexpensive–Moderate.*

The Arts and Nightlife

The Arts

Galleries

The **Art Gallery of Greater Victoria** is considered one of Canada's finest art museums and is home both to large collections of Chinese and Japanese ceramics and other art and to the only authentic Shinto shrine in North America. The gallery hosts about 40 different temporary exhibitions yearly. *1040 Moss St., Victoria, tel. 604/384–4101. Admission: $3 adults, $1.50 students and senior citizens, children under 12 free; free Thurs. after 5, though donations are accepted. Open Mon.–Wed. and Fri.–Sat. 10–5, Thurs. 10–9, Sun. 1–5.*

The **Emily Carr Gallery** (under the auspices of the Greater Victoria Gallery) presents the art of and films about this renowned artist, who was a contemporary of the Group of Seven. *1107 Wharf St., Victoria, tel. 604/384–3130.*

Among the numerous commercial galleries, the **Fran Willis North Park Gallery** (200–1619 Store St., tel. 604/381–3422) is a good bet. In a gorgeously restored warehouse near the waterfront, it shows contemporary paintings and sculpture by local artists; music is performed from time to time. For a further look at what's going on in Victoria's art scene, try the **Winchester Galleries** (tel. 604/595–2777), the **Nunavut Gallery** (tel. 604/598–1344), and the **Barton Leir Gallery** (tel. 604/383–6477).

Music

The **Victoria Symphony** has a winter schedule and a summer season, playing in the recently refurbished **Royal Theatre** (805 Broughton St., Victoria, tel. 604/361–0820) and at the **University Centre Auditorium** (Finnerty Rd., Victoria, tel. 604/721–8480). The **Pacific Opera Victoria** performs three productions a year in the 800-seat **McPherson Playhouse** (3 Centennial Sq., tel. 604/386–6121), adjoining the Victoria City Hall. The **Victoria International Music Festival** (tel. 604/736–2119) features internationally acclaimed musicians, dancers, and singers each summer from the first week in July through late August.

The **Victoria Jazz Society** (tel. 604/388–4423) organizes an annual **JazzFest International** in late June, which in the past has featured jazz, blues, and world-beat artists such as Dizzy Gillespie, Frank Morgan, Ellis Marsalis, and Aster Aweke.

For listings of clubs and restaurants featuring jazz during the year, call **Jazz Hotline** (604/658–5255).

Theater Live theater can be seen at the **Belfry Theatre** (1291 Gladstone Ave., Victoria, tel. 604/385–6815), **Phoenix Theatre** (Finnerty Rd., tel. 604/721–8000) at the University of Victoria, **Victoria Theatre Guild** (805 Langham Ct., tel. 604/384–2142), and **McPherson Playhouse** (3 Centennial Sq., tel. 604/386–6121).

Nightlife After 8 PM, **Tudor House Hotel Pub** (533 Admirals Rd., tel. 604/389–9943) becomes a pub attracting the younger set. There's a dance floor and large screen for disco and video entertainment nightly.

Harpo's (15 Bastion Sq., tel. 604/385–5333) features live rock, blues, and jazz, with visits from internationally recognized bands.

Excursion to Whistler

Important Addresses and Numbers

Tourist Information Contact the **Whistler Resort Association** (4010 Whistler Way, Whistler V0N 1B4; in Whistler, tel. 604/932–3928; reservations, tel. 604/932–4222; in the U.S. and Canada, tel. 800/944–7853). In Whistler Village an information booth at the front door of the Conference Center is open 8:30–8.

A provincial government **Travel Infocentre** (tel. 604/932–5528) is on the main highway, about 1 ½ kilometers (a mile) south of Whistler.

Emergencies Dial 0 for **police, ambulance,** or **poison control.**

Arriving and Departing by Car

By Car Arriving time from Seattle to Vancouver is about three hours. Whistler is 1½ to two hours north of Vancouver via Route 99, the Sea-to-Sky Highway.

Getting Around

By Bus **Maverick Coach Lines** (tel. 604/932–5031) has buses leaving every couple of hours from the bus depot in downtown Vancouver. The bus stops at Whistler Village and the fare is under $14 one way. During ski season, the last bus leaves Whistler at 10PM.

Perimiter Bus Transportation (tel. 604/266–5386) has daily service, November–April and June–September from Vancouver Airport to Whistler. Reservations are necessary 24 hoursin advance; the ticket booth is on the arrivals level of the airport.

By Train **BC Rail** (tel. 604/932–2134) travels north from Vancouver to Whistler along a beautiful route. The Vancouver Bus Terminal and the North Vancouver Station are connected by bus shuttle.

Exploring Whistler

If you think of skiing when you hear mention of **Whistler,** British Columbia, you're thinking on track. Whistler and Blackcomb mountains, part of the Whistler Resort Association, are the two biggest ski mountains in North America; there's summer glacier skiing, the longest vertical drop in North America, and the most advanced lifts in the world. At the base of the mountains is Whistler Village—a small community of lodgings, restaurants, pubs, gift shops, and boutiques. With more than 60 hotels, most of which are arranged within a five-minute walk between the mountains, the site is frenzied with activity. Culinary options within the village range from burgers to French, Japanese to deli cuisine; and nightly entertainment runs the gamut from sophisticated piano bars to casual pubs.

In the winter, the village buzzes with skiers taking to the slopes in vibrantly colored attire, but as the scenery changes from winter's snow-white to summer's lush-green landscapes, the mood of Whistler changes, too. Things seem to slow down a bit, and the resort sheds some of its competitive edge and welcomes a more relaxed, slower-paced environment. Even the local golf tournaments and the triathlon are interspersed with Mozart and bluegrass festivals.

Adjacent to the area is the 78,000-acre (31,579-hectare) **Garibaldi Provincial Park,** with dense mountainous forests splashed with hospitable lakes and streams. But even if you don't want to roam much farther than the village, there are five lakes for canoeing, fishing, swimming, and windsurfing, and many nearby hiking and mountain-bike trails.

No matter what the season, though, Whistler Village is very accessible to the pedestrian. Anywhere you want to go within the resort is at most five minutes away, and parking lots are just outside the village. The bases of Whistler and Blackcomb mountains are also just at the edge; in fact, you can ski right into the lower level of the Chateau Whistler Hotel, and all 2,700 of the village's hotel rooms are less than 1,000 feet from the lifts.

If you are interested in a tour of the area, **Alpine Adventure Tours** (tel. 604/932–2705) has a Whistler history tour of the valley and a Squamish day trip.

Scenic Drives

Completion of a new highway opened the **Coast Mountain Circle,** linking Vancouver to Cariboo Country. This 702-kilometer (435-mile) route takes in spectacular Howe Sound, the deep-water port of Squamish, Whistler Resort, and Pemberton Valley before heading back to Vancouver through scenic Fraser Canyon and Harrison Hot Springs. The loop makes a comfortable two- to three-day journey. For more information contact the **Tourism Association of Southwestern B.C.** (304–828 W. 8th Ave., Vancouver V52 1E2, tel. 604/876–3088 or 800/667–3306).

Sports and the Outdoors

Canoeing and Kayaking You'll see lots of canoes and kayaks at the many lakes and rivers near **Whistler.** If you want to get in on the fun, rentals are available at Alta Lake at both **Lakeside Park** and **Wayside Park.** Another spot that's perfect for canoeing is the **River of Golden Dreams,** either from Meadow Park to Green Lake or upstream to Twin Bridges. Kayakers looking for a thrill may want to try **Green River** from Green Lake to Pemberton. Call **Whistler Outdoor Experience** (tel. 604/932–3389) or **Sea to Sky Kayaking** (tel. 604/8989–5498) for equipment or guided trips.

Fishing **Whistler Backcountry Adventures** (tel. 604/938–1410) or **Whistler Fishing Guides** (tel. 604/932–4267) will take care of anything you need—equipment, guides, and transportation. All five of the lakes around Whistler are stocked with trout, but the area around **Dream River Park** is one of the most popular fishing spots. Slightly farther afield, try **Cheakamus Lake, Daisy Lake,** and **Callaghan Lake.**

Golf Arnold Palmer designed the par-72 championship **Whistler Golf Course** (tel. 604/932–4544), which is said to be a "good four-iron shot from the village." The course is very scenic, fairly flat, and challenging for the experienced, but pleasant for beginners. The relatively new **Predator Ridge Golf Resort** (360 Commonage Rd., Vernon, tel. 604/542–3436) is a very challenging public course. The area's newest offering, the **Robert Trent Jones Jr. Golf Course** (4599 Chateau Blvd., tel. 604/938–8000), is equally scenic, nestled at the foot of the mountain on the opposite side of Whistler Village.

Skiing
Downhill Whistler Resort has more than 200 runs along with hotels and restaurants, and, like Whistler, is in the process of rapidly expanding. The vertical drops and elevation at **Blackcomb** and **Whistler** mountains are, perhaps, the most impressive features to skiers. Blackcomb has a 5,280-foot vertical drop (North America's longest); Whistler has a 5,020-foot drop. The top elevation is 7,494 feet on Blackcomb and 7,160 on Whistler. These mountains also have the most advanced ski-lift technology, with lift capacity on Blackcomb being 26,350 skiers per hour; on Whistler, 22,295 per hour. Blackcomb and Whistler have more than 100 marked trails each and receive an average of 450 inches of snow per year; Blackcomb is open June–August for summer glacier skiing. **Whistler Ski School** (tel. 604/932–3434) and **Blackcomb Ski School** (tel. 604/932–3141) offer lessons to skiers of all levels.

Heli- and Snowcat Skiing In Whistler, **Mountain Heli-Sports** (tel. 604/932–2070 or 604/932–3512), **Tyax Heli-Skiing** (tel. 604/932–7007), and **Whistler Heli-Skiing** (tel. 604/932–4105) have day trips with up to four glacier runs, or 12,000 vertical feet of skiing for experienced skiers; the cost is about $300.

Dining and Lodging

For prices *see* Dining chart for Vancouver, *above.*

Dining **Il Caminetto Di Umberto; Trattoria di Umberto; Settebello's.** Umberto Menghi is Vancouver's best-known restaurateur because of his fabulously successful Italian restaurants. Now there are three in Whistler. Il Caminetto and the Trattoria are in the village, and Settebello's is in Whistler Creek, about 3 kilometers (about 2 miles) south. Umberto offers home-style Italian cooking and specializes in pasta dishes like crab-stuffed cannelloni or a four-cheese lasagna that mix well with the relaxed atmosphere. The Trattoria has a Tuscan-style rotisserie, featuring a pasta dish served with a tray of chopped tomatoes, hot pepper, basil, olive oil, anchovies, and Parmesan so that you can mix it as spicy and flavorful as you like. Settebello's specialty is lean grilled beef and chicken, and Il Caminetto, perhaps the best restaurant in the Whistler area, is known for its veal, osso buco, and zabaglione. *Il Caminetto: 4242 Village Stroll, tel. 604/932–4442; Trattoria: Mountainside Lodge, tel. 604/932–5858; Settebello's: Whistler Creek Lodge, tel. 604/932–3000. Reservations advised for dinner. Dress: neat but casual. AE, DC, MC, V. Expensive.*

★ **Les Deux Gros.** The name means "the two fat guys," which may explain the restaurant's motto, "Never trust a skinny chef." Portions of the country French cuisine are generous indeed. The spinach-and-warm-duck salad, steak tartare, juicy rack of lamb, and salmon Wellington are all superbly crafted and presented, and the service is friendly but unobtrusive. Located just southwest of the village, this is the spot for that special romantic dinner; request one of the prime tables by the massive stone fireplace. *1200 Alta Lake Rd., tel. 604/932–4611. Dinner only. Reservations advised. Dress: neat but casual. AE, DC, MC, V. Expensive.*

The Wildflower Cafe. Although this is the main dining room of the Chateau Whistler, it's an informal, comfortable restaurant. Huge picture windows overlook the ski slopes and let in the bright sun reflected off the snow. The rustic effect of the Chateau Whistler lobby continues in the Wildflower—more than 100 antique wood birdhouses decorate the room, and chairs and tables have that farmhouse look. Although there is an à la carte menu that focuses on Pacific Northwest cuisine, the restaurant features terrific breakfast, lunch, and dinner buffets that may include fresh crepes and omelets, sweet potato–and–parsnip soup, barbecued salmon, smoked halibut, artichoke-and-mushroom salad, pepper salad, seafood pâté, pasta in a spicy tomato sauce, and cold meats. *Chateau Whistler Hotel, tel. 604/938–8000. Reservations advised for dinner. Dress: neat but casual. AE, DC, MC, V. Expensive.*

Lodging

All lodgings can be booked through the Whistler Resort Association (tel. 604/932–4222 or 800/944–7853).

For prices *see* Lodging chart for Victoria, *above*.

★ **Le Chamois.** Sharing the prime ski-in, ski-out location at the base of the Blackcomb runs is this elegant, new luxury hotel. Of the 50 spacious guest rooms with convenience kitchens, the most popular are the studios with Jacuzzi tubs set in the living room in front of bay windows overlooking the slopes and lifts. Guests can keep an eye on the action also from the glass elevators and the heated outdoor pool. *4557 Blackcomb Way, tel. 604/932–8700; in the U.S. and Canada, 800/777–0185; fax 604/938–1888. 50 suites and studios, rooms for the disabled. Facilities: 2 restaurants, outdoor heated pool, Jacuzzi, fitness room, laundry room, complimentary valet skilocker, parking, shuttle to village. AE, DC, MC, V. Very Expensive.*

Chateau Whistler. Whistler's most extravagant hotel is a large and friendly looking fortress, just outside the village. It was built and run by Canadian Pacific Railway. It is the same style as the Banff Springs Hotel and the Jasper Park Lodge; the marvelous lobby is filled with rustic Canadiana, handmade Mennonite rugs, enormous fireplaces, and enticing overstuffed sofas. Floor-to-ceiling windows in the lounge, the health club, and the Wildflower Cafe overlook the base of Blackcomb Mountain. It's possible to schuss from there right into the basement of the hotel. The standard rooms are called premier and are fairly small, but the suites are fit for royalty, with specially commissioned quilts and artwork, and are complemented by antique furnishings. Both the Wildflower Cafe (*see* Dining, *above*) and La Fiesta, a tapas bar, are very good choices for a meal. Look for summer rates that drop by 50%. *4599 Chateau Blvd., Box 100, V0N 1B0, tel. 604/938–8000; in the U.S., 800/828–7447; in Canada, 800/528–0444; fax 604/938–2020. 303 doubles, 40 suites, rooms for the disabled. Facilities: 2 restaurants, bar, indoor-outdoor pool, indoor and outdoor Jacuzzis, morning stretch classes for skiers, 3 covered tennis courts, golf course. AE, DC, MC, V. Expensive.*

Pension Edelweiss. The Edelweiss is one of seven charming and very European bed-and-breakfasts around Whistler, and it's within walking distance of Whistler Village. Rooms have balconies and fireplaces and that crisp, northern European spic-and-span feel, in keeping with the Bavarian chalet style of the house. Each morning a different breakfast (included in room rate) is served: Scandinavian, American, French, German. *7162 Nancy Greene Way, Box 850, tel. 604/932–3641, fax 604/932–3776. 8 rooms, all with private bath. Facilities: sauna, Jacuzzi, transportation to lifts. MC, V. Inexpensive–Moderate.*

Index

Abigail's (B&B), *163–164*
A Contemporary Theatre, *84*
Admiral Motel, *166*
Adriatica (restaurant), *71*
Ainsworth's (shop), *132*
Air tours, *116*
A. Jay's (restaurant), *69*
Alexis (hotel), *74–75*
Alfred Sung (shop), *133*
All-City Dance Club, *88*
Allegro Dance Company, *85*
Alma Street Cafe, *154*
American Express, *7–8*
Amusement parks, *129–130*
Anne Hathaway's Cottage, *159*
Annex Theatre, *84*
Annie Steffen's (shop), *93*
Anthony's Home Port (bar), *86*
Antique Importers, *61*
Antiques shops
Seattle, *61*
Vancouver, *131–132*
Victoria, *160–161*
Apartment and Villa Rentals, *35*
Aquariums
Seattle, *51*
Vancouver, *123–124*
Arboretums, *57*
Armadillo & Co. (shop), *61*
Arnie's (bar), *86*
Arriva Ristorante, *142*
Artemis (shop), *132*
Art galleries and museums
Gallery Walk program, *58*
San Juan Islands, *98*
Seattle, *50–51, 57, 58, 61*
Vancouver, *117, 126, 127, 132*
Victoria, *166*
Art Gallery of Greater Victoria, *166*
Arts Club Theatre, *152*
ATMs (automated teller machines), *7*
Auctions, *131*
Avalon Ballroom, *88*

Baby-sitting services, *16*
Bacchus Lounge, *153*
Bacci (shop), *133*
Bach Choir, *153*
Back Alley Theatre, *152*
Backstage (club), *87*
Backstage Lounge, *153–154*
Bahn Thai (restaurant), *74*
Bainbridge Island, *88–90*
tourist information, *89*
transportation, *89*
Bainbridge Island Chamber of Commerce, *89*
Bali Bali (shop), *133*
Ballard Firehouse (club), *87*
Ballard Locks, *60*
Balloon flights, *50*
Ballroom dancing, *88*
Baren Haus (restaurant), *107*
Bars and lounges
Seattle, *86–87*
Vancouver, *153–154*
Victoria, *167*
Baseball, *31*
Seattle, *64*
Vancouver, *135*
Basketball, *31*
Seattle, *64*
Bay Cafe, *99*
Beaches, *31–32*
San Juan Islands, *99*
Vancouver, *135*
Beacon Hill Park, *158*
Beaconsfield Inn, *164*
Bead Works (shop), *61*
Beatles Museum, *130*
Bed-and-breakfasts, *33–34*
Bedford Hotel, *164*
Belfry Theatre, *167*
Bellevue Square shopping center, *61*
Bergman Luggage Co., *62*
Bicycling, *28*
San Juan Islands, *98*
Seattle, *63*
Vancouver, *133*
Whidbey Island, *93*
Big Time Brewery, *59*
Bilbo's Festivo (restaurant), *99*
Bishop's (restaurant), *144*
Bite of Seattle festival, *5*
Blackberry Books, *132*
Blackfish Studio, *93*
Blair House (B&B), *102*
Blethering Place (restaurant), *162*
Bloedel Preserve, *90*
Blues/R&B clubs, *87*
Boating and sailing, *28–29*
San Juan Islands, *98–99*
Seattle, *64*
Vancouver, *134*
Whidbey Island, *93*
Boardwalk Bookstore, *98*
Boat racing, *64*
Boboli (shop), *132, 133*
Boeing Field, *57*
Bombay Bicycle Club (bar), *151*
Bond's (shop), *132*
Bookshops, *132*
Books on Pacific North Coast, *18–19*
Border-crossing procedures, *9, 22*
Boutique Europa, *62*

Boy's Co. (shop), *132*
Bread Garden Bakery, Café & Espresso Bar, *140*
Breweries
Seattle, *57, 59*
tours, *59*
Vancouver, *127*
Brew pubs, *59*
Bridges (restaurant), *127, 153*
British Columbia Ferry Corporation, *25*
Brockton Point, *123*
Bruce Lee's grave site, *60*
Buchan Hotel, *151–152*
Bumbershoot festival, *5*
Buschlen-Mowat Gallery, *132*
Business hours, *27*
Bus travel, *22*
Leavenworth, *105*
regional service, *24*
Seattle, *46, 47*
Vancouver, *111, 114*
Victoria, *155*
Whistler, *167*
Butchart Gardens, *160*
Byrnes Block building, *121*

Cabezon Gallery, *98*
Cafe Dilettante, *61–62*
Cafe Juanita, *70–71*
Cafe Mexico, *163*
Caffe de Medici (restaurant), *142*
Camcorders, travel with, *11*
Cameras, travel with, *10–11*
Camilles (restaurant), *162*
Campagne (restaurant), *69*
Camping, *34*
Canada Day, *5*
Canada Place Pier, *119*
Canada West (shop), *132*
Canadian Craft Museum, *119*
Canadian Imperial Bank of Commerce headquarters, *120*
Canadian Pacific Station, *120*
Canlis (restaurant), *65*
Canoeing, *168–169*
Canrailpass, *14*
Cantata Singers, *153*
Capers (restaurant), *141–142*
Capilano Fish Hatchery, *130*
Captain Whidbey Inn, *95*
Carnegie's (club), *154*
Carousel Theater, *152*
Carpenter's Hall, *88*
Car rentals, *13–14*
Car travel, *21–22*
insurance, *24*
Leavenworth, *105*
San Juan Islands, *95*
Seattle, *46, 47*
service organizations, *24–25*
Snoqualmie Falls, *103*
speed limits, *24*
Vancouver, *111, 114*
Victoria, *155*
Whidbey Island, *90*
Whistler, *167*
winter driving, *24*
Casa-U-Betcha (restaurant), *72*
Cash machines, *7*
Casinos, *154*
CBC Orchestra, *153*
Cemeteries, *60*
Central Tavern, *87*
Chapy's (shop), *132*
Charles and Emma Frye Art Museum, *58*
Charles H. Scott Gallery, *126*
Charlotte Martin Theatre, *58–59*
Chartwell (restaurant), *139*
Chateau Victoria, *164*
Chateau Whistler (restaurant), *170–171*
Chau's Chinese Restaurant, *69*
Chez Daniel (restaurant), *161*
Chez Pierre (restaurant), *161*
Chez Thierry (restaurant), *141*
Chicago's (club), *87*
Childers/Proctor Gallery, *93*
Children, traveling with, *15–16*
Seattle attractions, *58–59*
Vancouver attractions, *5, 127, 129–130*
Victoria attractions, *159–160*
Chimera Gallery, *98*
Chinese Cultural Center, *122*
Chinese Freemasons Building, *121–122*
Chinese Times Building, *122*
Chiyoda (restaurant), *143*
Chocolate shops, *61–62*
Christ Church Cathedral, *117*
Christina's (restaurant), *99*
Churches
Vancouver, *117*
Cipriano's Ristorante & Pizzeria, *143*
Civic Light Opera, *85*
Cliff House (B&B), *94*
Climate, *4–5*
Clothing shops
Seattle, *62*
Vancouver, *132–133*
Club Monaco (shop), *132, 133*
Colleges and universities
Seattle, *57*
Vancouver, *126*
Colophon Books, *132*
Comedy clubs
Seattle, *88*
Vancouver, *154*
Comedy Underground (club), *88*
Commodore Ballroom (club), *154*
Cooper's Northwest Alehouse, *59*
Cornish College of the Arts, *83–84*

Cougar Inn, *106*
Coupeville, WA, *91*
Crafts shops, *62*
Craigdarroch Castle, *159*
Craigmyle Guest House, *166*
Crocodile Cafe (club), *87*
Cruises, *26*
Vancouver excursions, *116*
Crystal Gardens, *158*
Cuisine of Pacific North Coast, *32*
Currencies of Canada and United States, *8*
Currency exchange services, *7*
Customs regulations, *10*

Daily Planet (shop), *61*
Dance
Seattle, *85*
Vancouver, *153*
Dance clubs, *88*
Danish Bakery, *107*
Darvill's Rare Print Shop, *98*
Dashwood Manor (B&B), *164*
Days Inn, *150–151*
Deadman's Island, *123*
Deception Pass State Park, *91, 93*
Deer Harbor Inn, *103*
Delaurenti Wine Shop, *62*
Delta Pacific Resort & Conference Center, *148*
Delta Place (hotel), *148*
Delta River Inn, *148–149*
Der Ritterhof (hotel), *107*
Diane Farris Gallery, *132*
Dimitriou's Jazz Alley, *87*
Disabled travelers, hints for, *16–18*
Doc Maynard's (club), *87*
Dr. Sun Yat-sen Gardens, *122*
Doe Bay Village Resort, *101*
Dog House Backdoor Restaurant, *94*
Don Mee's (restaurant), *162*
Doubletree Inn, *81–82*
Doubletree Suites, *81–82*
Dragon Boat Festival, *5*
Duck Soup Inn, *100*
Du Maurier International Jazz Festival, *5*
Dusty Strings (shop), *61*
Duthie's (shop), *132*

E. A. Lee (shop), *132*
Early Music Guild (Seattle), *85*
Early Music Society (Vancouver), *153*
Eastsound Village, WA, *96*
Ebey's Landing National Historical Reserve, *91*
Ecomarine Ocean Kayak Center, *127*
Eddie Bauer (shop), *62*
Edelhaus (restaurant), *106*
Edelweiss Hotel, *106*
Edenwild (B&B), *100*
Edgewater (hotel), *78*
Edward Chapman, (shop), *132*
86th Street Music Hall, *154*
Elderhostel program, *18*
Elliott Bay Book Company, *58*
El Puerco Lloron (restaurant), *72*
Emergencies
Seattle, *47*
Vancouver, *114*
Victoria, *154*
Whistler, *167*
Emily Carr College of Art and Design, *126*
Emily Carr Gallery, *166*
Emmet Watson's Oyster Bar, *73*
Empress Hotel, *156, 163*
Empty Space Theater, *84*
Enda B. (shop), *133*
English Bay, *124*
English Bay Café, *140, 153*
English Bay Inn, *151*
Equinox Gallery, *132*
Ernie's Bar and Grill, *86*
Evergreen Motel, *108*

Ferry service, *25–26*
Bainbridge Island, *88*
San Juan Islands, *95–96*
Seattle, *47*
Vancouver, *111, 114*
Victoria, *155*
Whidbey Island, *91*
Festivals and seasonal events, *5–6*
Fifth Avenue Musical Theater Company, *84*
Film
Seattle, *51*
Vancouver, *153*
Finn's (shop), *132*
Fireworks Gallery, *62*
Fishing, *29*
San Juan Islands, *99*
Seattle, *63*
Vancouver, *133*
Whidbey Island, *93*
Whistler, *169*
Fish Ladder, *60*
Fitzgerald's on Fifth (club), *88*
Flea markets, *131*
Flying Shuttle Ltd. (shop), *62*
Folkart Interiors (shop), *132*
Folk clubs, *87*
Football, *31*
Seattle, *64*
Vancouver, *135*
Ft. Casey State Park, *91*
Fort Vancouver Days, *5*
Four Seasons (hotel, Vancouver), *147*
Four Seasons Olympic Hotel (Seattle), *75*

Frank & Dunya Gallery, *61*
Freedman Shoes (shop), *133*
French Connection (restaurant), *162*
Friday Harbor, WA, *97*
Friday's (hotel), *102*
Friends of Chamber Music, *153*
Front Street Ale House (restaurant), *100*
Fuller's (restaurant), *72*
F. X. McRory's (bar), *86–87*

Gallery Lounge, *153*
Gallery Walk program, *58*
Garden Court (bar), *86*
Garden Lounge, *153*
Gardens
Seattle, *57, 60*
Vancouver, *122, 128, 129*
Victoria, *158, 160*
Whidbey Island, *91*
Garibaldi Provincial Park, *168*
Garibyan Brothers Café Langley, *93*
George Straith (shop), *132*
Gérard Lounge, *153*
Gift shops, *133*
Giggles (club), *88*
Glass House (shop), *61*
Glass Knight (shop), *93*
Glass Slipper (club), *154*
Golf, *29*
Leavenworth, *105*
Seattle, *63*
Vancouver, *133*
Victoria, *161*
Whistler, *169*
Gordon Southam Observatory, *130*
Granville Island, *125–127*
Granville Island Brewery, *127*
Granville Island Information Centre, *126*
Granville Island Public Market, *125–126*
Grayling Gallery, *98*
Great Canadian Casino, *154*
Great Gallery, *57*
Great Windup (shop), *62*
Greenbank, WA, *91*
Griffin's (restaurant), *142–143*
Group Theater, *84*
Guess Where (shop), *61*
Guest House Cottages (B&B), *94*

Harpo's (club), *167*
Harrison Festival of the Arts, *5–6*
Harry Rosen (shop), *132*
Haus Rohrbach (B&B), *108*
Health and fitness clubs, *134*
Health insurance, *11–12*
Heffel Gallery, *132*
Helicopter tours, *116*
Hendrix, Jimi, *60*
Henry Art Gallery, *57*
The Herbfarm (restaurant), *104*
Hiking, *29–30*
Leavenworth, *105–106*
Vancouver, *134*
Hill's (shop), *132*
Hillside House (B&B), *102*
Hiram's at the Locks (bar), *86*
Hockey, *31*
Vancouver, *135*
Holiday Inn Sea-Tac (hotel), *82*
Holland House Inn, *164*
Holt Renfrew (shop), *132*
Home exchanges, *34*
Homefires Bakery (restaurant), *107*
Horseback riding, *106*
Horse racing, *31*
Hotel Europe, *121*
Hotel Georgia, *151*
Hotel Grand Pacific, *165*
Hotels, *33*
Leavenworth, *107–108*
San Juan Islands, *100–103*
Seattle, *74–83*
Snoqualmie Falls area, *104*
Vancouver, *145–152*
Victoria, *163–166*
Whidbey Island, *94–95*
Whistler, *170–171*
Hotel Vancouver, *117, 149*
Hotel Vintage Park, *75*
Houseboat communities, *126*
Hunt Club (restaurant), *72*
Hunting, *30*
Hyatt Bellevue (hotel), *82*
Hyatt Regency (hotel), *149*

Il Caminetto di Umberto (restaurant), *169–170*
Il Giardino di Umberto (restaurant), *142*
Il Terrazo Carmine (restaurant), *70*
Imagination Market, *132*
Inn at Langley, *94–95*
Inn at Swifts Bay, *100*
Inn at the Market, *79*
Inns, *33*
Insurance, *11–13*
automobile, *24*
International Bathtub Race, *6*
Intiman Theater, *84*
Isadora's (restaurant), *136*
Island County Historical Museum, *91*
Island Woods & Weaving (shop), *98*

J&M Cafe (bar), *86*
Japanese Deli House, *144*
Jazz clubs
Seattle, *87*
Vancouver, *154*
Jeffrey-Michael (shop), *62*
Jewelry shops, *62*
Jimi Hendrix's grave site, *60*
Joe Fortes (bar), *153*
Jogging. *See* Running and jogging
Joseph Abboud (shop), *62*

Kakali (shop), *127*
Kaplan's Deli, Restaurant and Bakery, *140*
Kayaking
instruction in, *127*
Seattle, *64*
Vancouver, *134*
Kells (restaurant), *70, 87*
Keystone, WA, *91*
Kids Only Market, *127*
Kingdome stadium, *54*
Kingston (hotel), *152*
Kirin Mandarin Restaurant, *136*
Kitsilano Beach, *135*
Klondike Gold Rush National Historical Park, *53*

La Bodega (bar), *153*
Ladies Musical Club, *85*
Langley, WA, *91, 93*
Languages, *11*
Laptops, travel with, *11*
Larry's (club), *87*
Latona Tavern, *87*
La Vie en Rose (shop), *133*
La Ville d'Is (restaurant), *162*
Lawrence Books, *132*
Leavenworth, WA, *104–105*
hotels, *107–108*
restaurants, *106–107*
sports, *105–106*
tourist information, *105*
transportation, *105*
Le Chamois (hotel), *170*
Le Crocodile (restaurant), *141*
Lee, Bruce, *60*
Le Gavroche (restaurant), *141*
Legislative Parliament Buildings, *156, 158*
Le Meridien (hotel), *147*
Leone (shop), *132*
Le Petite Saigon (restaurant), *162*
Les Deux Gros (restaurant), *170*
Le Tastevin (restaurant), *69–70*
Lime Kiln Point State Park, *97*
Linderhoff Motor Inn, *108*
Linyen (restaurant), *65, 69*
Lions Gate Bridge, *124*
Littler's (shop), *62*
Local Brilliance (shop), *62*
Loganberry Farm, *91*
Lopez Island, *96, 98, 99, 100–101*
Lost Lagoon, *122*
Luggage
airline rules on, *6–7*
insurance for, *12*
Luggage shops, *62*
Lumberman's Arch, *123*
Lynn Canyon Suspension Bridge, *130*

Mackaye Harbor Inn, *100–101*
McLeod's (shop), *132*
McPherson Playhouse, *166, 167*
Magic Mouse Toys, *62*
Mail service, *27*
Malinee's Thai (restaurant), *145*
Maplewood Farms, *130*
Margareta (shop), *133*
Marine Building, *119*
Mario's (shop), *62*
Maritime Market, *127*
Maritime Museum (Vancouver), *128*
Maritime Museum of British Columbia (Victoria), *159*
Mayflower Park Hotel, *79–80*
Meany Hall for the Performing Arts, *85*
Meany Tower Hotel, *80*
Medical services
Seattle, *47–48*
Vancouver, *114–115*
Victoria, *154*
Meerkerk Rhododendron Gardens, *91*
Metropolitan Grill, *65*
Michael Pierce Gallery, *61*
Miniature World, *156*
Mondo Uomo (shop), *132*
Money, *7–8*
Monorail, *47*
Moore Theater, *86*
Moran State Park, *97*
Motels/motor inns, *33*
Mountaineering, *29*
Mt. Constitution, *96*
Mulberry Manor (B&B), *165*
Murphy's Pub, *87*
Museum of Anthropology, *128*
Museum of Flight, *57*
Museum of History and Industry, *57*
Museums. *See also* Art galleries and museums
anthropology, *57, 128*
aviation, *57*
Beatles, *130*
children's, *58*
crafts, *119*
gems, *119*
history, *57, 91, 97, 128, 158*
maritime history, *128, 159*
natural history, *57, 158*
Oriental history and culture, *56*

in San Juan Islands area, *97*
science, *128*
in Seattle, *51, 54, 56, 57, 58*
in Vancouver, *119, 128*
in Victoria, *156, 158, 159*
whales, *97*
in Whidbey Island, *91*
Music, classical
Seattle, *85–86*
Vancouver, *153*
Victoria, *166–167*
Music, popular
festivals, *5*
Seattle, *87–88*
Vancouver, *154*

Naam Restaurant, *142*
Nazarre BBQ Chicken, *136*
Net Loft, *127*
New City Arts Center, *84–85*
Newcombe Theatre, *158*
New Orleans Creole Restaurant, *87*
Nightclubs. *See* Bars and lounges
Night Court (bar), *153*
Nikko (restaurant), *71*
Nine O'Clock Gun, *123*
Nippon Kan Theater, *56*
Nitobe Garden, *128–129*
Noor Mahal (restaurant), *140*
Northgate Mall, *61*
Northwest Chamber Orchestra, *85*
Northwest Folklife Festival, *5*

Oak Bay Beach Hotel, *165*
Oak Bay Village, *161*
Oak Harbor, WA, *91*
Oakridge Shopping Center, *131*
Ocean Pointe Resort, *165*
Odlin County Park, *96*
O'Doul's (hotel), *149–150*
Odyssey Contemporary Maritime Museum, *51, 54*
Off-Ramp Music Cafe (club), *87*
Okazuya (restaurant), *57*
OK Hotel (club), *87–88*
Old Country Mouse Factory (shop), *132*
Older travelers, hints for, *18*
Old Timer's Cafe, *87*
Olympia Fish Market and Oyster Co. Ltd. (restaurant), *145*
Omnidome Film Experience, *51*
On the Boards (dance company), *85*
Opening and closing times, *27*
Opera
Seattle, *86*
Vancouver, *153*
Victoria, *166*
Orcas Hotel, *101*
Orcas Island, *96–97, 99, 101, 103*
Orcas Performing Arts Center, *103*
Out to Lunch Series, *58*

Pacific Center Mall, *130*
Pacific Cinémateque Pacifique, *153*
Pacific National Exhibition, *6*
Pacific Northwest Ballet, *85*
Pacific Northwest Brewing Co., *59*
Pacific Opera Victoria, *166*
Pacific Plaza (hotel), *80*
Pacific Spirit Park, *129*
Pacific Undersea Garden, *156*
Package deals, *3–4*
Packing, *6–7*
Pagliacci's (restaurant), *162*
Painted Table (restaurant), *72–73*
Pan Pacific (hotel), *147–148*
Paramount Theater, *86*
Parker's (club), *88*
Park Inn Club & Breakfast, *81*
Parks, historical
San Juan Islands, *97*
Seattle, *54*
Parks, state
San Juan Islands, *96, 97*
Whidbey Island, *91, 93*
Passports, *9*
Pelican Bay (bar), *153*
Pension Anna, *107*
Pension Edelweiss (hotel), *171*
Periklis (restaurant), *162*
Pewter Pot (restaurant), *106*
Phnom Penh Restaurant, *136*
Phoenix Theatre, *167*
Pier 70 (club), *88*
Pike & Western Wine Merchants, *62*
Pike Place Market, *51*
Pink Pearl (restaurant), *136, 139*
Pink Peppercorn (shop), *132*
Pioneer Park, *54*
Place Pigalle (restaurant), *65*
The Planetarium, *130*
Planetariums and observatories
Vancouver, *130*
Plane travel, *19–21*
charter flights, *20–21*
children, *16*
discount flights, *19–21*
Leavenworth, *105*
luggage, rules on, *6*
regional service, *23*
San Juan Islands, *95*
Seattle, *46*
smoking, *21*
from United Kingdom, *22*

Plane travel *(continued)*
Vancouver, *110–111*
Victoria, *154–155*
Whidbey Island, *90*
Point Grey Beaches, *135*
Powerboating, *31*
Prices, *8–9*
Prospect Point, *124*
Puget Sound and Snoqualmie Valley Railway, *103*

Queen Elizabeth Park, *129*
Queen Elizabeth Theatre, *153*
Quilicum (restaurant), *144*

Radio stations, *26*
Rafting
Leavenworth, *106*
Vancouver, *134*
Rail passes, *14*
Railroads
Snoqualmie Falls area, *103*
Vancouver, *129*
Rainier Brewery, *57*
The Raintree (restaurant), *144–145*
Ravenhouse Art, *98*
Ray's Boathouse (restaurant), *73, 86*
Re-Bar (club), *88*
Recreational Equipment, Inc., *58*
Red Barn (airplane factory), *57*
Red Lion Bellevue (hotel), *82*
Red Lion/Sea-Tac (hotel), *81*
REI (shop), *62*
Reid, Bill, studio of, *127*
Reiner's Gasthaus (restaurant), *106–107*
Resorts, *34*
Restaurants, *32*
American, *65, 136*
Asian, *65*
Cambodian, *136*
Chinese, *65, 69, 136, 139*
Continental, *139–140*
delis, *69, 140*
East Indian, *140–141*
French, *69–70, 140*
Greek, *141*
health food, *141–142*
Irish, *70*
Italian, *70–71, 142–143*
Japanese, *71, 143–144*
Korean, *144*
in Leavenworth, *106–107*
Mediterranean, *71*
Mexican, *72, 144*
nouvelle, *144*
Pacific Northwest, *72–73, 144–145*
in San Juan Islands area, *99–100, 103*
seafood, *73, 145*
in Seattle, *56, 64–74*
Snoqualmie Falls area, *104*
Southwest, *73*
Thai, *74, 145*
in Vancouver, *120, 124, 135–145*
in Victoria, *161–163*
Vietnamese, *74, 136*
in Whidbey Island, *93–95*
in Whistler, *169–170*
Richard's on Richards (disco), *154*
Richmond Nature Park, *130*
Ridge Theatre, *153*
Roche Harbor, WA, *97*
Roche Harbor Resort, *101–102*
Rock clubs
Seattle, *87–88*
Vancouver, *154*
Rosario Spa & Resort, *101*
Rover's (restaurant), *70*
Royal Bank building, *120*
Royal British Columbia Museum, *158*
Royal Diamond Casino, *154*
Royal London Wax Museum, *156*
Royal Theatre, *166*
Royal Vancouver Yacht Club, *123*
Rubina Tandoori (restaurant), *140*
Running and jogging
Seattle, *63*
Vancouver, *134*

Saigon Gourmet (restaurant), *74*
Sailboarding, *30, 64*
Sailing. *See* Boating and sailing
Ste. Michelle Winery, *59*
Saleh Al Lago (restaurant), *70*
Salish (hotel), *104*
Salty's (bar), *86*
Sam Kee Building, *121*
San Juan Community Theatre, *103*
San Juan Historical Museum, *96*
San Juan Inn, *102*
San Juan Island, *97, 100, 101–102*
San Juan Island National Historic Park, *97*
San Juan Islands, *95–103*
the arts, *103*
beaches, *99*
guided tours, *96*
hotels, *100–103*
restaurants, *99–100, 103*
shopping, *98*
sightseeing, *96–97*
sports, *98–99*
tourist information, *95*
transportation, *95–96*
Santa Fe Cafe, *73*
Scarlet Tree (club), *87*
Scenic drives, *168*
Science World, *128*
Scuba diving, *30*
Seafair festival, *5*
Seasons in the Park (restaurant), *139*
Seattle, WA, *45–46*
the arts, *83–86*
children, attractions for, *58–59*
climate, *4*
downtown, *50–51, 54–56*
emergencies, *47*
excursions, *88–108*

festivals, *5*
free attractions, *57–58*
Fremont area, *61*
guided tours, *48–50*
hotels, *74–83*
International District, *54, 56*
nightlife, *86–88*
Pioneer Square, *54*
restaurants, *56, 64–74*
shopping, *61–62*
Skid Row, *54*
sports, *62–64*
tourist information, *47*
transportation in, *47*
transportation to, *46*
Underground Tour, *49*
Seattle Airport Hilton (hotel), *81*
Seattle Aquarium, *51*
Seattle Art Museum, *50–51*
Seattle Center, *56*
Seattle Children's Museum, *58*
Seattle Children's Theater, *58–59*
Seattle Hilton (hotel), *78*
Seattle International Youth Hostel, *80*
Seattle/King County Convention and Visitors Bureau, *47*
Seattle Mariners, *64*
Seattle Marriott (hotel), *82*
Seattle Opera, *86*
Seattle Repertory Theater, *85*
Seattle Seahawks, *64*
Seattle Sheraton Hotel and Towers, *78*
Seattle SuperSonics, *64*
Seattle Symphony, *85*
Seattle-Tacoma International Airport, *46*
Seattle Visitor Information Center, *50*
Second Beach, *124*
Seoul House Korean Restaurant, *144*
Settebello's (restaurant), *169–170*
Shaw Island, *96*
Shijo Japanese Restaurant, *143–144*
Ship travel. *See* Cruises
Shopping, *27–28. See also specific types of shops*
San Juan Islands, *98*
Seattle, *61–62*
Vancouver, *130–133*
Victoria, *160–161*
Whidbey Island, *93*
Sinclair Centre, *120, 131*
Siwash Rock, *124*
Six-Mile-House (restaurant), *163*
Sixth Avenue Inn, *80*
Skating, *63*
Skid Row, *54*
Skiing, *30*
Leavenworth, *105*
Seattle, *63*
Vancouver, *134*
S. Lampman (shop), *133*
Snoqualmie Falls, *103–104*
hotels, *104*
restaurants, *104*
sightseeing, *103–104*
tourist information, *103*
transportation, *103*
Snoqualmie Falls Forest Theater, *103–104*
Snoqualmie Pass, *104*
Snoqualmie Winery, *104*
Soft Rock Cafe, *154*
Sorrento (hotel), *78–79*
Southcenter Mall, *61*
Space Needle, *56, 86*
Space Needle Lounge, *56*
Spencer Spit State Park, *96*
Splashdown Park, *129–130*
Sports. *See also specific sports*
Leavenworth, *105–106*
participant, *28–31*
San Juan Islands, *98–99*
Seattle, *62–64*
spectator, *31*
Vancouver, *133–135*
Victoria, *161*
Whidbey Island, *93*
Whistler, *168–169*
Sportsbooks Plus, *132*
Springtree Eating Establishment and Farm, *100*
Stanley Park, *122–124*
Stanley Park Zoo, *124*
Star Bistro, *93*
Steam train, miniature, *129*
Stouffer Madison Hotel, *79*
Student and youth travel, *14–15*
Swan Lake Christmas Hill Nature Sanctuary, *160*
Swan's Cafe, *161–162*
Swiftsure Race Weekend, *5*
Sylvia Hotel, *152*
Szechuan Chongqing (restaurant), *139*

Takara (restaurant), *71*
Taxes, *8–9, 28*
Taxis
Seattle, *47*
Vancouver, *111, 114*
Teahouse Restaurant at Ferguson Point, *124, 139*
Telephone service, *26*
Tennis, *63*
Theater
children's, *58–59*
Seattle, *58–59, 84–85*
Vancouver, *152*
Victoria, *167*
Theater buildings, *56*
Theatresports, *152*
Thomas Burke Memorial Washington State Museum, *57*
Three Girls Bakery, *69*
Tipping, *27*
Tojo's (restaurant), *143*
The Tomahawk (restaurant), *145*

Topanga Cafe, *144*
Toronto-Dominion Bank building, *120*
Totem poles, *123*
Touchstone Theatre, *152*
Tour groups, *2–4*
Tourist information, *2*
Leavenworth, *105*
San Juan Islands, *95*
Seattle, *47*
Snoqualmie Falls, *103*
Vancouver, *114*
Victoria, *154*
Whidbey Island, *90*
Whistler, *167*
Town Pump (club), *154*
Toy shops, *62*
Train travel, *22. See also* Railroads
rail passes, *14*
regional service, *23*
Seattle, *46*
Vancouver, *111*
Whistler, *167*
Trattoria Mitchelli (restaurant), *71*
Trattoria di Umberto (restaurant), *169–170*
Travel Bug (shop), *132*
Traveler's checks, *7*
Triple's Seafood Bistro (bar), *86*
Trolleyman (brew pub), *59*
Trolleys, *47*
Tudor House Hotel Pub, *167*
Turgeon-Raine Jewelers, *62*
Turtleback Farm (B&B), *101*
Twickenham House (restaurant), *94*

University of Washington, *57*
University Plaza Hotel, *81*

Vancouver, B.C., *110*
the arts, *152–153*
beaches, *135*
Blood Alley, *121*
Cathedral Place, *117, 119*
children, attractions for, *5, 127, 129–130*
Chinatown, *121–122, 131*
climate, *4–5*
downtown, *117–122*
East Indian shopping district, *131*
embassies, *114*
emergencies, *114*
festivals, *5–6*
free attractions, *129*
Gaoler's Mews, *121*
Gastown area, *120–121*
Granville Island, *125–127*
guided tours, *115–116*
hotels, *145–152*
Italian community, *131*
Japantown, *131*
nightlife, *153–154*
opening and closing times, *115*
restaurants, *120, 124, 127, 135–145*
Robson Square, *117*
shopping, *130–133*
sightseeing, *116–129*
sports, *133–135*
Stanley Park, *122–124*
subway system, *114*
tourist information, *114*
transportation in, *114*
transportation to, *111, 114*
travel agencies, *115*
West End, *124*
Vancouver Art Gallery, *117*
Vancouver Chamber Choir, *153*
Vancouver Children's Festival, *5*
Vancouver Club, *119*
Vancouver East Cultural Centre, *152*
Vancouver International Airport, *110–111*
Vancouver International Film Festival, *154*
Vancouver Kidsbooks, *132*
Vancouver Museum, *128*
Vancouver Opera, *153*
Vancouver Playhouse, *153*
Vancouver Public Aquarium, *123–124*
Vancouver Recital Society, *153*
Vancouver Rowing Club, *123*
Vancouver Sea Festival, *6*
Vancouver Symphony Orchestra, *153*
Van Dusen Botanical Garden, *129*
Vassilis Taverna (restaurant), *141*
Victoria, B.C., *154*
the arts, *166–167*
Bastion Square, *158–159*
children, attractions for, *159–160*
Chinatown, *159*
guided tours, *155*
hotels, *163–166*
Market Square, *159*
nightlife, *167*
restaurants, *161–163*
shopping, *160–161*
sightseeing, *156–159*
sports, *161*
tourist information, *154*
transportation, *154–155*
Victoria Day, *5*
Victoria International Music Festival, *166*
Victoria Regent Hotel, *165*
Victoria Symphony, *166*
Victoria Theatre Guild, *167*
Village Theater, *85*
Visas, *9*
Vogue (club), *88*

Wah Mee Club, *54, 56*
Walking, *63*
Warwick Hotel, *79*
Washington Dance Club, *88*
Washington Park Arboretum, *57*
Washington State Ferry System, *26*
Waterfront Centre Hotel, *120, 150*

Waterfront Theatre, *152*
Waterworks Gallery, *98*
Wax museums, *156*
Wear Else? (shop), *132, 133*
Weather information, *5*
Wedgewood Hotel, *150*
West Coast Bellevue Hotel, *83*
WestCoast Camlin Hotel, *80*
West End Beaches, *135*
West End Guest House, *151*
Western Union, *8*
Westin Bayshore (hotel), *148*
Westin Hotel, *75, 78*
Westlake Center, *50, 61*
Whale Museum, *96*
Whale-watching, *97*
Whidbey Island, *90*
beaches, *93*
hotels, *94–95*
restaurants, *93–95*
shopping, *93*
sightseeing, *91, 93*
sports, *93*
transportation, *90–91*
Whidbey Island Naval Air Station, *91*
Whistler, *167–171*
emergencies, *167*
hotels, *170–171*
restaurants, *169–170*
scenic drives, *168*
sightseeing, *168*
sports, *168–169*
tourist information, *167*
transportation, *167–168*
Wild Ginger (restaurant), *65*
Wildlife viewing, *31*
William Hoffer (shop), *132*
William McCarley (shop), *132*
William Tell (restaurant), *139–140*
Windsurfing, *134*
Wineries
Seattle, *59–60*
Snoqualmie Falls area, *104*
Wine shops, *62*
Wing Luke Museum, *56*
Woodland Park Zoo, *56–57*
Woodmark Hotel, *82–83*
World Wide Books and Maps, *132*

YMCAs/YWCAs, *34*
Seattle, *80*
Youth hostels, *15*
Seattle, *80*

Zig Zag (shop), *133*
Zoos
Seattle, *56–57*
Vancouver, *124*

Personal Itinerary

Departure *Date*

Time

Transportation

Arrival *Date* *Time*

Departure *Date* *Time*

Transportation

Accommodations

Arrival *Date* *Time*

Departure *Date* *Time*

Transportation

Accommodations

Arrival *Date* *Time*

Departure *Date* *Time*

Transportation

Accommodations

Personal Itinerary

Arrival *Date* *Time*

Departure *Date* *Time*

Transportation

Accommodations

Arrival *Date* *Time*

Departure *Date* *Time*

Transportation

Accommodations

Arrival *Date* *Time*

Departure *Date* *Time*

Transportation

Accommodations

Arrival *Date* *Time*

Departure *Date* *Time*

Transportation

Accommodations

Personal Itinerary

Arrival *Date* *Time*

Departure *Date* *Time*

Transportation

Accommodations

Arrival *Date* *Time*

Departure *Date* *Time*

Transportation

Accommodations

Arrival *Date* *Time*

Departure *Date* *Time*

Transportation

Accommodations

Arrival *Date* *Time*

Departure *Date* *Time*

Transportation

Accommodations

Personal Itinerary

Arrival *Date* *Time*

Departure *Date* *Time*

Transportation

Accommodations

Arrival *Date* *Time*

Departure *Date* *Time*

Transportation

Accommodations

Arrival *Date* *Time*

Departure *Date* *Time*

Transportation

Accommodations

Arrival *Date* *Time*

Departure *Date* *Time*

Transportation

Accommodations

Addresses

Name

Address

Telephone

Name

Address

Telephone

Name

Address

Telephone

Name

Address

Telephone

Name

Address

Telephone

Name

Address

Telephone

Name

Address

Telephone

Name

Address

Telephone

Name

Address

Telephone

Name

Address

Telephone

Name

Address

Telephone

Name

Address

Telephone

Name

Address

Telephone

Name

Address

Telephone

Name

Address

Telephone

Name

Address

Telephone

Addresses

Name

Address

Telephone

Name

Address

Telephone

Name

Address

Telephone

Name

Address

Telephone

Name

Address

Telephone

Name

Address

Telephone

Name

Address

Telephone

Name

Address

Telephone

Name

Address

Telephone

Name

Address

Telephone

Name

Address

Telephone

Name

Address

Telephone

Name

Address

Telephone

Name

Address

Telephone

Name

Address

Telephone

Name

Address

Telephone

Special Series

Fodor's Affordables

Caribbean

Europe

Florida

France

Germany

Great Britain

London

Italy

Paris

Fodor's Bed & Breakfast and Country Inns Guides

Canada's Great Country Inns

California

Cottages, B&Bs and Country Inns of England and Wales

Mid-Atlantic Region

New England

The Pacific Northwest

The South

The Southwest

The Upper Great Lakes Region

The West Coast

The Berkeley Guides

California

Central America

Eastern Europe

France

Germany

Great Britain & Ireland

Mexico

Pacific Northwest & Alaska

San Francisco

Fodor's Exploring Guides

Australia

Britain

California

The Caribbean

Florida

France

Germany

Ireland

Italy

London

New York City

Paris

Rome

Singapore & Malaysia

Spain

Thailand

Fodor's Flashmaps

New York

Washington, D.C.

Fodor's Pocket Guides

Bahamas

Barbados

Jamaica

London

New York City

Paris

Puerto Rico

San Francisco

Washington, D.C.

Fodor's Sports

Cycling

Hiking

Running

Sailing

The Insider's Guide to the Best Canadian Skiing

Skiing in the USA & Canada

Fodor's Three-In-Ones (guidebook, language cassette, and phrase book)

France

Germany

Italy

Mexico

Spain

Fodor's Special-Interest Guides

Accessible USA

Cruises and Ports of Call

Euro Disney

Halliday's New England Food Explorer

Healthy Escapes

London Companion

Shadow Traffic's New York Shortcuts and Traffic Tips

Sunday in New York

Walt Disney World and the Orlando Area

Walt Disney World for Adults

Fodor's Touring Guides

Touring Europe

Touring USA: Eastern Edition

Fodor's Vacation Planners

Great American Vacations

National Parks of the East

National Parks of the West

The Wall Street Journal Guides to Business Travel

Europe

International Cities

Pacific Rim

USA & Canada